# KATHARINE CORNELL

Katharine Cornell as Masha in *The Three Sisters* (1942). The Billy Rose Theatre Collection, The New York Public Library for the Performing Arts, Astor, Lenox and Tilden Foundations.

# KATHARINE CORNELL

## A Bio-Bibliography

Lucille M. Pederson

Bio-Bibliographies in the Performing Arts, Number 46

GREENWOOD PRESS
Westport, Connecticut • London

**Library of Congress Cataloging-in-Publication Data**

Pederson, Lucille M.
    Katharine Cornell : a bio-bibliography / Lucille M. Pederson.
        p.   cm.—(Bio-bibliographies in the performing arts, ISSN
    0892-5550 ; no. 46)
    Includes index.
    ISBN 0-313-27718-4 (alk. paper)
    1. Cornell, Katharine, 1893-1974.   2. Cornell, Katharine,
1893-1974—Bibliography.   3. Actors—United States—Biography.
I. Title.   II. Series.
PN2287.C62P43   1994
792'.028'092—dc20
    [B]           93-32102

British Library Cataloguing in Publication Data is available.

Library of Congress Catalog Card Number: 93-32102
ISBN: 0-313-27718-4
ISSN: 0892-5550

First published in 1994

Greenwood Press, 88 Post Road West, Westport, CT 06881
An imprint of Greenwood Publishing Group, Inc.

Printed in the United States of America

The paper used in this book complies with the
Permanent Paper Standard issued by the National
Information Standards Organization (Z39.48-1984).

10 9 8 7 6 5 4 3 2 1

This book is dedicated to the members of my family
who gave me encouragement and inspiration.

# Contents

*Photo Essay Follows Page 29*

# Preface

The importance of Katharine Cornell, one of the leading lights in the theatre in the first half of the twentieth century, has been largely overlooked in recent decades. She had a significant influence on the theatre from the early twenties until her retirement in 1961, which was prompted by the death of her partner and director-husband, Guthrie McClintic. Soon after ending her career she began suffering from heart failure, but with medication was able to live a fairly normal life until her death, from pneumonia, in 1974. Because she had appeared briefly in only one motion picture (*Stage Door Canteen,* 1942) and in only two television productions (*The Barretts* 1956; *There Shall Be No Night* 1957) she is not known to younger generations.

Katharine Cornell went to Broadway when an increase in new theatres was a reflection of a nationwide boom. During the first two decades of the century the theatre, as well as vaudeville and burlesque, were popular modes of entertainment. Unfortunately, a theatrical syndicate, consisting of six men, controlled most of the theatres and forced their terms and booking arrangements on actors and rival managers. Actors who refused to comply with the demands of these men were excluded from syndicated theatres. Because financial profit motivated the managers, plays that appealed to the masses received priority. Consequently, plays were not "exclusively crass" but they were largely lacking in artistic quality (Taubman, 1965, p. 133).

Broadway welcomed the great international stars, such as Parisian-born Sarah Bernhardt and Italy's foremost actress, Eleanora Duse, who intrigued and inspired Americans and drew them to the theatre. At her father's theatre, as a child, Kit (nickname for Katharine) saw the stars' photographs in the lobby and became fascinated with the world of the theatre.

While American audiences were being entertained by European stars they were also seeing the emergence of native actors and actresses. Among the women were Ethel Barrymore, Mary Pickford, Lillian Gish, Ruth Gordon, Maude Adams, Laurette Taylor, Ina Claire, Theda Bara, Lenore Ulric, "a tot named Helen Hayes" and many others (Taubman, 1965, p. 132). When she was very young, Kit was inspired by Maude Adams in her role of *Peter Pan* to become a part of the theatre.

Although acting was in her blood from early childhood, Katharine Cornell did not wholeheartedly commit herself to the theatre until she fell in love with Guthrie McClintic. After the completion of her schooling at Oaksmere finishing school in Mamaroneck, New York, she was unsure of what she wanted to do, so she returned to Oaksmere to coach drama and athletics. New York beckoned, but she was in no hurry to get there until

Edward Goodman's off-hand invitation to look him up when she came sounded as though he had a part for her.  At any rate, her career had a rather late start.  When Guthrie McClintic entered Kit's life he became her "force," providing the drive and direction she needed.  He saw in her extraordinary qualities that "seemed to crystallize" on stage; he knew she belonged there (McClintic, 1955, p. 193).  He taught her a great deal about acting, especially how to listen.  During apprenticeship years with the Washington Square Players and Jessie Bonstelle's stock company some critics saw in Miss Cornell a unique quality not unlike that of the great Italian actress Eleanora Duse.  Being poor at first readings, Katharine Cornell did not impress casting directors, but those who saw her after she had developed a role recognized her talent.

Soon after her entrance onto Broadway in *Nice People* (1921), Katharine Cornell was acknowledged to have great promise.  With hard work, diligence, discipline and the guidance of Guthrie McClintic, who was becoming one of the principal Broadway directors, she began to take a prominent place among actresses whose qualities were quite different from hers.  Harold Isaacs of *Newsweek* reported that, although she lacked the "facility of Helen Hayes, the uninhibited genius of Judith Anderson, or the enameled brilliance of Lynn Fontanne," Miss Cornell had "a distinctive emotional quality" in her acting and in her person.  "She does not scintillate, she shines.  She does not sparkle, she glows," he wrote (Isaacs, 1948, p. 83).

Critical acclaim came when she played Jo in *Little Women* (1919) in London.  By a stroke of luck, British actor Alan Pollock had seen her in the London production and insisted on casting her as Sydney in *The Bill of Divorcement (1921)*.  She was a hit and received her first significant attention from critics.

After a string of parts in which she received plaudits for pathetic or sinful roles, Miss Cornell was cast in the title role in *Candida* (1924), which enabled her to demonstrate her ability.  Her outstanding portrayal made Candida a star role when, in earlier productions, the play's characters were considered to be of equal importance and merit.  Following *Candida*, she played Iris March in *The Green Hat* (1925) with such success that she became a star.  This meant that her name appeared in lights on the marquee and that the play had a long run--her first.

Iris, a sensational role, was followed by others of the same type, which pleased the public but not her critics.  Shocked and angered when she appeared in *Dishonored Lady* (1930), the critics predicted Miss Cornell's demise unless she turned from tarnished women to roles worthy of her ability and plays of "richer dramatic substance" (Young, 1927, p. 208).

Despite the competition of movies, the decade of the twenties brought a creative drive, new works, a new group of critics, designers, and directors as well as an increase in the number of Broadway plays, of which an immoderate amount were trash.  As motion pictures increased, drawing actors and good talent to Hollywood, road show business dwindled.  Meanwhile, in New York, a movement for better drama, which had been rumbling for some time, gathered momentum.  The Actors' Equity was formed and, after a strike in 1919, producers gave in to shabbily treated performers.  The twenties stimulated the formation of new cooperative groups such as the Actors' Theatre, the Dramatists Theatre and other organizations "dedicated to artistic production" (Hughes, 1951, p. 390).

The critics' outburst over Miss Cornell's selection of plays coincided with her purchase of the rights to *The Barretts of Wimpole Street* (1931) for Guthrie.  He insisted that she play Elizabeth, but they could find no producer who would take the risk of investing in the play.  The time seemed right for her to gain control over her performances, as leading actresses Mrs. Fiske and Eva Le Gallienne had already done by forming their own companies. The McClintics organized the C. & M. C. Company (for Cornell and McClintic) in 1930, with Miss Cornell as actress-manager and McClintic as director. Their first venture, *The Barretts of Wimpole Street* (1931), was the greatest success of her career, artistically, financially and emotionally. It launched her as an actress-manager and enabled her to produce plays of high quality. Furthermore, the feat was accomplished with the nation in the depths of the Great Depression. Miss Cornell had now become a strong part of the intellectual force and commitment that not only enabled theatre to survive the war, the encroachment of movies and the Depression but, also, to enjoy its best years from 1920 to 1940.

During the remainder of her career she appeared in classics, plays by American and European dramatists, and several plays written specifically for her. To each production the McClintics gave their best, choosing the finest actors available and sparing no expense to achieve excellence.

Katharine Cornell experienced the peaks of success and the valleys of failure with grace. Many of the critics praised her magnetic "presence," and when plays such as *Lucrece* and *Alien Corn* disappointed them, they faulted the plays, not her. Of course, she had her detractors but they were outnumbered by her devotees and a loyal public.

After *The Barretts* Miss Cornell's next triumph was Juliet in *Romeo and Juliet* (1934). For it she received a four-star rating and the New York Drama League Award. She had been preceded by many fine actresses: Eva Le Gallienne, whose Juliet was excellent; Jane Cowl's Juliet, in 1923, who had been hailed as the greatest of her generation; and Ethel Barrymore's portrayal which, running concurrently with Cowl's performance, had failed. Brooks Atkinson saw Cornell's Juliet as "a complete re-creation--with the suppleness of an actress and the imperious quality of an artist who plays from within" (*New York Times,* 12/21/34). Other critics agreed that she was unequaled by other Juliets of her generation. Even the lovely Vivien Leigh, who played Juliet with "grace and eloquence" six years later, did not attain the distinction of Cornell's Juliet. The production was disappointing and a financial disaster for Miss Leigh and Laurence Olivier who played Romeo (Vickers, 1988, p. 124).

Miss Cornell's next play, *Flowers of the Forest* (1935), was not a success. Critics applauded the acting but found the author did not forcefully carry through with his theme or give it emotional depth (Atkinson, 4/9/35). Cornell proved her resiliency by reaching her zenith in her following production, *Saint Joan* (1936). Critic John Anderson claimed that she played with "an inner glow," letting "that quality of sheer faith shine through as the sun would if she were a stained-glass saint instead" (Anderson, 3/10/36).

Her next role, Oparre in *The Wingless Victory,* was so exhausting that she decided to take a year's sabbatical for rest and introspection. The time-consuming task of making up her entire body, the weight of the child she carried up and down the stairs and the emotional intensity of her role had depleted her.

Revitalized by her leave, Miss Cornell returned to do *Herod and Mariamne* (1938). The beauty of the production, particularly the last scene, and Miss Cornell's luminosity were praised, but the drama itself was criticized for its long speeches and distracting details. A failure on the tryout, it was not taken to New York.

Guthrie, to whom failure meant "try again," urged her to do *No Time for Comedy* (1939), an unlikely choice inasmuch as she had a real fear of comedy. Despite her trepidation, it was a great hit and her third largest money-maker.

After the long run and 31-week tour of *No Time for Comedy,* Miss Cornell appeared in *The Doctor's Dilemma (1941).* This, too, was successful but, with the outbreak of World War II, she began having more financial losses. The plays she chose, particularly *Rose Burke* (1942), did not appeal to wartime audiences. However, critics were enthusiastic about the benefit revival of one of her finest roles, the lead in *Candida* (1942) and her production of *The Three Sisters* (1942) which achieved the longest run of any Chekhov play in the United States. The play's success was a credit to the brilliant all-star cast and McClintic's artistry. Ironically, Ruth Gordon, who had urged Guthrie to do *The Three Sisters* so she could play Masha, the role he gave to Miss Cornell, received the most praise for her Natasha.

The most moving experiences in Katharine Cornell's life came when she took *The Barretts* to the servicemen in the European War Theater. Despite objections of the Special Services Division and other authorities that a romantic love story would not appeal to men at war, the GIs loved the play and loved Miss Cornell for bringing it to them.

Following the overseas tour, Miss Cornell undertook to do *Antigone* (1946) which she had seen in Paris. The production was a mixture of classical and modern. Some of the acting was excellent even though characters were poorly drawn, but the play did not have appeal for the critics or the public. Because of poor box office receipts, it was played in repertory with *Candida* and closed after a short run.

Next, the McClintics did a lavish production of Shakespeare's *Antony and Cleopatra* (1947). Although in 1907, Constance Collier had set a record of 90 productions, the recent endeavors of Jane Cowl and Tallulah Bankhead to do the Shakespearean play had been failures. Some critics felt that Miss Cornell lacked passion and wickedness in her portrayal of Cleopatra, but it was generally judged to be one of her "crowning achievements" (Moss, 1974, p. 96). With 251 performances giving the play the longest run in its history, Miss Cornell far surpassed Collier's record. However, the play lost money because of the high production costs.

Her second comedy, *The Constant Wife* (1951), which had been one of Ethel Barrymore's greatest successes, became Miss Cornell's most profitable venture. Critics who thought the production lacked the brightness of Barrymore's hit were outnumbered. The proof of its appeal was in the box office receipts.

The decline of her popularity came with the rise of psychological realism, a new type of drama embraced by New York audiences, but not yet accepted by road audiences. They demonstrated their gratitude for her years of bringing theatre to them by remaining devoted and loyal until the end of her career.

As she grew older, suitable roles for her were not being written; her grand style of acting and the kind of plays she preferred had become passé. By 1960, the 12 million dollars she had grossed and put back into her productions was depleted. Seven of her last eight plays had lost money and she decided it was time to stop.

Had she been more flexible or had she been willing to play repellent women, anti-heroines, she might have withstood the changes of time. However, she would not compromise, said her stage manager Gertrude Macy in our interview, for she felt that she could affect or influence someone's life if she reached that person emotionally. Letters from fans attested to the effect she had on many of them. One stated that she had been "lifted out" of herself when she saw *Antigone* (1946). A second wrote that "there is always nobility in your acting." Another thanked her for always being "a constructive force and influence for good in American life."

By 1960 the years of hard work and the diligence it took to maintain her high standards had taken their toll. She was weary and, after Guthrie's death in 1961, she lost her desire to continue.

For three decades as actress-manager Katharine Cornell was one of the leading ladies of the theatre. She had strived for excellence, taking good plays to audiences throughout America. She never lost consideration or respect for her audiences and fellow actors, nor did she choose plays for the money they would make or seek the limelight for herself. To the end she remained the gracious lady that her fans desired her to be.

In the foreword of *Leading Lady: The World and Theatre of Katharine Cornell* Martha Graham, modern dance pioneer who has been acclaimed as a foremost artist of our century, paid a fitting to tribute to her friend Kit. Of her, Miss Graham wrote, "she has this once left something even her exit cannot take away: the innocence of greatness" (Mosel and Macy, 1978, p. vi).

## The Format of This Book

This book is intended as a reference for Katharine Cornell's distinguished theatrical career from the 1920s through the 1950s. The major aspects of her career encompass her early years of apprenticeship, her early Broadway years, her years as actress-manager, several radio presentations, the one film in which she appeared, two television dramas, a few recordings, and the roles she could have played, but did not. Finally, an extensive bibliography, her honors and awards as well as her publications are included.

My interest in Katharine Cornell began in my high school years and continued through my study of drama in college and The Neighborhood Playhouse, School of the Theatre, in New York. The details I have been able to assemble are from articles, reviews, interviews, books, letters, her autobiography and my own observations from seeing her in several productions. Many of these materials, retained in scrapbooks and boxes at the Performing Arts Research Center at Lincoln Center in New York City, are yellowed and brittle. Sources of many reviews and articles have crumbled away or were only partially recorded, making  some documentation incomplete. The most useful sources consulted for the biography were Katharine Cornell as told to Ruth Woodbury Sedgwick, *I Wanted to Be An Actress: The Autobiography of Katharine Cornell*; Guthrie McClintic, *Me and Kit*; Tad Mosel and Gertrude Macy, *Leading Lady: The World and Theatre of Katharine Cornell*; Gladys Malvern, *Curtain Going Up*; Linda Towle Moss, "A Historical Study of Katharine Cornell As An Actress-Producer, 1931-1960." Additional major sources include reviews and articles by Brooks Atkinson, John Mason Brown, Edith J. R. Isaacs, Louis Kronenberger, Burns Mantle, S. J. Woolf, Alexander Woollcott, Stark Young and many other critics as well as theatre historians.

To begin, the brief biography and chronology are intended to highlight the major events of Katharine Cornell's life and career. The biography is also meant to convey the dedication, self-discipline, professionalism and sensitivity of a woman who took seriously her responsibility to her audiences and fellow actors. Her ability to maintain high standards and integrity through failure and despite criticism was one of her most admirable qualities. Another stellar quality was her sense of fairness and protectiveness of an actor's vulnerability.

The next section, focusing on Stage Appearances, is divided into the early years of her apprenticeship, her Broadway years, and her years as actress-manager. Her radio, film and television appearances, and recordings are combined because of their limited number.

Career events are listed chronologically in each section and numbered consecutively. For example, stage appearances in the early years begin with S0l,

S02,...etc. and continue through the Broadway years with S21,...etc.; radio appearances with R01,... etc., and recordings with D01,...etc.

The chapter following her major career events consists of an annotated bibliography of reference sources (books, magazines, periodicals, trade papers, newspaper articles and reviews, unpublished material and collections) providing information on Katharine Cornell. Bibliographic items are prefixed with entry codes B001, etc.

Appendix A lists her awards and honors. Roles that she could have played (mostly film) appear in Appendix B. Her own publications are listed in Appendix C. The subject index, which refers to both page and entry numbers (such as S10), concludes the book.

Your suggestions for additions, corrections or embellishments for future editions are welcome. They may be sent to me in care of Greenwood Press, Westport, Connecticut.

## Acknowledgments

I wish to express my gratitude to the following institutions and individuals who have been helpful in my research for this book: the University of Cincinnati for a grant in the 1970s which eventually led to this work, the Performing Arts Research Center of the New York Public Library at Lincoln Center, the Cincinnati Public Libraries, the Langsam Library at the University of Cincinnati and all staff members who have been of invaluable assistance.

Among the individuals who have been helpful over the years are Gertrude Macy and Mildred Natwick, who graciously granted me interviews in the 1970s. I am especially grateful to Tad Mosel and Gertrude Macy for their extensive biography and to Miss Macy for saving Miss Cornell's fan letters that I had the privilege of reading. To Linda Towle Moss for her historical study of Miss Cornell's actress-producer years, Gladys Malvern for her biography, and Guthrie McClintic for his autobiography, I express my gratitude. My appreciation also goes to colleagues, former students and friends who have given me support and encouragement: Ernest Weiler, Rudolph Verderber, Warren Lashley, Mary Heider, Cynthia Berryman-Fink, Teresa Sabourin, Hector Currie, Joyce Maurer, Mary Jo Cranley, Leona Cox and others whose names I may have unintentionally omitted.

I give my special thanks to Mary Blair, who invited me to undertake this project and gave me invaluable feedback as well as encouragement; to Marilyn Brownstein, Ann Le Strange, George Butler, and James Robert Parish who have seen this to completion and to Marilyn Schwiers, Evelyn Schott and Victoria Rogers for their help. I am especially indebted to Nancy Jose for her interest, dedication and computer assistance.

I am deeply grateful to my family for their support, especially to my daughter who urged me to undertake this, and to my husband for being so patient and helpful.

# KATHARINE CORNELL

# Biography

When a daughter was born to the Cornells, in Berlin, Germany, on December 16, 1893 (some records give the date as 1898), little did her parents dream that she would become a beautiful woman and renowned actress. They named the tiny girl, who weighed scarcely three pounds, Katharine. She cried, rather screamed, incessantly, no doubt in protest of her early entrance into the world. Her parents' attempts to quiet her were in vain, and the unwelcome gestures of other residents in the pension forced the Cornells to move several times. Their concern for the child's survival and the uncharitable environment prompted Dr. Cornell to cut short his study of medicine in Berlin. When Katharine was almost eight months old, the Cornells sailed to the United States and went home to Mariner Street in Buffalo, New York.

Under the traumatic circumstances of her first months the Cornells could hardly have contemplated a bright future for their daughter. That the frail child possessed the potential of a magnetism and elegance that would project beyond the footlights was unimaginable to the Cornells. Nor did they dream that critics would call her "the most absorbing personality" of the stage and predict that she would be one of the "great American actresses" (B014, p. 108; B251, p. 207; B162, p. 17). They had no expectation that a critic would one day declare their daughter to be "one of the few young women of our American theatre who has in her an understanding of what is called the art of acting" (B166, p. 51). The unprepossessing Cornell child gave her parents no inkling of her potential in those first few months and years of her life.

She grew to have a dedication and the discipline, as well as the physical endowments, to strive for excellence in her endeavors. Once she was firm in her commitment, she willingly sacrificed everything else for the theatre. She worked hard, lived a Spartan existence when performing, maintained her privacy, and abandoned herself to the demands of each role she played. Guided by Willa Cather's concept that art is "a mould in which to imprison for a moment the shining, elusive element which is life itself," she prepared painstakingly for a part (B199, p. 82). No matter how much praise she received, she always felt that she could have done better. In essence, she became dedicated in her quest of perfection as an actress (B074, p. 17).

Out of her sensitivity, innate shyness and the unhappiness she experienced under the harsh discipline of her father, the thoughtless remarks of her grandmother and the early and tragic death of her mother, Katharine Cornell developed a compassionate understanding and responsibility toward others. Her compassion became one of her most striking traits and affected whatever she did. She approached characterizations, as well as her fellow actors and audiences, not to be judgmental, but with the intent of understanding why they behaved as they did (B199, p. 82; B092, p. 20).

Her sensitivity to an actor's fragile ego enhanced her belief that, to stay at the top, "one must have a human and understanding relationship with one's associates" (B047, p. 165). If an actor working for her were to have an illness or experience some personal crisis, she was sympathetic and supportive. If an actor missed rehearsals or gave less than what she considered his best, she reprimanded him tactfully, but firmly, in private.

Christopher Plummer, who became a well-known film star in *The Sound of Music*, other movies and television dramas, played Count Zichy in *The Dark is Light Enough*. Having encountered her discipline and as well as her forgiveness for missing rehearsals and being late for a matinee, he gained a keen appreciation of her as a person and actress. He believed that "she hired people who had a sense of life..." and "gave back the essential quality that people brought to her. Without compromising herself or her standards, she was what you wanted her to be...." (B163, p. 493).

Katharine Cornell forged her way by forming her own company when producers refused to undertake the kind of play she believed had substance and moral integrity. She took this risk even with America in a deep depression. Although road tours had diminished to a few second-rate companies, she uncovered America's hunger for good theatre. By opening the doors of playhouses that had been closed for a generation, she demonstrated that even classics would find an audience if they were played well (B046; p. 29). Her success motivated other road companies to follow her example. Her faith in the public's appreciation for drama was repaid by devoted, loyal fans who would travel miles to see her for as long as she took her plays on the road.

Because of her respect for drama, Katharine Cornell surrounded herself with superior actors (B284). Disliking the star system, she chose supporting casts to enrich the play, not to make herself look better (B040). She and her director husband always focused on "the quality of the play as a whole, its 'higher value'" (B065).

She extended her range to classics, and nurtured new aspiring American actors, playwrights, designers and other artists. She felt it was her responsibility to contribute a sense of well-being to her audiences, to keep fellow actors employed and to be charitable with her talent. Taking first-rate casts to audiences in the hinterlands of America, the European battlefront, and to Israel, she introduced good theatre to many who had never seen a play. Had not Ray Henderson's death thwarted the world tour he was arranging for her, she would have enriched the lives of people in as many as 33 countries. These endeavors affirmed her dedication, sensitivity, integrity and intelligence. Finally, her portrayals provided experiences that lifted those in her audience out of the monotony of their everyday lives. One of her most notable contributions, the 1933-34 repertory tour, occurred at a time "when morale desperately needed a lift" (B218, p. 244).

Fans rewarded her by expressing their gratitude in letters to her. After seeing *The Barretts* overseas, a GI wrote: "We were transported by your magic spell into a different and timeless world." A night police reporter who had seen *Saint Joan* confessed that "night police reporters are traditionally hard-boiled, not given to weeping at plays or writing fan letters but that is what I did and am doing now." Another member of her audience paid her tribute, saying that "...your distinguishing quality is the ability to draw the audience out of themselves so completely that they follow you unresistingly where the playwright leads and they come back infinitely refreshed....Seeing you is like coming onto a high, windy place on a sultry day" (B513).

She set many records in boxoffice receipts and audience attendance. In 1932, *The Barretts* exceeded previous house records in Philadelphia, Baltimore, Detroit and San

Francisco, and made its most outstanding record at the Boston Opera House with its 3000 seats, on March 17, 1945. In Baltimore, Washington, D.C., Boston and Chicago, *Romeo and Juliet* set boxoffice records for classical drama in 1935. *Saint Joan* surpassed all previous attendance at the Shubert in Boston and tied a record in San Francisco. A boxoffice record was broken by *The Wingless Victory* at the National Theatre in Washington, D.C. New house records were set in Buffalo, Toronto, Cincinnati and Cleveland by *The Dark is Light Enough* (Moss, pp. 168-169). Moreover, on her repertory tour, attendance and boxoffice receipts in many one-night stands exceeded past performances.

In spite of formidable successes, there were critics who thought she was not a great actress but a stage personality. She dealt with their criticism by looking ahead and working hard on the next role she was doing. Having learned that the rewards of the stage could be sweet and its penalties bitter, she continued on the path she had chosen, undaunted by the disparaging comments and her failures (B296). Such was to be the future of Katharine Cornell whose uncertain start in life seemed to hold little promise.

Katharine's mother, Alice Plimpton Cornell, was the granddaughter of a successful businessman who had hoped Alice's father, George Plimpton, could eventually take over the family's affairs. However, George had little talent or interest in business. Fortunately, the family had sufficient money to support him while he did as he pleased, which included considerable travel abroad. That meant that his daughter Alice had spent a great deal of her young life in Europe. A pretty woman with a good sense of humor and a love of life, she must have found Buffalo a bit stifling, particularly since she didn't take to the Cornells' proclivity for acting.

Katharine's father, Peter Cortelyou Cornell, was the eldest child of Colonel S. Douglas Cornell, a graduate and later a trustee of Hobart College where his grandfather had once been professor of mathematics. Colonel Cornell had remained in the family house on Delaware Avenue and carried on the lead works built by his father. The Colonel was a popular, likable man with a passion for amateur theatre. He loved to direct plays and had set up a complete theatre in the attic of the Delaware Avenue house when his children were small. In Cobourg, Ontario, where the family spent their summers, an outdoor area at the back of their residence, Hadfield House, served as a stage. In bad weather they took their plays to the town hall or the Cobourg Opera House.

It was natural that Katharine, like her grandfather, her father and his sister Lydia, who developed a repertoire of sketches to perform for charities and social events, would have acting in her blood. In fact, she first appeared as an infant being wheeled across the stage in a baby carriage in *Alice in Wonderland.* As a child, from her lookout on the stairway where she was allowed to watch rehearsals, she became intrigued with the magic world of make-believe.

Because she looked like a boy after losing her hair with scarlet fever, her mother or grandmother began calling her Kit, the name that was used throughout her life by those close to her. It conveyed their respect and affection. Although she was not a pretty child, her Grandmother Plimpton insisted she was beautiful. When her Grandmother Cornell objected to the exaggerated claim, the maternal grandparent retorted that there was "nothing repulsive" about her (B163, p. 19). No doubt her grandmothers had the best of intentions, but that comment and other similar ones left their mark on the sensitive child. Their impact, Kit said in her autobiography, was "seared" in her consciousness. She grew up having no illusions about herself; she knew she was not attractive. Shy and insecure, she found consolation with her imaginary friends.

When Kit was eight years old her father's career change turned her interest more strongly in the direction of the theatre. At that time Peter Cornell gave up his medical career, to which he had not been unduly devoted, to enter professional show business as manager of the Star Theatre. His success in this venture (it seemed everything he touched turned to money) resulted in his managing the Majestic Theatre as well. His new profession provided the opportunity for Kit to see many plays behind the scenes and out front. She studied the posters in the lobby with the glamorous photographs of the great stars and met many of them personally. One of her most treasured possessions was the copy of Sarah Bernhardt's autobiography which the author autographed and gave to her. Jessie Bonstelle, who brought a season of stock to Dr. Cornell's theatre every year, was especially taken with the child and allowed her to watch rehearsals. One day she said, "Hurry and grow up and play Jo [in *Little Women*] for me (B047, p. 8).

At the time, Kit's insecurity prevented her from daring to dream of a career in acting, so when she was asked what she wanted to be when she grew up, she always said "a trained nurse" (B163, p. 37). However, it is clear in her autobiography with Sedgwick and Malvern's biography of her that Kit was always drawn to the theatre (B047, B139).

She was at ease only when she was outdoors or engaged in sports. A natural athlete, she learned tennis and became runner-up for the city championship. She was also amateur swimming champion of Buffalo. She rode horseback, climbed trees and raced through the lobby of her father's theatre on roller skates. An expert gymnast, she took part in a circus for charity. On the program was a professional acrobat whose performance on the slack wire fascinated her. Her interest in wanting to learn the art prompted him to make her a present of his slack wire.

Keeping it secret from her father, she strung the wire up in the backyard and, after hours of practice, could balance with a parasol. She became the attraction of neighborhood friends, mostly boys, who soon prevailed upon her to teach them. When rumors of mishaps reached her father, he quickly brought an end to her acrobatic escapades.

After the banishment of the slack wire, she dared the neighborhood boys to match her exploits in the streets. They followed her leadership until they evidently became tired of being outdone by a girl and bullied her to prove that she was, after all, just a girl. Again, she took refuge in her backyard, playing dress-up with her imaginary friends.

Her athletic pursuits and make-believe world enabled her to endure her father's unexplained restrictions and punishments that added to her sense of inadequacy. Despite the family's financial comfort and other advantages, a childhood that should have been happy was not. She was never able to please her father. Even after she became a success and he boasted of the pride he took in her, she never overcame the feeling that she hadn't measured up to his expectations. Nor did he ever demonstrate his confidence in her by offering financial backing for any of her plays, a gesture he could have well afforded.

In her autobiography she told Ruth Woodbury Sedgwick that it was seeing Maude Adams in *Peter Pan,* in 1905, that left her stagestruck. When the plain little woman, who did not possess the beauty of the other stars, burst through the window and flew about the stage, Kit knew that she wanted to devote her life to the theatre.

After kindergarten Kit attended St. Margaret's School where she appeared in school pageants. At age fourteen she wrote a play entitled "Patty en tension" in French which was given before a large audience at St. Margaret's School. She also directed and appeared in the play. An article in the *Buffalo Commercial* praised the presentation and commended the acting ability and talent of Dr. and Mrs. Peter Cornell's daughter. At the end of her eighth grade, which was also the twentieth anniversary of the School's founding, Kit appeared as the Live Snowman, the star in "An Arctic Carnival," and played the title role in "Mr. Kris Kringle." Her experiences with amateur theatricals made her want to know more about plays; she could frequently be found in the library with her face buried in a book of them.

As Mosel and Macy noted in their biography of her, somewhere in her teens Kit seemed to go suddenly "from plain and homely straight to beautiful with no stops between..." (B163, p. 41). Boys were aware of it; she was not. In fact, she carried the insecurity about her looks throughout her life. In her autobiography she admitted that the fear and shyness resulting from her unattractiveness had to be overcome each time she went before an audience or met new people.

In 1908, at the end of the eighth grade, Kit was sent to Oaksmere, a finishing school for preparing young women for social life, in Mamaroneck, New York. There, the headmistress, Mrs. Merrill, encouraged her to develop her athletic abilities and theatrical talents, the things she loved most.

Her continued participation in sports gave her the grace, agility and physical responsiveness that were to be her greatest assets in acting. Her favorite subjects were history of the novel, the Bible and psychology, which gave her an understanding of people. She pursued her dramatic interests by writing pantomimes, acting in them, directing them and preparing the sets. She was most intense about directing, especially outdoor productions staged against the rocky coast. She also became a voracious reader and reveled in the opportunity to see Broadway plays.

In 1911, Kit was graduated from Oaksmere and her Aunt Lucy Plimpton took her abroad as a graduation gift. She considered applying for entrance into Bryn Mawr, but changed her mind when she saw the entrance exams. She seemed not to know what she would do when Mrs. Merrill invited her to return to Oaksmere to teach drama and coach athletics. She accepted the opportunity.

At this time the little theatre movement had begun and there was great interest in amateur theatre. With the general public interest and Kit's enthusiasm, drama flourished at Oaksmere.

During her years of teaching, she frequently visited Buffalo to attend to her mother whose alcoholism had claimed her beauty and was taking her life. Unfortunately, Alice Cornell had sunk too far to respond to her daughter's loving care. She died of a heart attack on June 19, 1915, shortly before her forty-fifth birthday. Her death left Kit with a deep sadness and a great compassion for others as well as sufficient money to become independent of her father.

She returned to Oaksmere in the fall of 1915, and threw herself into a heavy schedule of a new play every two weeks. Outside directors were brought from New York. Kit played Napoleon in Shaw's *Man of Destiny*, and Malvolio in *Twelfth Night* with Theresa Helburn, who played the role of Sir Toby Belch and directed the show. Kit also wrote a comedy, entitled "Play," which Edward Goodman of the Washington Square Players directed. At the end of the production Goodman made a comment which she interpreted as practically "an engagement" when he said, "If you're thinking of going into the theatre, let me know when you come to New York" (B047, p. 9). The invitation gave her the impetus to leave Oaksmere at the end of the term and go to New York.

Once she had finally made the move to New York, accompanied by Aunt Lucy Plimpton as chaperon, Kit haunted the business offices of the Washington Square Players in the Comedy Theatre. The warm welcome she anticipated from Eddie Goodman was not forthcoming but he did finally invite her to join some other actors who were going to be reading, if she liked. Always a miserable first reader she became paralyzed and could not utter a sound. Of course, she was dismissed.

Not to be defeated, she decided that she needed some coaching in acting and sought the help of Florence Enright who, as a visiting director at Oaksmere, had been very kind to her. Miss Enright suggested that Kit watch rehearsals and prevailed upon Eddie Goodman to allow her to watch *Bushido* which he was directing. Goodman asked her to substitute for one of the girls who played Shusai, a Japanese mother whose part was only four words. Kit seized the opportunity and when the girl left the show, she got the part. Her debut in a semi-professional show just off Broadway occurred in December, 1916. Later, she did the offstage cries of a mother in childbirth in Andreyev's *The Life of Man* (1916).

Her first real part was in *Plots and Playwrights* (1917), a Harvard prize play by Edward Massey, which opened March 26, 1917. Heywood Broun in the *New York Tribune* and Burns Mantle in the *New York Evening Mail* made favorable comments. Mantle saw her as "the most promising actress of the present season" (B163, p. 68). Another unofficial critic in the audience, Guthrie McClintic, who was working for producer Winthrop Ames, saw the show and scribbled on his program next to the name of Katharine Cornell: "Interesting--monotonous--watch" (B149, p. 160).

During the run of *Plots and Playwrights*, Kit was introduced to William Faversham who asked her to play the leading woman's role in his play, *The Old Country*. Knowing that she was not ready for a big part, she refused the offer. It was probably a wise decision as the show ran for only 15 performances.

The Washington Square Players asked her to return for a second season with them. She played Mis' Cary Ellsworth in Zona Gale's *Neighbors* (1918), and Mrs. Frank Darrel in Grace Latimer Wright's *Blind Alleys* (1918). *The New York Times* reviewer commented on her "distinguished spirits, marked intelligence and increasing skill" (B163, p. 70). That season she also appeared in *Yum Chapab* (1918) and *The Death of Tintagiles* (1918).

In the spring of 1918, Jessie Bonstelle approached her with an offer to play the "fifth business" woman in her company which would open in Buffalo and move to Detroit. She was expected to play any part other than the lead, the heavy, the character woman or the ingenue. The opportunity was too good to turn down even though the Washington Square Players would have liked her to finish out their season.

Kit's first job as a paid professional (she made $50 a week) was the role of Grace Palmer in *Cheating Cheaters* (1918), which Marjorie Rambeau had played with success on Broadway the previous season. Since the part was a straight one, Grace Palmer's appearance was important, so for her first appearance in Buffalo Kit went into debt for an elegant dress. The local paper carried an editorial the next morning about Miss Katharine Cornell of whom, it said, both Buffalo and Dr. Peter Cornell could be proud.

*Cheating Cheaters* was followed by *Seven Chances* (1918), a play described as "a David Belasco nothing" (B163, p. 75). In the third week of the season Kit played Signora Vannucci in *Romance* (1918) by Edward Sheldon. The Signora was a middle-aged Italian lady-in-waiting to a famous opera singer who had one good scene in the play, at the opening of the last act. Kit went to the University of Buffalo for coaching in Italian diction and drew laughs throughout the scene. Reviewers were enthusiastic about her ability.

*Pals First* (1918) followed *Romance*. She played an aging southern spinster who was deaf. The part was slight but as a reviewer wrote, it was "...one of the funniest things in the play" (B163, p. 76). In her fifth week she had what she considered to be one of her better roles and one she loved playing--Dora, a cockney girl. Again, she won plaudits from reviewers.

After 14 plays in Buffalo the company went on to Detroit where they opened with *The Man Outside* (1918) at the Garrick Theatre. Kit delighted the audience and reviewers compared her acting to the manner of Lynn Fontanne.

The season ended October 20, 1918, after 10 performances a week and a new play every Monday. Having had the best training in the best stock company, Kit returned to New York, but the Washington Square Players had closed. She was making the rounds of agents' offices when Jessie Bonstelle called to tell her she had a part for her in a play she was directing for Grace George. When Kit was handed the script and asked to be the first reader, the fear that she always experienced on first readings gripped her; she mumbled inaudibly. Stopping her, Miss George asked, "You don't think you can do this part, do you, Miss Cornell?" (B047, p. 17). Kit left in tears; in fact, she disappeared for two days. Upon her return, she learned that Miss George had asked her to read again and had concluded, from Kit's disappearance, that she didn't have "the right stuff in her" (B047, p. 18).

Not liking to be told she was wrong about talent, Jessie Bonstelle gave Kit a tongue-lashing, then ordered her to try out as a replacement for Marcelle in William A. Brady's third road company of *The Man Who Came Back* (1918). Kit followed her mentor's orders and John Cromwell, the director, hired her. The show opened in Providence five days later. Reviewers were complimentary and treated her as the star although she was the second lead. It was her first touring experience and she loved it.

At the end of the tour she returned immediately to Bonstelle's company. That spring and summer she played second leads in Buffalo and Detroit. The opening show was *Ann's Adventure* (1919), later played by Grace George as *Ruined Lady*. Reviews were more than kind to Kit and she and the leading lady, Esther Howard, became good friends.

With the ending of World War I and the Actors' Equity strike, William Brady, at the insistence of Jessie Bonstelle, was staging his London production of *Little Women* (1919) and asked Kit to play the part of Jo. Tired from the rigorous schedule of summer stock, Kit had already refused Brady's offer to do the long tour of *The Man Who Came Back*. She said "no" to Brady, but could not withstand Bonstelle's persuasion and finally accepted the role.

Once in England, the after-effects of the war created problems and delays for the production and, adding to the tension, Miss Bonstelle was particularly demanding and critical of Kit in rehearsals. This especially rankled Leslie Faber, who played the Professor, so much that he confronted Miss Bonstelle about what he perceived to be her unfair treatment of Miss Cornell. Having overheard the confrontation, Kit went to her distraught mentor to assure her that she understood that Miss Bonstelle was only helping her and that the English actors simply didn't appreciate that. Miss Bonstelle confessed that she was pushing Kit to do her best because she wanted her "to be a truly great actress," not a stock actress who, like herself, hadn't succeeded. Her mentor's concern and expectations increased Kit's admiration of her. Miss Bonstelle pulled herself together and the show went on (B139).

It opened November 10, 1919, at the New Theatre in London with a series of matinees (no evening performances) forced upon them by the crowded theatre bookings. However, the demand for *Little Women* was so great that the regularly scheduled show closed, giving the evenings over to *Little Women*. Londoners flocked to see Kit; they loved the vitality and spice she gave to a play that they could have otherwise ridiculed for its sentimentality. Word of her success, of course, reached America, but did not particularly impress casting directors.

When *Little Women* was about to close in London, Kit received a cable from Brady and Bonstelle asking her to stay on to play Marcelle in the London production of *The Man Who Came Back* if Mary Nash, who had been given first choice, refused the role. Nash accepted it, so Kit sailed for home to join the stock company, this time to alternate leads with Jessie Bonstelle. Bonstelle had hired a new director for her 1920 season--his name was Guthrie McClintic.

Sometime between 1917 and 1919, Kit and Guthrie had met at a meeting where organization of the Theatre Guild was being discussed. Each reported the date differently but they did remember their impressions of one another. She recalled that he was "a pale, frail creature" (B047, p. 12); he was struck by her "mystic aura" and "curious, haunting luminosity". From the time of their first meeting he felt her greatness as a woman. (B149, p. 193).

They met again in Brady's office when they signed their stock company contracts. This time there was no doubt in McClintic's mind that he would someday marry her. First, he had to dissolve the clandestine marriage he had entered with Estelle Winwood, a British actress he called "this lady," and whose name he would not disclose. She was ten years his senior (B149, p. 109).

As he got to know Kit, Guthrie appreciated her "warm generosity," and respected her "discipline and capacity for work." He also became aware of her "acute shyness and diffidence." He felt, that around her, there was "an eerie sensation of distillation of spirit--something you find away from the haunts of man, deep in a forest...or in the middle of the ocean at the dead of night" (B149, p. 193).

During the season with Bonstelle, Kit and Guthrie fell in love. He directed all the plays in which she appeared and, because she was such a slow study, coached her privately to save time in rehearsals for the other actors. He delighted in watching the development of her technique and her projection of the "womanly greatness" that had first struck him.

The first play of the season was *Heaven* (1920) which John Golden had asked Jessie Bonstelle to try out for him so that he could see Kit in the lead role. The audience went wild over her performance but she didn't get the part, which wasn't too much of a disappointment for her as she didn't think she was ready for it. Later, the play was shown in New York as *Seventh Heaven* and in Hollywood with Janet Gaynor.

In *Daddy-Long-Legs* (1920) she was, as she admitted, "miscast and incredibly bad" in the Ruth Chatterton part (B047, p. 28). That was followed by *Too Many Husbands* (1920), one of the few roles in which she felt comfortable, and *Lombardi, Ltd.* (1920), a farce she enjoyed. When they closed the season with *Civilian Clothes* (1920), she had begun to feel that she couldn't make it. The hectic schedule and Bonstelle's disapproval of Guthrie had been stressful. She also knew she worked too slowly to become a good stock actress.

She had worked hard and learned a great deal but when she returned to New York, there was no job waiting for her and, again, she had to make the rounds of agents' offices. However, this time was different; one great change had occurred in her. From the time that she fell in love with Guthrie, she had no doubt about her commitment to acting. Guthrie provided the drive and direction she needed to succeed in her desire to be an actress.

She made her Broadway debut as Eileen Baxter-Jones on March 1, 1921, in Rachel Crothers' *Nice People* with Francine Larrimore and Tallulah Bankhead, who had the daring, unconventional qualities that suited her perfectly for the role. The play was a big success and fun for Kit even though she did not make a "lasting" impression. She had hopes that the next season would be better, and it was.

While waiting for Guthrie's divorce to become final, they leased and sublet a house at 23 Beekman Place, in Manhattan, that would be their home when they married. Guthrie had also found a play, *Dover Road*, to direct and he wanted her to play the role of Anne but she was hesitant about the part. Then they read *A Bill of Divorcement* and she knew immediately that she wanted to play Sydney Fairfield.

Guthrie suggested the play to Winthrop Ames, who learned that the British actor Allan Pollock owned the rights to the play. Fortunately for her, Pollock was looking for an American actress to play the role when two elderly Scot ladies from his home in Scotland, who had seen *Little Women*, were dining with him and mentioned that the girl who played Jo would be a wonderful Sydney. As it happened, Pollock had also seen the show but couldn't remember the name of the actress who played Jo. His friend Leslie Faber supplied it and, about two weeks after the McClintics read the play, the Dillingham office notified Kit that Pollock wanted her for the part.

As the story is told in her biography by Mosel, Dillingham's casting director, Fred Latham, was unimpressed with Kit in *Nice People,* advised Pollock against using her and urged him to wait until he arrived in New York and could see her again. However, Pollock was adamant in his decision so Latham had no choice but to hire her.

On September 8, 1921, Kit and Guthrie were married in Cobourg at the home of her Aunt Lydia Cornell, despite her father's strong disapproval. Dr. Cornell finally relented, attended the ceremony and, eventually, the two men became friends.

The day after their wedding *A Bill of Divorcement* (1921) went into rehearsal. The director, Basil Dean, gave Kit the week-end off for a honeymoon. It was taken as a generous gesture but, in reality, after hearing her bad first reading, Dean had hoped she wouldn't return. Anyway, he wanted Meggie Albanesi, who had played the part in London, but Dean's hopes were not fulfilled; Pollock didn't fire Kit.

Opening reviews of *A Bill of Divorcement* were poor. There were five openings that night and only three of the first-string critics were present to see *A Bill of Divorcement*. Their reviews were discouraging. However, good fortune prevailed. Carl Van Vechten, author and music critic, was in the audience and thought the play was wonderful. He called Alexander Woollcott, urging him to see it and to do something to save the play. Rushing to the matinee, Woollcott agreed with Van Vechten. Immediately he spread the word to other critics and wrote an excellent review for *The New York Times*. Soon, requests for tickets were so great that the management, who had cancelled the theatre after the opening, had to find another theatre. The play was a hit and ran for 173 performances. It marked the end of Kit's apprenticeship.

After her success as Sydney Fairchild, a number of managers made offers to the promising newcomer. Al Woods wanted her to sign a contract that would make her a star but she refused because she didn't like the star system.

When *A Bill of Divorcement* and Guthrie's production of *The Dover Road* closed, the McClintics took a vacation abroad. In England, Kit met Clemence Dane (pen name of British actress Winifred Ashton), and asked her to play Mary Fitton in *Will Shakespeare* (1923), also by Dane. She accepted it as her next role.

Mary Fitton, a part calling for physical agility, was well suited to Kit's gymnastic expertise, even though critic Heywood Broun thought her bouncing about needed more restraint lest she break a table or chair. Critics did not like the play and, after 80 performances, it closed on March 11, 1923.

Immediately she went into rehearsal for *The Enchanted Cottage* (1923), written by Sir Arthur Wing Pinero and directed by Miss Bonstelle. Kit thought that Laura

Pennington was "an exquisite person to play," but the show was badly stage-managed (B047, p. 56). Moreover, neither the critics nor the audiences were enthusiastic. It, too, had a short run.

In 1923, just when their finances were at their lowest because of the two failures that each had experienced (Guthrie's *Gringo* and *The Square Peg*), 23 Beekman Place went up for sale. The McClintics managed to scrape together a down payment to buy it. Also that year, Kit had committed herself to do *Casanova* (1923), which meant she could not be considered for the world premiere of Shaw's *Saint Joan* that the Theatre Guild was planning.

Kit was eager to play the role of Henriette in *Casanova* even though it was a very small part. It offered the opportunity of a dual characterization as the mistress of Casanova and as their young daughter. The press was kind to her, but to Lowell Sherman, who played Casanova, they were "rotten" (B047, p. 62). The play opened at the Empire on September 26, 1923, and closed 77 performances later on December 2, 1923.

Kit's next venture was *The Way Things Happen* (1924), written by Clemence Dane and directed by McClintic. Her role as Shirley Pride had one good scene. On opening night, Kit received 21 curtain calls for that scene. However, the play, which had gone well in the Philadelphia tryout, ran only 24 performances in New York.

As a favor to William Harris, Jr., Kit replaced the leading actress in *The Outsider* (1924), a role she had turned down because of her commitment to *The Way Things Happen*. Furthermore, the play had already received bad reviews in its Baltimore tryout. With only six days of rehearsal, a run-through in Stamford, and one dress rehearsal, the play opened in New York, March 3, 1924. The play seemed doomed, but the insight and compassion Kit gave to the crippled Lalage won her critical acclaim. Of all her plays thus far, this was the most successful financially. After a 13-week run, the late-season hit was closed by the Actors' Equity strike.

For the next season, David Belasco offered Kit the role of Suzanne in *Tiger Cats* (1924), an adaptation of a French play, *Les Félines*. Although the play was disagreeable and Suzanne was "the most horrible" woman she had known, Kit took the part for the discipline it would require and to avoid typecasting (B047, p. 67). The play was a miserable experience for her. She couldn't play the part as Edith Evans had done it in England, which was what the author wanted, and she didn't get along well with the leading man, Robert Loraine. Through Belasco's intervention she was allowed to play the role as she felt it should be, and the author admitted it was an improvement. Much to Kit's relief, the play expired after 48 performances.

The group that made up Actors' Theatre, which had been formed by Francis Wilson during the strike of 1919, decided that the great actors of the stage should have the opportunity of playing their favorite roles in a few special matinees as "a kind of intramural activity" (B163, p. 179). The problem was that few great actors had the time.

In 1924, someone had the idea of doing *Candida* because it required only six players, none of whom were considered to be in starring roles. Kit played the role of Candida. After three weeks of special matinees, the demand for tickets was so great that *Candida* was made a full bill at the Forty-Eighth Street Theatre. Cornell made Candida so successful that the part became a star role thereafter. As an additional jewel in her crown, one of Kit's admirers, A. Conger Goodyear, arranged to have artist Eugene Speicher paint a portrait of her as Candida.

Before she finished with *Tiger Cats*, Kit had signed a two-play contract with Belasco to do *The Green Hat* and another play. Because the other play had not yet been selected, she was released to do *Candida* and was already rehearsing *The Green Hat* during the *Candida* run. Peggy Wood filled her place when Kit had to leave before the end of *Candida's* run to begin *The Green Hat*.

Guthrie disliked *The Green Hat* and did not want her to do it, but the role of Iris fascinated her. So determined was she, that she violated her contract with Belasco on the grounds that he had not yet found the second play for her. The violation was resolved amicably and Guthrie finally consented to direct. The contrast between her intellectual Candida and her passionate Iris March convinced the critics of her versatility and superb acting ability. *The Green Hat* opened in New York on September 15, 1925, and ran for 29 weeks there, 8 weeks in Boston and then went on tour. When it closed it had run for over two years--her first long run and the first time her name appeared in lights over the theatre. While she was having huge success in New York, Tallulah Bankhead's production in London was not so fortunate (B035, p. 12).

For her next season, Kit was faced with choosing between Eugene O'Neill's *Strange Interlude* and Somerset Maugham's *The Letter*. She chose *The Letter* (1927), not because she liked it but because the author-producer, Messmore Kendall, pursued her until she finally accepted. On opening night, a sensation was created by people blocking traffic to get a glimpse of the star. Although reviews were mixed, the play ran for 13 weeks. Cornell now had her own following.

Stark Young of the *New Republic* panned the play but complimented Miss Cornell. He wrote: "She is moving toward her prime as a woman, she grows more and more effective as a brilliant theatrical presence as she moves on the stage, and more telling as an instrument by which feeling and excitement may be conveyed." He recommended that she should take the risk of doing plays with "richer dramatic substance" (B251, p. 208).

During one of the performances of *The Letter* Miss Cornell received a note from Gertrude Macy, a young woman she and Guthrie had met aboard ship on one of their trips. Kit received her backstage after the show and the outcome of that visit was that Guthrie asked Miss Macy to accompany Kit on a trip abroad when he was unable to do so. Gert jumped at the chance and, soon after, went to work for Miss Cornell, eventually becoming her "General Representative." That, according to Kit, meant that she ran "the whole shooting match," particularly the financial part (B047, p. 84).

At some point during 1928, friends and advisers persuaded Kit to drop five years from her age. Her candidness in disclosing her age and her late entrance into the theatrical world was, they argued, a disadvantage, particularly in playing younger roles. Furthermore, she looked younger than her age. She reluctantly obliged but always felt guilty about the deception which was not revealed until friends gathered to celebrate her 75th birthday and found, much to their surprise, that it was her 80th.

After *The Letter* had closed, Al Woods asked the McClintics to do an adaptation of *Jealousy* by Louis Verneuil. The lead was "another lurid, sensational part" and Kit wanted to do something different, so she did not accept the offer (B047, p. 83).

As it happened, she had bought an adaptation by Margaret Ayer Barnes of Edith Wharton's *The Age of Innocence* in the event that Gilbert Miller would not find her a play for the next season. Her intuition served her well; Miller had not found her a play and told her to go ahead with *The Age of Innocence* (1928). Adjustments were made to meet Miss Wharton's objections to the dramatization of her novel and McClintic directed.

During the pre-Broadway tryout Miss Cornell proved herself to be a real trouper. Despite the excruciating pain she suffered from several mishaps that occurred before the opening in which she fractured a rib and burned her arm, she insisted the show should go on. When the play proceeded to Cleveland, another accident occurred; the joint of a finger was smashed in the limousine door and, again, she refused to give in to the pain. To disguise the bandaged finger she wound a chiffon scarf around it and incorporated the scarf into her characterization. The audience was unaware of the sheer grit it took to play the serene Ellen Olenska (B163, p. 230).

The play opened in New York on November 8, 1928, went to Pittsburgh for a week and returned to New York where it ran for 26 weeks before beginning a 9-week tour.  The critics, happy that she was not playing another tawdry woman, were enthusiastic about *The Age of Innocence* and her beauty, which was enhanced by the stunning period costumes.  Miss Wharton, too, was delighted with the play's success.

If the critics thought Miss Cornell was finished with tawdry women, they did not anticipate her next play, *Dishonored Lady* (1930), which Ned Sheldon and Margaret Ayer Barnes had written for Ethel Barrymore.  When Miss Barrymore had procrastinated in making a decision to do the play, Guthrie bought it for Kit.

*Dishonored Lady* was a sordid exaggeration of the well-known 1857 Glasgow murder case of Madeleine Smith who had killed her secret lover so that she could marry another man.  Despite the unpleasant character, it was an exciting part for Miss Cornell and a popular play with audiences.  It ran for 16 weeks in New York and did a long tour which took her to the Pacific Coast for the first time.

In Los Angeles and San Francisco she played to "sensational business, and a beautiful press" (B047, p. 89)  Many of those in her audience were stars and movie offers came frequently.  Irving Thalberg, a top Metro-Goldwyn-Mayer executive and talent developer, was particularly interested in making a picture with her, but she didn't think she could act in both stage plays and pictures.  Thalberg tried on several occasions to persuade her to do Elizabeth and Juliet.  Eventually his wife, Norma Shearer, played the roles.

Although the audiences liked her in *Dishonored Lady*, the critics did not.  Richard Dana Skinner, in *The Commonweal,* stated that her first-class talent could not "withstand the corrosion of theatrical rubbish" (B212).  According to Mosel, the critics were both shocked and angered that she played the trashy woman so well.  Underlying their anger, Mosel perceived, was the fact that she had tarnished their image of Katharine Cornell (B163, p. 240).

The critics' dissatisfaction with her trashy parts coincided with the decision the McClintics had made which was to be a "cornerstone" in their stage partnership.  When Kit was returning to Los Angeles to finish the tour of *Dishonored Lady*, she read a play that she found so exciting she bought the rights to it for Guthrie.  He shared her enthusiasm but insisted that she play the lead, Elizabeth, in *The Barretts of Wimpole Street.*  She insisted it wasn't right for her, but he was adamant that it was.  Finally, she consented, then continued the tour of *Dishonored Lady.*

When the McClintics decided to do *The Barretts*, their friends Stanton Griffis and A. Conger Goodyear, who had suggested that Kit go into management if she ever found a play she liked, offered to provide the money for the play.  Griffis was a partner in a stock exchange firm, Hemphill and Noyes, and later became a United States ambassador to Poland, Egypt, Argentina and Spain.  Goodyear, former head of the Albright Museum in Buffalo, became founder of the Museum of Modern Art in New York in the 1930s. Gertrude Macy became the third partner.  Griffis and Goodyear advised her that this was the time to become her own manager, a venture that she, Guthrie and Gert Macy had been considering.  Thus, the C. and M. C. (for Cornell and McClintic) Productions was organized for the purpose of allowing Miss Cornell the freedom to do plays she wanted to do, not for making money.  The modest initial investment of $30,000 in *The Barretts* was the beginning of her financial success.

Despite the caveats of well-meaning friends that *The Barretts* would not appeal to the playgoing public, it was so successful that the three investors (Griffis, Goodyear and Macy) were paid back almost immediately. Furthermore, Katharine Cornell was to gross over 12 million dollars during her years as actress-manager. Everyone received a salary, not a percentage, and all of the profits from productions were put back into the business to insure against failures in the future.

The McClintics practiced the policy of discussing business, artistic and casting matters, but Guthrie made most of the final decisions. His artistic decisions were especially meritorious. He was a brilliant director with a true sense of color and a gift for bringing out the actors' talents and setting them to their best advantage. In fact, John Tillinghast, who studied McClintic's directing, remarked that McClintic's ability to give actors the confidence to achieve their best was his greatest asset as a director (B514, p.166). He also had "an eye for stage grouping and a sense of life throbbing through a spacious script," observed Brooks Atkinson (B284). A perfectionist, McClintic spent eight days with the actors sitting around a table reading their parts to establish the overall design and action of the play before they rehearsed on their feet. Having chosen actors who he believed were right for the parts, he saw it as his job "to meld them into a harmonious whole" as much as possible (B149, pp. 243-44).

Kit admired the way Guthrie built up an actor without imposing his own perception of the role so that he destroyed what the actor was "groping for," and she always trusted his judgment (B047, pp. 100-101). One of his great fans, Ruth Gordon, who McClintic had directed in a number of plays, said she "owed half her career" to him because of his guidance (B079, p. 430).

The McClintics' capacity for supporting one another made them a remarkable combination. In fact, they became one of the twentieth century's "most famous and creative" teams, stated theatre historian Garff Wilson (B240, p. 127). Norris Houghton, director and designer, observed that the Cornell-McClintic team was "more than a twosome." They had a penchant for selecting the right people to work with them: their respective general managers, Gertrude Macy and Stanley Gilkey, their press agent Ray Henderson, and several stage managers. They were "a closely knit group of loyal and congenial ladies and gentlemen" and there was "just enough tension to keep everyone on his toes," said Houghton (B101, pp. 121-122). When a play was ready for presentation, it was smooth in "its detail and the overall shape and polish of its action" (B240, p. 247).

As usual, the cast for *The Barretts* (1931) was carefully selected. Guthrie had gone to London to get Brian Aherne, who was to play a captivating Browning. Charles Waldron would play the dour Edward Moulton-Barrett. The greatest casting difficulty came in finding Flush who had to have a good disposition. Finally, an eight-month old cocker spaniel proved to be not only a perfect Flush but, also, the most popular dog of the year.

At the opening night of their first production, February 9, 1931, for the first time "Katharine Cornell Presents--" shone on the marquee. That night *The Barretts* appeared to be a failure. In fact, Stanton Griffis predicted that the McClintics would be "crucified" in the reviews the next morning. Two of the three reviews following the Cleveland tryout had been derogatory and, for the New York opening, a torrential downpour had delayed the arrival of a rain-soaked, disgruntled audience who trickled in and banged down seats during most of the first act. At the beginning of the play only 52 people were seated in the main floor. What's more, Flush had almost walked away with the show when he jumped down from the sofa to investigate the people sitting in the boxes. As his mistress rescued him, the audience applauded. Flush's curiosity dispelled their irritation with the weather and turned their dampened spirits into a general mood of congeniality and receptiveness.

After the show, while the McClintics dejectedly awaited the reviews at 23 Beekman Place, Alexander Woollcott knocked at the door to announce that they had a smash hit. The reviews were laudatory. In fact, *The Barretts* was to break all records at the Empire Theatre.

The critics found fault with the play but had extravagant praise for Miss Cornell. Again, offering her a handsome salary and other enticements, Irving Thalberg tried to lure her to Hollywood to play Elizabeth for MGM. He was so persuasive that she said "yes," then later, panicked and withdrew from the commitment. She did not want future audiences to laugh at her as they had done with the movie of Bernhardt in *Camille*. Moreover, she wanted to play to audiences in the theatre who responded to her and she to them. Among the movie titles she continued to refuse were *The Good Earth* and *For Whom the Bell Tolls*.

Although the role of Elizabeth did not appear to be difficult, it was taxing simply because, dressed in heavy fabrics over several petticoats, she lay with her feet upon the sofa for most of the play. Masses of false curls fell to her shawl-draped shoulders and her lower body was covered with a wool afghan. She was on stage for nearly three hours--for all but the last three minutes of the play--portraying an ill woman who had to project her voice to the last rows. By midsummer the play had been running for six months, and the heat had become oppressive. A lump developed at the base of her skull and she felt a vibration in her head. Fearful that she would be unable to go on with the show and thus jeopardize the jobs of 60 people, they omitted Saturday performances to give her a 3-day week-end for rest at her Sneden's Landing home, 30 miles outside of New York. Doctors could find no physical causes for her ailment except emotional and mental exhaustion. The cast was paid for a 6-week lay-off so that she could rest.

In the middle of the Depression prognosticators said that no show could survive a lay-off, but the show re-opened to a long line of playgoers waiting to buy tickets, and the boxoffice was deluged with mail orders. It appeared that *The Barretts* could run for years. However, Miss Cornell's symptoms and anxiety persisted with more intensity. The McClintics decided to close the New York show in February and, on a week-to-week basis, tour with it through June. After playing 370 performances, the play was closed. A forfeit was paid to the theatre because it was playing to full capacity and, at the announcement of its premature closing, hundreds had to be turned away.

During the run of *The Barretts*, it had been decided to hire Ray Henderson, who had been press representative for Winthrop Ames and a number of the "greats" in the theatre, as press agent for Miss Cornell. Because of his instinct for what the public wanted, his news releases gave her "a public voice" and kept her name before them. When she returned to the theatre after a 6-week lay-off, her audiences were waiting for her. To meet the cost of the production on the 1932 tour of *The Barretts,* the third year of the Depression, the top ticket prices ($3.30) were set slightly higher than those of most touring companies. Even so, every performance played to standees.

Miss Cornell's symptoms, which had subsided temporarily, returned and, this time, she became even more panicky about her condition. A physician at Johns Hopkins finally diagnosed the problem. The position in which she was sitting on the sofa throughout the play had caused the congestion and vibration in her head by putting pressure on a particular vertebra. He suggested changing the position of the sofa, which she refused to do. Somehow, knowing the cause of the problem miraculously cured it, or at least made it tolerable.

Another problem occurred on the tour which made a good story for one of Ray Henderson's press releases. Flush was so well-behaved on stage--he slept through performances--that well meaning elderly ladies were convinced that he was being drugged, and they filed reports with the Society for the Prevention of Cruelty to Animals. When examiners arrived at the theatre they found a bouncy, tail-wagging dog that simply became somnolent in the spotlight. The problem of the kind little ladies was solved by parading Flush amid the theatregoers during intermission where his frolicking dispelled any thought of drug addiction.

A most memorable event of the tour for Miss Cornell was the benefit performance Henderson suggested for the Chicago schoolteachers who were practically destitute. The proceeds of a final matinee, given in the Civic Opera House at a dollar a ticket, were donated to the Teachers' Sick Fund. Within an hour all of the tickets were sold, hundreds were turned away and the teachers received $2,761.

Members of the company also received and witnessed other gestures of Miss Cornell's generosity. Basil Rathbone, who had played Miss Cornell's leading man in each of the plays (Browning, Romeo and the Reverend James Morell) was particularly touched by her consideration of fellow actors and her audiences. During the tour he was suffering some health problems and Miss Cornell insisted that he and his wife take the drawing room on her special coach so that he could be more comfortable. Another instance of her consideration came at the end of the tour when she gave every member of the company an extra week's salary in appreciation of their work. Moreover, her generosity toward her audiences explained why they became loyal fans. As an actress, she always gave them her best. Rathbone had high praise for the leading ladies she played in the tour. Of her Elizabeth, he said that it was "not only the greatest performance of her life, it was also one of the greatest performances by an actress that I have ever seen" (B197, p. 120).

As Alexander Woollcott reported, Miss Cornell had taken the finest troupe she could assemble on her repertory tour that ended in San Francisco, July 2, 1932. The audiences were large and enthusiastic, making it a profitable venture, and proving the viability of touring. "It was," in Woollcott's words, "a venture so personal and so isolated in the springs of its motive, that it would be easy to exaggerate its importance as the harbinger of a new day" (B244, pp. 70-71). Morton Eustis credited her with paving the way for a rebirth of the once prosperous road (B066, p. 944).

Following the tour Herr Hirth and his wife Joanna welcomed the McClintics that summer as paying guests at their country house near Grainau, Bavaria, a place to which Miss Cornell returned for five consecutive years. There she found relaxation and time to study her roles.

In 1931, the McClintics had taken a two-year lease on David Belasco's Forty-Fourth Street Theatre after his death earlier that year. Miss Cornell chose *Lucrece* (1932), translated by Thornton Wilder from André Obey's version of Shakespeare's *The Rape of Lucrece*, for her first show in the Belasco Theatre. She produced the play because she believed in "its moral grandeur" (B114). The best talents in American theatre contributed to the production which was lavished with both money and love. The play opened December 20, 1932, and ran only 31 performances. Miss Cornell said that the play was too beautiful, that the audience thought she was "going arty." She would have liked to do it again and it pleased her when producer Arthur Hopkins told her it was her "most successful failure" (B047, pp. 117-118).

From the start, Brian Aherne, who played Tarquin, had been dubious about pantomiming the rape scene.  It had been done so effectively with stylized ballet movement and vocal orchestration by the Jacques Copeau Company in the French production that he could not visualize it otherwise.  Miss Cornell was not satisfied with the scene, and later conceded that it probably should have been done by dancers.  In Aherne's opinion, the production was a "costly beautiful bore and a monumental flop" (B004, p. 196).  Critics agreed that the literary quality of the play did not match the acting, and that some of the artistic devices got in the way.  However, contrary to Miss Cornell's disappointment with the rape scene, John Anderson thought it was played with "power and brilliance" (B257).

At any rate, the bad notices after the opening of *Lucrece* were "unnerving."  As Aherne explained, "...failure undermines the actor's faith in his own judgment and this can be a painful wound.  We were all very depressed while the play lasted" (B004, p. 199).

In her next production Miss Cornell played Elsa Brandt, a young talented pianist, in Sidney Howard's *Alien Corn* (1933).  The flaws in the play were overlooked because of Miss Cornell's "presence."  She felt that it was one of the best things she had done. It opened at the Belasco February 12, 1933, and prospered even at the lowest point of the Depression.  When the banks and most of the theatres were closed, Miss Cornell ordered the box-office to accept any kind of payment, even IOU's.  All of them were made good, reaffirming her trust in people.  The play was closed May 15, 1933.

For some time Ray Henderson had been suggesting that Miss Cornell do a Shakespearean play.  She had not felt she could try Shakespeare.  However, the long speech she had delivered in *Lucrece* had planted the thought that perhaps she was ready for the challenge, if she could do it simply, without bravura.  Even though she wanted to do Rebecca West in Ibsen's *Rosmersholm,* everyone wanted her to play Juliet.  When H. T. Parker, drama critic of the *Boston Transcript,* called on her in Boston during the run of *Alien Corn* to urge her to do Juliet, she agreed.  She realized that, at her age, if she were ever to play Juliet, it had to be then, but with one condition--that she could take time to perfect the part before presenting it in New York.

Henderson already had devised a plan for a transcontinental repertory which would provide the opportunity for her to polish the role of Juliet.  The tour would consist of *Candida, The Barretts* and *Romeo and Juliet*, extend through her 1933-34 season and demonstrate her belief that the road was still viable.

At the termination of their 2-year lease of the Belasco Theatre, the McClintics chose not to renew or pick up the option to buy. Instead, they moved their offices to the new RKO building in Rockefeller Center where they began arrangements for the tour. Gert Macy became stage manager, Guthrie set about the difficult task of finding actors who could fulfill the roles in three plays, and Miss Cornell went to Garmisch to work on her part.

The tryout opening for *Romeo and Juliet* was scheduled for November 29, 1933, in Buffalo, New York.  Even though they took pride in her, Buffalo playgoers did not patronize *Romeo and Juliet* but they did fill the house to capacity for *The Barretts*. Henderson had forewarned the McClintics that Shakespeare was not popular and, for this reason, he had insisted on alternating it with *Candida* and *The Barretts* to finance the tour. Audiences did not go to a Shakespearean play, he said, until word got around that it was a "good" production.

In November, 1933, the troupe headed west from Buffalo in two Pullman and two baggage cars, to cover 17,000 miles and to play 225 performances.  In addition to most of the original cast in *The Barretts*, the troupe included Orson Welles, Alice Johns and

Martha Graham, who directed the dances. Between Duluth and Seattle they made no stops. The movie theatre owners in Montana had become so fearful of competing with live theatre that they closed all theatres to road companies.

*The Barretts* was scheduled to play in Seattle, Guthrie's hometown, on Christmas night but a continuous 23-day downpour of rain caused washouts and long delays. When the troupe finally arrived in Seattle three hours past curtain time, the entire audience, over a thousand people, was still waiting. Immediately, the cast and crew went into action and the curtain was pulled to allow the audience to watch the stagehands and electricians unpack and assemble the set, while Guthrie entertained them with explanations, anecdotes and whatever he could conjure, including frequent entrances and exits by Flush. At five minutes past one the play began, and when the curtain fell at four a.m., the inspired actors received more curtain calls than they had ever had. The story of the thrilling event was broadcast to the nation on the airways by Woollcott as "The Town Crier." The event became legendary and almost as famous as Dicken's *Christmas Carol.* Retelling the story of *The Barretts* in Seattle became an annual radio Christmas tradition for a number of years (B201).

Although *Romeo and Juliet* was doing well, McClintic knew that it did not reflect his best directorial abilities nor Miss Cornell's real capability as Juliet. A remark made by a lady to her companion in a San Francisco audience which he overheard gave him a clue to the problem: the forthcoming tragedy was predictable when the curtain opened! McClintic dashed from the theatre to get an unmarked copy of the play and read it with new insight--as the exhilarating, gay, hot-blooded drama of reckless youth. Before the end of the tour, the play was dropped from the repertory because it was difficult to set up for one-night stands, all of the costumes and sets were given to a theatre in Cincinnati and preparations for a new production began.

To work anew on the part of Juliet, Miss Cornell went abroad again to Garmisch. Although she had already played the role for over a year, she pored over all the prompt books and references she could find. This time she went to Vicenzo, outside Verona, to see the walled garden and high balcony where the story of Juliet, according to legend, had occurred. As soon as she returned to New York, rehearsals for their second *Romeo and Juliet* (1934) began. After three years of preparation, the new production opened in Detroit on December 3, for a week's run, then went to Cleveland for four performances and on to Pittsburgh for a week. Two performances were given in Toronto before it opened at the Martin Beck in New York on December 20, 1934.

Basil Rathbone was still cast in the role of Romeo, Brian Aherne as Mercutio, and Edith Evans as Nurse. Several replacements were made in both cast and crew as well as new sets and costumes. This time Mielziner's sets were done in the style of a thirteenth century Italian artist, Giotto di Bonsone, who was noted for lightness and gaiety (B514, p. 93). The curtain rose on a vibrant setting; the action was swift, impetuous, exciting. When the curtain fell, there was silence, then a wild burst of applause.

Critics wrote rave reviews. Burns Mantle called her "the greatest Juliet of her time" and Brooks Atkinson said Miss Cornell "has hung another jewel on the cheek of theatre nights" (B163, p. 354; B284). In *The Commonweal* Grenville Vernon reported that "we have gradually become aware that perhaps alone among American actresses Katharine Cornell has been touched by the wand of genius" and that "...no Juliet of this generation has equaled her" (B229). The reviews prompted McClintic to proclaim that "The century's third Juliet had arrived!" (B149, p. 307). Indeed, she received the greatest critical acclaim of her career for her portrayal of Juliet (B512, p. 214). For 77 performances every seat was sold and there were hundreds of standees.

Soon after the New York opening, news came from England that George (Guy) Booth, husband of Edith Evans had died. The news shocked and saddened members of the cast, for Miss Evans' portrayal of the Nurse had not only been a triumph for her, but had also contributed to the play's great success. Miss Cornell, who had found Miss Evans to be "an absolute dream to work with," was especially affected. She immediately released the grief-stricken actress from her contract and found a replacement. Brenda Forbes played the Nurse until Blanche Yurka could take the role (B163, p. 357; B069, p. 162).

The show had been scheduled for 6 weeks and Guthrie was appalled that a production that was so heavily in debt should close at the height of a profitable run. However, both Ray Henderson and Miss Cornell had reasons for wanting to close: Henderson because the closing date had been announced and Miss Cornell because a cough that had been plaguing her made the death scene in the tomb particularly difficult. McClintic was appeased by extending the run for 3 weeks. The following fall (1935) the show was taken on a tour which closed with a special return engagement in New York at Christmastime.

For her performance as Juliet, Miss Cornell received the New York Drama League Award. That same year the University of Buffalo honored her with the Chancellor's Medal. Yale, however, refused to confer an honorary degree upon her because a woman, especially an actress, could not be considered for such recognition. Her profitable production, which grossed over $566,000 despite the highest ticket price ($3.85) ever charged at that time for a Shakespearean production, began a renascence of Shakespearean plays. Moreover, in three seasons she had played Juliet 232 times, outnumbering performances of other actresses since Julia Marlowe had played Juliet.

She had reached the peak of her career and tasted the sweetness of success; disappointments and failures lay just ahead. Two nights after *Romeo and Juliet* closed, *The Barretts* (1935) was revived with all five of the principal actors. The press liked it better than the original, but the audiences did not return. It was closed after 24 performances.

Fortunately, Miss Cornell had already begun rehearsals on John van Druten's *Flowers of the Forest* (1935). Auriol Lee owned the production rights and van Druten insisted that she direct. Miss Cornell was very uneasy that Guthrie would not be directing so it was finally agreed to let him supervise. That was the first strike against *Flowers of the Forest*. The second strike was McClintic's dislike of the play and the third was Miss Lee's tendency to fall asleep during rehearsals, which proved to be the early symptoms of encephalitis. Altogether, the experience was painful for everyone. They managed to get through 40 performances before closing in May, 1935. It was Miss Cornell's second failure of the decade.

When the C. & M. C. Productions was chartered with a capital of 600 shares, Miss Cornell received 200 shares for her interest in *The Barretts*, Griffis and Goodyear 180 shares each and Gert Macy 40 shares. No profits were to be paid to shareholders but were saved for future productions. The government, however, would not allow them to retain the large amount of capital that *The Barretts* had earned. They were forced to declare $100,000 in dividends, with $11,000 to go to Gert, and the rest split in halves to Griffis and Goodyear which they used to establish the Katharine Cornell Foundation. It had been stipulated that, upon the dissolution of the company, assets and properties were to be divided into three equal parts and distributed to the Museum of Modern Art to honor Goodyear, Cornell University's theatre department to honor Miss Cornell and the Actors' Fund of America to honor Griffis. The dissolution occurred in 1963.

From the time Miss Cornell had been unable to try out for *Saint Joan*, because of her earlier commitment to *Casanova*, the desire to play the Maid of Domremy had remained. When the German actress Elisabeth Bergner saw Miss Cornell's Juliet and urged her, as did others, to do *Saint Joan*, the time seemed right. Plans were made to begin rehearsals for *Saint Joan* after a tour of ten and one-half weeks with *Romeo and Juliet* (1935) in which Maurice Evans would play Romeo and then take the role of the Dauphin in *Saint Joan*.

Bad luck plagued the rehearsals, the out-of-town tryout and the opening. Miss Cornell caught the flu and developed laryngitis, necessitating a postponement of the New York opening. The delay was psychologically devastating to her not only because she was keyed up for the performance but, also, because of her feeling of responsibility toward her fellow actors and her audience.

When the show finally opened March 9, 1936, it was an instant success despite the delayed opening because of Miss Cornell's illness, the only time she had to postpone a New York opening. In order to keep on schedule with their tour, the McClintics paid a penalty to end the New York run of *Saint Joan* when boxoffice receipts were too high to warrant it.

Brian Aherne, who played Browning in *The Barretts* and was playing the role of Richard de Beauchamp in *Saint Joan* praised Miss Cornell's portrayal. In his autobiography he stated that "Katharine Cornell has given many performances in a wide range of parts but none, I think, better than her Saint Joan for which her gifts and qualities seemed ideally suited" (B004, p. 252). Calling the role Miss Cornell's "zenith," Mosel wrote that "Joan seems to have been the one great stage role she was fated to play from the beginning" (B163, p. 374).

An incident that arose during the play involved Tyrone Power, then an unknown who was playing Robert de Baudricourt. Power faced a dilemma when he received an offer for a Hollywood contract with Twentieth Century Fox. Although it was in the middle of the show's run, Maurice Evans (the Dauphin) advised Power to take the opportunity, exclaiming, "...Why, you might hit and go up like a rocket!" Power took his advice and went to Miss Cornell who graciously released him from his contract, even though she had to spend a good deal of time rehearsing a replacement. Power made a hit in Hollywood, and never forgot Miss Cornell's kindness. He said it was "the greatest thing anyone ever did for me" (B008, p. 85). Years later, when she asked him to play in *The Dark is Light Enough*, Power left Hollywood long enough to pay the debt he felt he owed her. He accepted just enough salary to meet his expenses (B004, p. 253).

Her next show, *The Wingless Victory* by Maxwell Anderson, opened on December 23, 1936. Miss Cornell played the sensuous, beautiful Oparre to an enthusiastic audience. Although some critics praised her for a brilliant performance, others, like Stark Young, castigated her for her "lack of distinguished instinct as an artist" and called the play "semi-tosh" (B246, p. 412). Edith J.R. Isaacs, on the other hand, judged the scene in which Oparre's husband allows her to leave Salem to be one of the finest she had ever done, "unless perhaps she surpasses herself in the final moment of this same play, as she dies forgiving" (B107, p. 95).

The physical and emotional demands of the Oparre role were exhausting. In addition to lifting and carrying her child about, she had to undergo hours of applying body makeup. As the show progressed and ticket demand slackened, the play alternated with *Candida* to give Miss Cornell some respite. *The Wingless Victory* was taken on tour after 110 performances, which proved to be even more taxing than the New York performances.

Miss Cornell was the first actress to receive Chi Omega's National Achievement Award. The presentation was made by the nation's First Lady, Eleanor Roosevelt, at the White House, March, 1937. On that occasion Miss Cornell's nervousness so overcame her that she was speechless when she rose to express her thanks. Mrs. Roosevelt graciously intervened and suggested that the guests adjourn as she extricated Miss Cornell from the kind of situation in which she was most uncomfortable.

The strain of playing Oparre and the twenty years of her indefatigable insistence on quality in theatre productions had taken a toll on Miss Cornell. Depleted and bored, she decided to take a year off. Her ennui concerned Ray Henderson who believed one could not stop at the peak of productive years. Not wanting to disappoint him, Miss Cornell assured him she was not stopping forever and suggested he begin making arrangements for the world tour he had planned for her. Retreating alone to her home Chip Chop on Martha's Vineyard, she began to rest, relax and take stock of herself.

An announcement of the world tour was made and Henderson set off to make arrangements in the 33 countries to be visited. En route from Egypt to London, he was drowned when his seaplane crashed near Athens on October 1, 1937. The plans for the world tour died with him and he was later replaced as press agent by Francis Robinson.

In September, 1938, *Stage* magazine began publishing Miss Cornell's life story as she told it to Ruth Woodbury Sedgwick. Entitled *I Wanted to be an Actress*, the story appeared in book form in 1939. *Time* reported that the book was acceptable but it had failed to convey Miss Cornell's "star" personality. "When that personality cannot be directly, physically communicated, as in her life story, it dries up like ink on a blotter," the reviewer wrote (B085).

The outcome of her year of introspection resulted in one certainty for Miss Cornell: the theatre was where she belonged. At the year's end she returned to the stage in *Herod and Mariamne* (1938) which was such a resounding failure that it was not opened in New York. During the tryout in Pittsburgh, Gert Macy bluntly told the McClintics the play was a flop and should be closed. Not ready to accept that indictment, Miss Cornell fired Gert on the spot, then retracted, admitting that Gert was not only right but that she was also indispensable to her. Gert stayed with the McClintics.

A failure to Guthrie meant that one would immediately try again, and he urged his wife to accept Robert Sherwood's invitation to join the Playwrights' Producing Company in *No Time for Comedy* (1939), a most unlikely selection for her. Her fear of comedy was no secret. Furthermore, S. N. Behrman had written the play for Ina Claire who hadn't accepted it, and it had also been offered and refused by Lynn Fontanne and Gertrude Lawrence. Finally persuaded to give it a try, Miss Cornell at least had the good fortune of being supported by Laurence Olivier, John Williams and Robert Flemyng, all masters of comedy.

After the opening of their out-of-town tryout in Indianapolis, Miss Cornell was so distraught over her performance that the author and members of the Playwrights' Company feared she would quit. However, she persisted and the show opened in New York, April 17, 1939, at the Ethel Barrymore Theatre. To the delight of everyone, *No Time for Comedy* was, in every sense, a great hit. Financially, it grossed over a million dollars, the third largest money-maker of her career. The play ran 24 weeks and then toured for 7 months in 57 cities.

During the show's New York run, the McClintics invited Laurence Olivier, who was playing the leading male role, to stay at their home during the show's New York run. Vivien Leigh was filming *Gone with the Wind* in Hollywood at the same time and she and Olivier were trying to keep their love affair from the public until their divorces were final and they could marry.  When Olivier received a frantic call from Hollywood that Miss Leigh was distraught from overwork and a change of directors, Miss Cornell released him from a rehearsal to fly to Hollywood to see her.  After her filming was completed, Miss Leigh also stayed with the McClintics until the closing of *No Time for Comedy* when she and Olivier would return to England.  It was another example of the McClintic's generosity and understanding for which Olivier expressed his gratitude and good fortune (B230, p. 109).

About this time Miss Cornell was introduced to Nancy Hamilton who had co-authored a revue, *One for the Money*, which Gert Macy produced.  Nancy Hamilton brought her gift for laughter into Miss Cornell's life, made a film and a tape that Miss Cornell narrated and proved to be a faithful friend when Miss Cornell most needed support after Guthrie's death.

For her 1941 season, Miss Cornell chose another of Shaw's plays, *The Doctor's Dilemma* (1941).  Although the role of Jennifer Dubedat is small, the author gave her a tremendous buildup for her entrance.  The breathtaking costumes, designed after those in 1903 fashion plates, set off Miss Cornell's beauty.  The play ran in New York for 15 weeks and then went on tour for another 14 weeks.  Beginning its second week in San Francisco, when Pearl Harbor was bombed, boxoffice receipts dropped dramatically, so the tour was concluded.

With the closing of *The Doctor's Dilemma* in San Francisco, the McClintics decided to remain on the west coast and immediately begin rehearsals there for *Rose Burke* (1942).  They planned to open it in San Francisco and then combine the 2 plays for a cross-country tour back to New York.  Unfortunately, *Rose Burke* did not fit the moods of wartime.  Although it was earning money, Miss Cornell would not disappoint her audiences and closed the tour.  It was the second time she had refused to impose an inferior play on her audiences.

With the country fully involved in war, Miss Cornell decided to revive *Candida* (1942) to benefit the Navy Relief Society and the Army Emergency Fund under the auspices of The American Theatre Wing War Services.  A star-studded cast was selected with Raymond Massey, Burgess Meredith, Mildred Natwick and Dudley Digges for this fourth and intended final version of *Candida*.  Everything was donated or waived: salaries for actors and stagehands, the theatre, the royalties.  The show was to run a week with four matinees and a Sunday performance but, to meet the great demand for tickets, it was extended another month in New York and taken to Washington, D.C. for a week at the National Theatre.  One thousand mail orders were rejected each day and there were 200 standees at each performance.  The Navy Relief Society and Army Emergency Fund each received over $35,000 and The American Theatre Wing almost $10,000.  For that show Miss Cornell had appealed to Private Burgess Meredith's commanding officer to give Meredith a leave long enough to play the important role of Marchbanks in a benefit performance of *Candida* for the Army and Navy.  The officer granted the leave and Meredith's performance was a triumph for him.  Meredith later recalled the lasting impression that Miss Cornell and McClintic had made on him.  She was "quite beautiful; a gentle-mannered lady, very quiet," he said.  Her husband seemed to have an "almost detached admiration of her gifts, a kind of stagedoor crush on her" (B151).

Headed by Judith Anderson, Ruth Gordon and Katharine Cornell (stars were listed alphabetically to avoid slighting them), the cast of her next production, *The Three Sisters*, (1942) was "glittering."  What was remarkable was that the stars did not try to upstage one another.  However, Kirk Douglas, then unknown and just trying to break into acting, had a bit part in *The Three Sisters* and tells the story in his autobiography of his attempt to make an impression. He wanted to make the most of his role as a servant so he entered with a flourish which was entirely out of character. His entrance would have led the audience to expect him to have important lines when, indeed, he had not a word to speak. After rehearsal, Miss Cornell drew him aside and "diplomatically" suggested he see the makeup man and play the part as a Russian peasant. He felt deflated, but after becoming a professional himself, he realized his scene-stealing had deserved far less tact than he had received from the "gracious, charming woman." Furthermore, he felt that playing "an unattractive dopey peasant" was well worth the privilege of being in a cast with great artists (B059, p. 102).

The tryout for *The Three Sisters* (1942) was in Washington, D.C., and the opening in New York at the Ethel Barrymore Theatre on December 21. The play ran for 122 performances before it went on the road to achieve the longest run of a Chekhov play in the United States and the longest run *The Three Sisters* had ever had. Critic John Anderson of the *New York Journal American* wrote that it "added greatly to her stature as an actress-manager" (B140). Burton Rascoe of the *New York World-Telegram* called it an "artistic event in the history of the theater" (B460).

For the war effort Miss Cornell made an exception to her avoidance of acting in movies. She appeared in the movie *Stage Door Canteen*, made in celebration of the American Theatre Wing's Center for enlisted men. Along with other prestigious contributors such as the Lunts, Edgar Bergen, Yehudi Menuhin and many others, she appeared in a short vignette, in which she handed an orange to Lon McAllister and recited a few lines from *Romeo and Juliet.*

Katharine Cornell's greatest experience was yet to come during World War II through her part in the war effort. While she was touring in *Lovers and Friends*, her name was suggested to the American Theatre Wing as being representative of the best in American theatre to take a production to the armed services overseas. Her first reaction was that she wasn't a comedienne and wasn't right for this venture. After reconsidering, she agreed to the offer if she could take *The Barretts* and if she could get Brian Aherne. Standing firm against the objections that GIs wouldn't want to see a costume play about a romantic love affair, she won the consent of the Special Services Division (SSD) and other Washington authorities, but only after a trial run at Mitchell Field. The response of 2500 GIs supported her conviction, and the play was approved with the stipulation that an alternate play be prepared in case *The Barretts* failed as the SSD was sure it would.

The size of the cast and stage crew was reduced to 17, still much larger than the average U.S.O. troupe. When the set, costumes and props were assembled, the weight allowance left them only 2 or 3 pounds for Flush. Because a cocker spaniel was too large, they found a Yorkshire terrier. On August 11, 1944, the cast and crew sailed aboard the S.S. *General Meigs* under orders to the North African Theater of the U.S. Army. They landed in Naples, Italy.

Of the experience with *The Barretts* overseas tour, Brian Aherne tells one story in his autobiography. During the bitter winter months they were entertaining the GIs in the Fifth Army who were holding the Forgotten Front in the mountains. The men were brought in trucks from their mucky foxholes to the outskirts of Florence. There they were given showers, a hot meal and a ticket to *The Barretts*, which was played in the daytime so the GIs could be back at their stations by dark. Being so near a city, few men were expected to attend the play. To the surprise of *The Barretts* company, the theatre was always packed.

One afternoon as the GIs were leaving the show "a tough, burley paratrooper" was overheard saying to his buddy, "Well...What I tell ya! Told ya it'd be better'n goin' to the cat house, didn't I?" The members of the show took the remark as a "supreme tribute" (B004, pp. 324-325).

Alec Guinness saw *The Barretts* on its tour of the warfront but could not be "as effusive as expected" of him. He thought everyone except Miss Cornell "played down to the troops" (B086, p. 130). On the other hand, Garff Wilson, who later became a theatre historian, saw the play with a truckload of GIs under the worst of circumstances and had quite another reaction. It was a bitterly cold night in December, 1944. He describes his vivid memory of it: "The crowded audience of soldiers was bundled to the eyebrows, like the actors, with scarves, overcoats, earmuffs, and woolen caps. Yet the men of that audience, most of whom had never seen a live stage play before, sat utterly entranced and spellbound....The evening was a revealing illustration of the magic that good theatre can exert, contrary to the skepticism of those who habitually underrate both living drama and American audiences" (B240, p. 280).

Upon her return home Miss Cornell told S. J. Woolf of *The New York Times* that "the sight of those truckloads of boys who were brought in to see us play was an inspiration in itself. I don't think I ever put more of myself into acting and I have never acted before keener, more discriminating or more appreciative audiences" (B243, p. 14). It was the most moving experience of her life and her greatest success.

During the tour the McClintics celebrated their 23rd wedding anniversary, and General Mark Clark gave a citation to the company "for excellence in performance, merit and discipline." The last performance, their 140th, was given in Rheims. On January 31, 1945, they sailed from London for home.

When the tour of the warfront was ended, the actors needed to replenish their finances so the McClintics took the GI production of *The Barretts* to Boston for a week. At the Boston Opera House it broke all records for legitimate drama. From Boston it played for 11 weeks in New York, and on the first night the audience gave Miss Cornell an ovation.

While touring for the GIs in Paris she had seen Jean Anouilh's version of *Antigone* and it appealed to her. In February, 1946, she opened in Lewis Galantiere's translation of Anouilh's text at the Cort Theatre with Sir Cedric Hardwicke as Creon. Breaking with traditional costuming, the men wore dinner jackets and the women wore robes. The stage was stark with three steps at the rear against a background of plain grey curtains and a few essential modernistic props.

In Detroit, the house was packed for the American premiere of *Antigone* (1946). The play opened in New York on February 18, where Miss Cornell won the respect of the critics but they did not find the play fulfilling. Lewis Nichols, in *The New York Times*, criticized it for lack of clarity, for anachronisms, poorly drawn characters, and a lack of logical motivation for Antigone's actions. Some of the acting, he said, was excellent but the story seemed empty and the characters "not quite living human beings" (B439).

For the fifth time she revived *Candida* (1946) with Marlon Brando as Marchbanks. Audiences received the play enthusiastically, but some reviewers criticized the play and the role of Candida herself. "Psychological realism" had caught on and was more appealing to audiences than romanticism, Miss Cornell's forte. Times were changing. Some critics were still appreciative of Miss Cornell's ennobling characterizations but her leading women were going out of style and there were no new plays for her.

While she waited for parts in new plays, Miss Cornell alternated *Antigone* with *Candida*, then took *The Barretts* on an 8-week tour of the west. She gave her 1000th performance of Elizabeth in San Francisco on February 7, 1947. By the end of the tour she had played the role 1019 times and had grossed at least $2,250,170 (B512, p. 82).

When no suitable play was forthcoming, she took the opportunity to play Shakespeare's Cleopatra, a part she had wanted to do for a long time. Because *Antony and Cleopatra* had a history of failures and was difficult to perform, Miss Cornell was not expected to succeed. The play had been rehearsed for 5 weeks and toured for a 7-week tryout period before it opened in New York on November 26, 1947, at the Martin Beck. However, to the surprise and perhaps chagrin of pessimistic well-wishers, the play succeeded beyond expectations. Brooks Atkinson, in his *New York Times* review, commented that Miss Cornell was too "well-bred and good mannered" for "the Egyptian dish" but that "she brings the style, authority and incandescence that become her best" to one of Shakespeare's best scenes (B287). William Beyer claimed that she "reaches the pinnacle of her greatness" and could no longer disclaim the title of First Lady of the Stage (B20, p. 86).

One of the actors in *Antony and Cleopatra*, Anthony Randall, who became well known film and television star Tony Randall, got his first acting job on Broadway after the war with "the great Katharine Cornell." In his autobiography he tells of a lesson he learned from her that has probably saved him a great deal of time. As a student of Method acting, he customarily spent three hours preparing for his entrance on stage. One night Miss Cornell suggested that he go on and do his part without all that preparation. He tried it and found that his acting was just the same (B196). As it happened, the McClintics, especially Guthrie, had little patience with the Method approach to acting because actors got so involved in their preparation.

The McClintics had spent $125,000 to stage a beautiful, quality production of *Antony and Cleopatra* that logged 251 performances--16 weeks in New York and a 9-week tour in 4 major cities. It set the record as the longest run the play had ever had. Even so, because of production costs, the show lost money.

After several years of poor health, Dr. Peter C. Cornell died in September, 1949. He left a trust which provided a lifetime income for his daughter and sufficient cash to pay for the house she and Guthrie had built at Sneden's Landing.

For her next endeavor Miss Cornell commissioned writer Kate O'Brien to dramatize her novel *For One Sweet Grape*. The play, entitled *That Lady* (1949) and set in the sixteenth century, was the story of Spanish princess Ana de Mendoza whose love affair with Philip II shook Spain's political world. Miss Cornell's performance was applauded as one of her finest, but Miss O'Brien's adaptation of her novel missed the mark of being good drama. *That Lady* was later (1954) made into a film with Olivia de Havilland as the star.

The heroine Ana was distinguished by the eye patch worn over one eye she had lost in a duel at the age of fourteen. Miss Cornell wore the patch with such glamour that young girls who had the misfortune of losing an eye came to her for help in wearing their patches. She graciously assisted them.

After the production of *That Lady* Miss Cornell opened *Captain Carvallo* (1950) in Buffalo. Directed by McClintic, the comedy was set in a country farmhouse kitchen in which Miss Cornell's role called for a good deal of cooking. Despite the lessons she took, she was not convincing, nor was the play appealing. It closed, the third production she had not brought to New York after the out-of-town tryout (B163, p. 501).

In the summer of 1951, the producers of the drama and opera festival in Central City, Colorado, invited Miss Cornell to play in Somerset Maugham's comedy *The Constant Wife* (1951) for 3 weeks. The play was so successful that the McClintics took it to New York. Again Miss Cornell proved that in a comedy she could attract audiences to the theatre. The production grossed more than all of her plays in the 29 years since she had become her own manager. Opening on December 8, 1951, it ran for 17 weeks in New York before making a 4-week tour of eastern states. The following season the company criss-crossed the country in a tour that extended for 31 weeks. It grossed over $1,000,000--her last financial success.

Finally, she was cast as a U.S. delegate to the United Nations in *The Prescott Proposals*, written by Howard Lindsay and Russel Crouse. It opened at the Broadhurst on December 16, 1953. More a melodrama of the lady delegate's personal life than a political play, it received mixed reviews. Brooks Atkinson was disappointed in the superficial political treatment but thought that Miss Cornell gave "a superb performance-- warm, beautiful, lady-like, forceful and good humored" (B276). A fan wrote that she made women realize middle age could mean "added charm," but other devotees detected a loss of grace in her movements (B513).

Her audiences of devoted fans were thinning and, although still loyal, they saw her beauty fading. She had no appeal for younger generations who could not identify with the characters or her elegance and so, in New York, her last few plays were financial failures.

The next suitable role that Miss Cornell undertook was the Countess Rosmarin Ostenburg in *The Dark is Light Enough* (1955) which Christopher Fry had written for Edith Evans. To repay his debt for her help in getting his career started, Tyrone Power took temporary leave of Hollywood to play her leading man. Set in an Austrian country house, McClintic gave the production the opulence characteristic of the company. It opened February 23, 1955, at the ANTA Theatre. Reviewers found flaws in the somber play and, although some praised her, they were also becoming more critical.

In 1955, she made her first television appearance. In celebration of the 25th anniversary of her Broadway opening, she played Elizabeth on N.B.C.'s *Producers' Showcase* with Anthony Quayle as Browning and Henry Daniell as Moulton-Barrett. The production was directed by Vincent J. Donehue. *Newsweek* reported that she was eager to do more television, particularly *Candida* and *The Doctor's Dilemma* (B082).

However, in 1955, she underwent lung surgery to cure the persistent cough that had begun to plague her in Juliet's death scene. At the end of her recuperation, in 1958, she made her second and last television appearance when she played in Robert Sherwood's *There Shall Be No Night* with Charles Boyer and Bradford Dillman, directed by George Shaefer. In each of these performances she played to 28 million viewers and found it exciting, but for some unexplained reason she did not continue in television.

Ward Morehouse remarked in *Theatre Arts Monthly* that Miss Cornell, healthy at 60, would undoubtedly stay on the stage as long as she could totter (B159). That year she opened in her second Christopher Fry play, *The Firstborn* (1958), which was directed by Anthony Quayle who also played Moses. She played Pharaoh's sister and the music was composed by Leonard Bernstein. Written as a salute to the new state of Israel on its 10th anniversary, the play opened on April 30, 1958, at the Coronet Theatre in New York, and closed May 31 because of low boxoffice receipts. Sponsored by the American-Israeli Committee, *The Firstborn* was taken to the 10th anniversary celebration in Israel for a week of performances in July, 1958. The financial loss for that venture was close to $100,000.

The final production of Miss Cornell's career, *Dear Liar* (1960), written by Jerome Kilty, was a presentation of the letters between George Bernard Shaw and Mrs. Patrick Campbell. McClintic was associate producer of *Dear Liar* with S. Hurok and, again, Brian Aherne played her leading man.

In the spring of 1959, the duo toured 18,000 in a Land Cruiser, taking *Dear Liar* to 66 cities, many of which were hard to reach by public transportation (B224, p. 61). The New York opening took place March 17, 1960. Although it had been a top boxoffice draw in Phoenix, the receipts in New York were poor. Miss Cornell closed the New York run on April 30, 1960, and took the play to Boston for a week. Reviewers criticized the tedium and wordiness of the letters as well as Miss Cornell's failure to capture the "audacity" of Stella Campbell. Miss Cornell was not comfortable in the role of Mrs. Campbell and Brian Aherne had the advantage of having better lines in the role of Shaw. Aherne thought it was his good fortune to have had one of his finest parts, which he considered Shaw to be, late in his career. Although he disliked touring, he consented to tour in *Dear Liar* largely because of his loyalty to Katharine Cornell. Of his association with her, he said, "Our relationship, both professional and personal, has been one of the enduring pleasures of my life" (B004, pp. 345, 318).

Cancer of the kidney took Guthrie's life on October 28, 1961, just several weeks after the McClintics' 40th anniversary. After his death, Kit could not return to the stage. He was her "force." She said, "I do not believe I would have done anything worth comment but for him" (B182, p. 56). She had always given him credit for his inspiration and invaluable counsel.

She sold her houses at Sneden's Landing and Chip Chop, moved to the Barn, just inland from Chip Chop, and bought a house in Manhattan around the corner from 23 Beekman Street. With the encouragement of Nancy Hamilton, she maintained an interest in her hobbies and the island community by restoring the 300-year-old Association Hall near Vineyard Haven with funds from the Peter C. Cornell Foundation.

Not long after Guthrie's death she began suffering from heart failure but, with medication and care, was able to lead a normal life which included some travel. In 1972, friends gathered to celebrate her 75th birthday and the long kept secret was out--it was her 80th. At the advice of several friends, she had dropped five years from her age in 1928. A birthday tape, prepared by Nancy Hamilton, expressed what Katharine Cornell had meant to so many people--"great and small, articulate and inarticulate" (B163, p. 517).

In February, 1974, she was presented with the American National Theater and Academy's (ANTA) National Artist Award, her final citation in a long list of awards. Two months later, in April, the dedication of the Katharine Cornell-Guthrie McClintic Room at the New York Library of the Performing Arts in Lincoln Center took place. An attack of flu prevented her from attending and, in early June, she was flown by hospital plane to her island retreat.

Katharine Cornell died on June 12, 1974, of pneumonia, at her home in Martha's Vineyard. A white marble bench marks the place where her ashes were buried behind the Association Hall near Vineyard Haven, which she had restored in 1971. Arrangements were made by Nancy Hamilton for a "walk-through" memorial service several days later in the Association Hall. As rain fell and bells tolled, friends, neighbors and others who wanted to pay their tributes greeted one another, exchanged memories and viewed the photograph of Miss Cornell. Intermittently, there was a hush in the soft music and the "brown velvet" voice of Miss Cornell from her recorded readings halted the conversations. Among those who mingled there were Mary Martin, Ruth Gordon, Garson Kanin, Brenda Forbes, Mildred Dunnock, her cousin Doug Cornell, Gertrude Macy, and Nancy Hamilton (B163, p. 519).

Miss Cornell's estate was $500,000, the bulk of which was left to Nancy Hamilton who had lived with her after Guthrie's death. With her gift of laughter Miss Hamilton had helped Kit to remain active and involved in her community hobbies and the island community.

When a reporter of the *Vineyard Gazette* asked at her memorial service why Katharine Cornell was loved so much, her friends responded, "her energy, her intelligence, her warmth, her generosity, her style..." (B114).

George Oppenheimer of *Newsday* wrote in her obituary that "...she possessed a kind of glamour....Hers was a combination of presence, an indefatigable air of mystery, an elegance and refinement that set her apart and an appeal that lay not alone in her beauty but in her voice, in her gestures and in her intelligence" (B178).

To every role Katharine Cornell had brought "a special kind of excitement" (B159, p. 10). As Morris Gelman expressed it in *The Theatre*, she was "imbued with a magnetic and inspirational something that marks a star of the brightest radiance" (B074, p. 48). In our interview Mildred Natwick, who acted with her in *Candida* and *The Firstborn*, described Miss Cornell's special quality as "a kind of glow." Her personal theatricality and all of her natural assets, especially her rich, velvet voice, suited her for the stage. She was not considered beautiful, but across the footlights her high cheekbones, wide-set eyes, generous mouth, dark hair, heart-shaped face and stateliness gave the effect of great beauty. She also possessed a sense of timing, rhythm, movement and line. Critic Alden Whitman found her acting to be "quite as remarkable for the carefulness of its design as for the fire of her presence" (B235, p. 1). Moreover, her talent for mimicry was sharpened by the discipline and concentration necessary in the portrayal of varied and challenging roles. Her husband remarked that, "She can be old or young, radiant or dull, splendid, drab, inspired, buoyant, harsh, grief-stricken--whatever she chooses to be" (B021, p. 174).

In early performances her "special radiance and grandeur shone only fitfully" and she was told that she was not suited for the stage (B064, pp. 38-39). She ignored the negative appraisals and proved her judges to be wrong. The encouragement of Bonstelle and Guthrie's conviction that she belonged on stage were enough to sustain her desire to be an actress. She said that her husband's belief in her and his brilliance as a director inspired her to turn her "face definitely toward the greater things of the theatre" (B182, p. 56). Their respect and admiration for one another's talents and their mutual dedication to the theatre were strong bonds in their enduring marriage (B243).

Acting did not come easily for her and she experienced extreme nervousness, especially on opening nights. She had not outgrown the feeling of being unattractive and her "instinctive fear of being hurt" which she suffered as a child. Her husband explained that she had developed a "psychic sensitiveness" as a result of her childhood experiences which was "her principal asset as an artist" (B021, p. 172).

She believed that acting is the creation of "an illusion of reality" and that "the essential thing is to make the audience believe all the time." She also believed that acting could not be reduced to a formula, and found it difficult to describe her approach to a role (B064, p. 38).

Guthrie taught her to attack each part "as if it were new and vital" (B064, p. 39). She painstakingly studied the character and then projected herself into it. During early rehearsals she concentrated on the other actors' lines and their interpretations. Reading her own lines without expression, she suspended her characterization until she had a feel for the relationship of her role to the other players. Consequently, her first readings were often so poor that directors and fellow actors doubted her ability. Once she had mastered the lines, she turned her attention to the development of the character, selecting what was significant, which, to her, was the mark of an artist (B064, p. 48). Jackson Harvey, in

*Theatre Magazine,* described her acting as a complete submerging of herself in a part. The outcome was "subtlety" and "conviction" (B089, p. 24).

Through her athletic pursuits her body was finely tuned to respond to her thoughts. She had a sense of theatre and an instinctive feel for the limits of the stage where she sometimes worked alone to master her character's movements such as the broad strides of Joan d'Arc and the swift-moving, youthful steps of Juliet. Believing that an actor must know at all times what he is doing, she rarely changed actions once they were set. Where some actors relied on the inspiration of the moment, she did not find sudden inspiration to be dependable. Nor did she have the electrifying moments that other actors experience (B064).

Despite her diligence in improving her art, some critics castigated her for mannerisms, her "taste for trailing skirts, sofas, and sufferings," and for being forty years behind the time. They also criticized her penchant for emotional parts and particularly, for her lack of versatility and brilliance (B067; B091). Some felt she was more of a great stage personality who was a "prisoner" of the public's fondness for "comforting esthetic images" than a great actress (B091, p. 206). Keenly sensitive to these criticisms and aware of her own inadequacies, she did not deny her love of costumes, her troublesome mannerisms and her discomfort with comedy, even though she had been successful with it. Changing what she could and dismissing what could not be changed, she endeavored to perfect the qualities that were uniquely hers. She had learned well a lesson taught her at the beginning of her career: you "always stay, stand the gaff, and hope, as long as there is any hope" (B047, p. 18).

Beyond her magnetism and grandeur, what was her legacy? She had spent four decades on the American stage and for much of that time was considered, along with Helen Hayes, to be a first lady of the theatre. Each disclaimed the honor, Miss Hayes contending that Miss Cornell was "the true claimant of the title" (B015, p. 94). When Miss Hayes returned to the New York stage after some time in Hollywood, Miss Cornell welcomed her would-be rival, saying the theatre needed Helen Hayes so much that it was good to have her return. From Miss Hayes' perspective Miss Cornell was "generous, always ready to hand out praise." She went on to describe Kit as "a very serious, romantic actress. With her tall, graceful figure, shining black hair, and creamy skin, she looked like a woman in a Renaissance painting," (B090, p. 262). It was a mark of their greatness that these actresses did not engage in rivalry, but respected and admired one another's talents and diversity (B015, p. 122).

As actress-manager, Miss Cornell had produced a wide variety of plays of high quality. Even when costs rose far in excess of receipts, she maintained the quality of her productions, and at no time pandered to low public taste. During her years on stage few actresses possessed her "power" to draw audiences to see plays like *Candida* and *The Barretts* (B179). She always worked, surviving the menacing forces of a stock market crash and moving pictures.

By taking good theatre to the outreaches of America she proved that the road was alive and that audiences would patronize good plays. At a time when the number of touring companies was declining, she travelled over 100,000 miles in 43 states and spent a total of 336 weeks on the road during her career. In many cities she set boxoffice records. Her most successful tour was to the front lines of the European war zone where she took *The Barretts* to battle-weary GIs in World War II.

To many fans, who demanded excellence and understanding of her, she was an inspiring force. Young people, in particular, confided their aspirations and their fears to her. They asked for advice and requested interviews which she frequently granted.

Among her most devoted admirers were the servicemen who had seen her overseas. They had an immediate audience with her.

She left to those who saw her in her finest roles the memories of Candida's understanding and tenderness, Juliet's innocence and impetuous love, Elizabeth's electric presence, and Saint Joan's radiant conviction. Unfortunately, these moments cannot be recaptured through film. That was her wish.

She had taken the risk of presenting classic plays, promoting new American playwrights and giving a start to many young aspiring actors, such as Tony Randall, Maureen Stapleton, Marlon Brando, Tyrone Power, Kirk Douglas, Burgess Meredith and Orson Welles. The actors who surrounded her in any cast were the finest available. Discipline, dedication, hard work and consideration for those who worked with her enabled her to leave a legacy undiminished by her declining years when her style of acting was no longer popular. She became a "genuine giant" in her field but, because she preferred live audiences, she is now "virtually forgotten" (B179).

Fellow actor Christopher Plummer epitomized her effect on her profession in these words: "She gave the theatre the romantic quality it should have--the dream of it was alive in her hands--the religion of it. There was a magic about the profession you were in--you should tiptoe across a stage--it wasn't just an ordinary hall, it was a theatre!" (B163, p. 493).

Katharine Cornell, like Helen Hayes and Judith Anderson, gave to her acting "an integrity, devotion, and a quality" resembling the ideals of the classic school" (B241, p. 457). Perhaps the key to her artistic development and her legacy is most aptly revealed in her favorite lines from *Will Shakespeare*: "...and we climb...not because we will, but because we must. There is no virtue in it; but some pride" (B136, p. 21).

As Jo in *Little Women* (1919). The Billy Rose Theatre Collection, The New York Public Library for the Performing Arts, Astor, Lenox and Tilden Foundations.

As Mary Fitton in *Will Shakespeare* (1923). The Billy Rose Theatre Collection, The New York Public Library for the Performing Arts, Astor, Lenox and Tilden Foundations.

As Mary Fitton playing Juliet in *Will Shakespeare* (1923). The Billy Rose Theatre Collection, The New York Public Library for the Performing Arts, Astor, Lenox and Tilden Foundations.

As Candida in *Candida* (1924). The Billy Rose Theatre Collection, The New York Public Library for the Performing Arts, Astor, Lenox and Tilden Foundations.

As Elizabeth Barrett Moulton-Barrett with Brian Aherne as Robert Browning in *The Barretts of Wimpole Street* (1931). The Billy Rose Theatre Collection, The New York Public Library for the Performing Arts, Astor, Lenox and Tilden Foundations.

As Juliet in *Romeo and Juliet* (1934). The Billy Rose Theatre Collection, The New York Public Library for the Performing Arts, Astor, Lenox and Tilden Foundations.

As Joan d'Arc in *Saint Joan* (1939). The Billy Rose Theatre Collection, The New York Public Library for the Performing Arts, Astor, Lenox and Tilden Foundations.

As Oparre in *The Wingless Victory* (1936). The Billy Rose Theatre Collection, The New York Public Library for the Performing Arts, Astor, Lenox and Tilden Foundations.

As Jennifer Dubedat in *The Doctor's Dilemma* (1941). The Billy Rose Theatre Collection, The New York Public Library for the Performing Arts, Astor, Lenox and Tilden Foundations.

As Elizabeth Barrett Moulton-Barrett in her last revival of *The Barretts of Wimpole Street* (1944). The Billy Rose Theatre Collection, The New York Public Library for the Performing Arts, Astor, Lenox and Tilden Foundations.

# Chronology

1893    **February 16** -- Katharine Cornell is born in Berlin, Germany.

1901    **Summer** -- First press notice appears in the *Cobourg Sun* as an editorial she writes about "The Hidden Treasure," a play she and Jo Pierce have written and presented.

1907    **June** -- Writes, directs and presents a French play at St. Margaret's School, the elementary school she attends.

1908    **Fall** -- Begins attending Oaksmere, a finishing school in Mamaroneck, Long Island.

1911    **Spring** -- Graduates from Oaksmere.

1915    **June 19** -- Her mother, Alice Plimpton Cornell, dies at the age of 44.

        **Fall** -- Returns to Oaksmere to coach drama and athletics.

1916    **Fall** -- Makes her debut with Washington Square Players at the Comedy Theatre in New York as Shusai in *Bushido*. Does offstage cries in *The Life of Man*.

1917    **March 26** -- Receives favorable reviews for her part in *Plots and Playwrights* with Washington Square Players in New York.

1918    **Spring** -- With the Washington Square Players in New York, plays in *Neighbors*, and *Blind Alleys* for which *The New York Times* gives her first honorable mention. Also appears in *Yum Chapab* and *The Death of Tintagiles*.

        **Summer** -- Joins Jessie Bonstelle's Stock Company in Buffalo. Performs in *Cheating Cheaters*, *The Gypsy Trail*, *Daybreak*, *Broken Threads*, *Capt. Kidd, Jr.*, *Lilac Time*, *Seven Chances*, *Romance*, *Pals First*, and *Fanny's First Play*.

**1918**    **June 23** -- Opens in *The Man Outside* with Jessie Bonstelle's Stock Company.

**Fall** -- Returning to New York, she gets her first real part, as Marcelle, in the touring company of *The Man Who Came Back*. Reviewers treat her as the star.

**1919**    **Summer** -- Plays second leads in Buffalo and Detroit with Bonstelle's Stock Company. Opens in *Ann's Adventure*, later retitled *Ruined Lady* and played by Grace George.

**November 10** -- British audiences give her a warm reception for her role as Jo in *Little Women* at the New Theatre in London where it runs for 2 seasons.

**1920**    **Spring** -- Returns to Detroit to play alternate leads with Jessie Bonstelle whose new assistant stage director is Guthrie McClintic.

**Summer** -- Appears in the world premiere of Austin Strong's *Heaven*, later named *Seventh Heaven*. Also acts in *Daddy-Long-Legs*, *Too Many Husbands*, *Lombardi, Ltd.*, and *Civilian Clothes*.

**1921**    **March 1** -- Makes her first Broadway appearance in *Nice People* with Francine Larrimore and Tallulah Bankhead. The play runs for 31 weeks at the Klaw Theatre in New York.

**September 8** -- Marries Guthrie McClintic and they sign a 3-year lease on the house at 23 Beekman Place, Manhattan, New York.

**October 10** -- Opens in *A Bill of Divorcement* in the George M. Cohan Theatre in New York. Reviews are splendid; the play becomes a hit. Closing after 173 performances, *A Bill of Divorcement* is taken on a short tour.

**1923**    **January 1** -- Plays Mary Fitton in *Will Shakespeare* which runs for 80 performances at New York's National Theatre.

**March 31** -- Opens at the Ritz Theatre in *The Enchanted Cottage* in the role of Laura Pennington, for an 8-week run.

**September 26** -- Appears as Henriette in *Casanova* at the Empire Theatre in New York. Despite kind reviews, the play lacks appeal for Broadway audiences.

**1924**    **January 28** -- In the role of Shirley Pride, appears in *The Way Things Happen*, her first play under McClintic's direction since stock days. The play runs for 25 performances at the Lyceum Theatre.

**March 3** -- At the Forty-Ninth Street Theatre, she replaces the lead in *The Outsider* and receives critics' acclaim. Of her plays thus far, it is the most successful, critically and financially.

1924    **October 21** -- In the role of Suzanne, opens in *Tiger Cats,* at the Belasco Theatre in New York to mixed reviews. The play closes after 48 performances.

**December 12** -- After playing in special matinees for the Actors' Theatre in New York, *Candida* officially opens and outruns its original production in America. Because of great ticket demand, a commercial run is done at the 48th Street Theatre.

1925    **September 15** -- *The Green Hat*, with Leslie Howard, already a hit before it opens in New York at the Broadhurst Theatre, makes her a star. Critics polled by *Vanity Fair* unanimously vote Cornell the leading lady of the next decade.

1926    **Fall** -- Sets out on a cross-country tour of *The Green Hat* which runs for 3 seasons.

1927    **September 26** -- Opens in *The Letter* at the Morosco Theatre in New York. Audiences consider it sensational, but the press responds unfavorably. After 13 weeks, it is taken on a 5-month tour.

1928    **Fall** -- On the first day of rehearsals for *The Age of Innocence*, Gertrude Macy goes to work for her.

**November 27** -- Opens in New York in *The Age of Innocence* at the Empire Theatre after a tryout in Albany and Pittsburgh. Most critics are happy with her in the role of Ellen Olenska but critical of the play.

1929    **Fall** -- Makes a successful 9-week tour in *The Age of Innocence*, starting in Washington, D.C. at the Poli Theatre and ending at the Shubert Teck in Buffalo.

1930    **February 4** -- Opens in *Dishonored Lady* at the Empire Theatre in New York to unkind reviews. It is the last play that reads "Katharine Cornell in ...."

**Summer** -- Begins a 17-week tour in *Dishonored Lady* to the Pacific Coast; enjoys sensational business in Los Angeles and San Francisco.

**December** -- Buys *The Barretts of Wimpole Street* for Guthrie.

1931    **January 5** -- Forms the Cornell-McClintic Corporation (C. & M. C. Productions, Inc.) with her as producer-manager and McClintic as director.

**February 9** -- Opens *The Barretts of Wimpole Street* at the Empire Theatre in New York, her first venture as actress-manager. It proves to be one of the greatest successes of her career.

**Spring** -- Hires Ray Henderson as her press representative. He gives her a "public" voice and establishes the tradition of addressing her as "Miss Cornell," which the press adopts.

| | |
|---|---|
| **1931** | **May 14** -- David Belasco dies. |
| | **August 31** -- The McClintics lease the Belasco Theatre in New York. |
| **1932** | **February 5** -- Jessie Bonstelle, who had taught her a great deal about acting and held high aspirations for her, dies at the age of 66. |
| | **December 20** -- *Lucrece* opens in New York at the Belasco Theatre and closes after 31 performances. |
| **1933** | **February 20** -- Presents *Alien Corn* at the Belasco Theatre in New York. The play prospers despite the bank crisis and does not close until July 2, in Chicago. |
| | **Summer** -- McClintics terminate their lease of the Belasco Theatre and Gert Macy becomes stage manager. |
| | **Summer** -- Kit vacations at Garmisch in Bavaria. |
| | **November 22** -- Begins a transcontinental repertory tour with *The Barretts*, *Candida* and *Romeo and Juliet*. The road company is identical to the original cast. |
| | **November 29** -- Makes her first presentation of *Romeo and Juliet* in Buffalo. On the tour the company gives 225 performances in 75 towns and cities, from Buffalo, New York, to Seattle, Washington, through the south to Amarillo, Texas, and Thomasville, Georgia, and northeast to Portland, Maine. |
| **1934** | **December 20** -- With the opening of a new production of *Romeo and Juliet* at the Martin Beck Theatre in New York, to marvelous reviews, she reaches the peak of her career. The play closes February 23, after 77 performances. |
| **1935** | **February 22** -- Receives the Chancellor's Medal from the University of Buffalo, the first woman and artist to receive it. |
| | **February 25** -- Revives *The Barretts* in New York with the original five principals for 3 weeks while rehearsing *Flowers of the Forest*. Although the press reception is better than for the first production, attendance for *The Barretts* is disappointing. |
| | **April 10** -- Appears in *Flowers of the Forest* under Auriol Lee's direction. One of her failures, it runs for only 5 weeks in New York. |
| | **May 17** -- Receives the New York Drama League Award (Delia Austrian Medal) for her distinguished performance of Juliet. |
| | **October 10** -- Begins a tour of *Romeo and Juliet* with Maurice Evans and Florence Reed through the midwest. At the end of the tour the play returns to New York. |

**1935**    **December 23** -- Opens in *Romeo and Juliet* for two weeks in New York.

Establishes the Katharine Cornell Foundation.

**1936**    **January** -- Plays Elizabeth in *The Barretts* for the 709th time and Juliet in *Romeo and Juliet* for the 253rd time.

**March 9** -- Opens in *Saint Joan* in New York, a financial success and personal triumph.

**Spring** -- Tours with Saint Joan to Boston, Philadelphia, Chicago, Los Angeles and San Francisco.

**May 1** -- At the end of a special benefit of *Saint Joan* a tribute is paid to Flush on his birthday. He has played 709 performances and travelled 25,000 miles with *The Barretts*.

**June** -- University of Wisconsin honors her with the Doctor of Letters degree.

**Summer** -- Buys property on Martha's Vineyard for her island retreat.

**December 23** -- Beginning with a 4-week tryout tour at the National Theatre in Washington, D.C., on November 24, *The Wingless Victory* opens at the Empire Theatre to mixed reviews. After 11 weeks, it plays in repertory with *Candida*. Having given 110 performances in New York, *The Wingless Victory* is taken on a short tour.

Buys *The Ivory Fan,* by Gustav Ekstein, for her world tour. It is to be one of 5 or 6 repertory plays.

**1937**    **Summer** -- Exhausted from 20 years of working without respite, she begins a sabbatical year and agrees to let Ray Henderson proceed with plans for a world tour which is announced in *Theatre Arts Monthly*.

**March 10** -- Second revival of *Candida* plays in repertory with *The Wingless Victory* in New York.

**March 20** -- Hobart College presents her with an honorary degree.

**March 28** -- *New York Times* reports that Miss Cornell might do a movie, possibly a film version of *The Wingless Victory* if the script satisfies her.

**March 30** -- First Lady Mrs. Eleanor Roosevelt presents her with Chi Omega Sorority's Gold Medal of the National Achievement Award at the White House. She is the first actress to receive it.

**June 14** -- Elmira College honors Katharine Cornell and Helen Hayes with Doctor of Letters Degrees.

1937    **June 15** -- Cornell University bestows on her an Honorary D. Litt. Degree.

        **June 21** -- Receives Doctor of Humane Letters from Smith College.

        **July** -- Flush dies. Wrapped in an actor's coat, he is buried at Sneden's Landing in The Palisades, 15 miles from New York. The Associated Press sends the story over its entire network.

        **October 1** -- En route from Egypt to London, Ray Henderson is killed when his plane crashes in the Mediterranean Sea. Plans for the world tour are abandoned.

1938    MGM offers her $300,000 to make one film. They fail to entice her.

        **February 16** -- Celebrates her 40th birthday (secretly her 45th).

        **May 24** -- Hobart College, where her grandfather and great grandfather had been trustees, presents her with an honorary degree.

        **May** -- *Stage* magazine grants her permission to publish her life story, *I Wanted to Be an Actress*, as she told it to their editor, Ruth Woodbury Sedgwick.

        **June 15** -- University of Pennsylvania bestows an honorary Doctor of Letters degree upon her.

        **October 26** -- Returning from her sabbatical, she presents *Herod and Mariamne* in Pittsburgh, a failure which is not taken to New York.

1939    **March** -- Her autobiography, *I Wanted to Be An Actress*, with Ruth Woodbury Sedgwick, is published.

        **April 17** -- Co-stars with Laurence Olivier in New York at the Ethel Barrymore Theatre in *No Time for Comedy* which becomes the third largest money-maker of her career.

        **Fall** -- *No Time for Comedy* sets out on a 7-month tour to play in 57 cities.

1940    **Spring** -- While the tour is in Chicago, Francis Robinson is hired to replace Ray Henderson as press representative. He later goes with Rudolf Bing at the Metropolitan Opera Company.

1941    **March 11** -- Appears in *The Doctor's Dilemma* and sets a record run (15 weeks) of the Shaw play in New York.

        **June 4** -- Receives Doctor of Fine Arts degree from Clark University.

        **Fall** -- Begins a 14-week road tour, visiting 12 cities, with *The Doctor's Dilemma*.

1942      **January 24** -- *Rose Burke* opens in San Francisco. She begins a cross-country tour with it. Not up to her standards, it is the 2nd play not taken to New York.

               **April 27** -- Presents an all-star revival of *Candida* for the benefit of the Army Emergency and Navy Relief Society. The Army and Navy each receive $37,817 and $10,000 goes to the American Theatre Wing.

               **December 21** -- Supported by Judith Anderson, Ruth Gordon and Gertrude Musgrove, Miss Cornell plays Masha in *The Three Sisters* at the Ethel Barrymore Theatre in New York. Breaks a record for the longest run of that play anywhere.

               Appears in the movie *Stage Door Canteen*, a film made in celebration of the American Theatre Wing's Center for servicemen on West 44th Street in New York City.

1943      **November 29** -- Opens in *Lovers and Friends* at the Plymouth Theatre in New York. Although panned by some critics, the play is profitable and runs for a total of 31 weeks.

1944      **August 11** -- Departs for the North African Theater of the U. S. Army to present *The Barretts of Wimpole Street*. The overwhelming reception of the armed forces overseas mades it the greatest success of her career. The company receives a citation from General Mark Clark "for excellence in performance, merit and discipline."

               **September 8** -- The McClintics celebrate their 23rd anniversary in Naples.

1945      **January 31** -- Leaving England, the company embarks for home from the warfront on the S.S. *Queen Mary*.

               **March 26** -- After taking *The Barretts* to Boston for one week, the play opens in New York.

               The U. S. Government awards Miss Cornell the Medal of Freedom for services during World War II.

1946      **February 18** -- Opens in *Antigone* in the Cort Theatre in New York.

               **April 3** -- Revives *Candida,* with Marlon Brando as Marchbanks, for the fifth and last time. It plays in repertory with *Antigone* in New York.

1947      **June 7** -- In San Francisco plays Elizabeth Barrett Browning for the 1,000th time. *The Barretts* has grossed at least $2,250,170.

               Receives an honorary degree from Ithaca College.

1947    **November 26** -- *Antony and Cleopatra* opens at the Martin Beck Theatre in New York and, with a total of 251 performances, succeeds beyond all expectations.

1948    **June 15** -- Princeton awards her an honorary Doctor of Fine Arts Degree.

    **September 26** -- Her father, Dr. Peter C. Cornell, dies, leaving her an inheritance, part of which goes toward payment of Peter Rock, her home at Sneden's Landing.

    The American Theatre Wing honors her with the Antionette Perry Award for a "distinguished performance" in *Antony and Cleopatra*.

1949    **November 22** -- Presents *That Lady* at the Martin Beck Theatre to unkind reviews. After a 10-week run in New York, the play makes a 14-week tour through Texas and the south.

1950    **February 6** -- Rockford College awards her the Jane Addams Medal for her distinguished contribution through her life and work. This award was first made in 1947.

    **December 6** -- Opens *Captain Carvallo* in Buffalo. Neither the critics or audiences thought it a suitable play for her; it is the third show she closes out of town.

    A special exhibit of Eugene Speicher's portrait of Miss Cornell as Candida is opened in the Albright Gallery in Buffalo.

1951    **January 10** -- Presents *The Barretts of Wimpole Street* on a radio show by the Council of the Living Theatre for the bicentennial of the American professional theatre.

    **May 6** -- She plays in *Candida* for "Theatre Guild on the Air," a *U.S. Steel Hour* production, with Alfred Ryder in the role of Marchbanks.

    **June 23** -- *The Washington Post* reports that Miss Cornell is still hedging about making a film on Florence Nightingale as had been announced earlier.

    **August 4** -- At the drama and opera festival in Central City, Colorado, she plays in *The Constant Wife* with great success.

    **November 27** -- Gives a performance of *The Constant Wife* to benefit a scholarship fund at The Neighborhood Playhouse, School of the Theatre in New York City.

    **December 3** -- She and Brian Aherne receive honorary degrees from Baylor University at the dedication of the Armstrong-Browning Library.

1951    **December 8** -- Opens *The Constant Wife* in New York, at the National Theatre, to gross over 1.5 million dollars. It is the greatest financial success of C. & M. C. Productions in its 29 years. After the New York run, it tours 3 eastern cities for 6 weeks. The following season, it tours 35 cities.

        **December 13** -- Does a benefit performance of *The Constant Wife* at the National Theatre, in New York City, to aid the Rivington Neighborhood Association.

1952    **January** -- Marks the 21st anniversary for Miss Cornell as actress-manager.

1953    **December 16** -- Appears in *The Prescott Proposals*, at the Broadhurst Theatre, in New York. Suffers a loss of over $100,000.

1955    **February 23** -- Opens in *The Dark is Light Enough* at the ANTA Theatre. Has heavy losses in New York but tours successfully.

        **June 14** -- Middlebury College confers an honorary degree upon her.

        **September 29** -- Enters hospital to undergo lung surgery which requires a 3-year period of recuperation.

1956    **June 11** -- Both she and Guthrie McClintic receive honorary Doctor of Literature Degrees from Kenyon College.

        **April 2** -- With Anthony Quayle as Browning, presents *The Barretts* on television for N.B.C.'s *Producers' Showcase,* her 25th anniversary as actress-manager.

1957    **March 17** -- Presents *There Shall be No Night* on N.B.C.-TV with Charles Boyer, Bradford Dillman and Phyllis Love.

1958    **April 30** -- Opens in *The Firstborn* at the Coronet Theatre to lukewarm reviews. A costly production, it fails financially.

        **July 3-12** -- Under the sponsorship of the American-Israeli Committee, presents *The Firstborn* in Tel Aviv and Jerusalem in celebration of Israel's 10th anniversary.

1959    **May 20** -- Accepts the Medal for Good Speech on Stage awarded by the American Academy of Arts and Letters.

        **December 29** --Receives a citation as Woman of the Year from the American Friends of the Hebrew University. The University of Jerusalem establishes a Katharine Cornell Chair of Comparative Literature, which is to be endowed for $100,000.

1960      **March 17** -- After touring for 27 weeks, *Dear Liar*, a theatrical reading of the letters between Shaw and Mrs. Campbell, opens in New York at the Billy Rose Theatre.

1961      **September 8** -- The McClintics' celebrate their 40th wedding anniversary.

               **October 29** -- Guthrie McClintic dies. Miss Cornell loses her desire to continue her acting career.

1963      The C. & M.C. Production Company is dissolved.

1969      **Summer** -- Kit takes a group of friends on a boat trip through the French canals and visits Joanna Hirth in Bavaria.

1971      She has the 300-year-old Association Hall near Vineyard Haven, Martha's Vineyard, restored.

1973      **February 16** -- In Naples, Florida, celebrates her 75th birthday (actually her 80th) and reveals the long deception that she is 5 years older than believed.

               **Spring** -- Shortly after her birthday she is hospitalized briefly.

1974      **January 10** -- Accepts the American National Theater and Academy's National Artist Award for her "incomparable acting ability" and for "having elevated the theater throughout the world."

               **April 24** -- The Katharine Cornell-Guthrie McClintic Room is dedicated at the New York Public Library's Theatre Collection at Lincoln Center. An attack of flu prevents her attendance.

               **June 12** -- Katharine Cornell dies of pneumonia at Martha's Vineyard. Her ashes are buried in the cemetery behind the Association Hall near Vineyard Haven, which she had helped to restore.

# Stage Appearances

This chapter is divided into three parts. Beginning with S01 each entry is numbered consecutively to the end of the chapter regardless of the division. The following divisions are made:

**The Early Years** cover Miss Cornell's apprenticeship years with the Washington Square Players and Bonstelle Stock Company (1916-1920) prior to her first Broadway appearances.

**The Broadway Years** include the period between 1921 and 1931, before she became manager of her own company.

**Actress-Manager Years** chronicle the major part (1931-1960) of her Broadway career, two major tours and several plays for which she found it necessary to accept outside financial backing.

## THE EARLY YEARS (1916-1920)

S01     *Bushido* (Washington Square Players, Comedy Theatre, off Broadway, New York, 1916). Kit spoke four words as Shusai, a Japanese mother.

S02     Her second performance that season was offstage when she made a series of cries as a mother giving birth in *The Life of Man.*

S03     *Plots and Playwrights* (Washington Square Players, New York, March 1917). In this prize play by Edward Massey she had her first real part, for which she received favorable comments from critics. Guthrie McClintic, who was in the audience, noted on his program that, although she was "monotonous," she was "interesting" enough to "watch." Critic Heywood Broun described her as "a dead-white, young American Duse" (B149, p. 160).

S04     *Neighbors* (Washington Square Players, 1918). Kit took the role of Mis' Cary Ellsworth in Zona Gale's play.

S05     *Blind Alleys* (Washington Square Players, 1918). She played Mrs. Frank Darrel, a New Englander. A *New York Times* reviewer commented on her personality, intelligence and skill.

S06     *Yum Chapab* (Washington Square Players, 1918). In this pantomime Kit played the drums.

S07     *The Death of Tintagiles* (Washington Square Players, 1918). She appeared swathed in gauze.

S08     *Cheating Cheaters* (Bonstelle Stock Company, Buffalo, 1918). Her first appearance in her hometown, Kit played a straight part for which she received a favorable editorial.

S09     *Seven Chances* (Bonstelle Stock Company, Buffalo, 1918). She played a part described as "sentimental" and "moonstruck" (B163, p. 75).

S10     *Romance* (Bonstelle Stock Company, Buffalo, 1918). Kit played Signora Vanucci, a middle-aged Italian lady-in-waiting to a famous opera singer. A Buffalo reviewer wrote that her acting "stamps her as an actress of much ability" (B163, p. 75).

S11     *Pals First* (Bonstelle Stock Company, Buffalo, 1918). A critic in a Buffalo paper applauded her portrayal of an aging southern spinster as "one of the funniest things in the play" (B163, p. 76).

S12     *Fanny's First Play* (Bonstelle Stock Company, Buffalo, 1918). Kit won much applause for her role of Dora, a cockney girl.

S13     *The Man Outside* (Bonstelle Stock Company, Garrick Theatre, Detroit, 1918). A local critic compared her acting to the manner of Lynn Fontanne.

S14     *The Man Who Came Back* (William A. Brady's 3rd road company. Shubert-Majestic Theatre, Providence, Rhode Island, January 6, 1919). She was graduated to second lead when she replaced Laura Walker in the part of Marcelle, an opium addict. The leading man was Conrad Nagel who was followed by three other leading men: Henry Hull, Frank Morgan and Arthur Ashley. The play went on tour and critics treated her as the star. Honors went to her when they played in Rochester, New York.

S15     *Ann's Adventure* (Bonstelle Stock Company, Buffalo and Detroit, 1919). Grace George later took the play to New York as *Ruined Lady* but did not ask Kit to be in the New York company.

S16     *Little Women* (London, England, 1919). Jessie Bonstelle, who staged William Brady's production, insisted that Katharine Cornell play the part of Jo. London audiences flocked to see her.

S17     *Heaven* (Bonstelle Stock Company, Buffalo and Detroit, 1920). Kit played the part of Diane and was considered for the Broadway production, but John Golden, the producer, thought she lacked sufficient sex appeal. The title was changed to *Seventh Heaven* and the role went to Helen Mencken. Janet Gaynor played the film role.

S18     *Daddy-Long-Legs* (Bonstelle Stock Company, Buffalo and Detroit, 1920). She believed she was miscast in the Ruth Chatterton role and played it badly.

S19     *Too Many Husbands* (Bonstelle Stock Company, Buffalo and Detroit, 1920). Kit felt comfortable in this role. Her husbands were played by Guthrie McClintic and Frank Morgan.

S20     *Lombardi, Ltd.* (Bonstelle Stock Company, Buffalo and Detroit, 1920). She loved the farce and played it with such zany abandon that the audience was convulsed with laughter.

S21     *Civilian Clothes* (Bonstelle Stock Company, 1920). Guthrie directed this last play of the season. He and Kit had fallen in love. They returned to New York--he to direct *Green Goddess* and she to look for a job.

## THE BROADWAY YEARS (1921-1931)

**S22      NICE PEOPLE**
(Opened: March 1, 1921, at the Klaw Theatre, New York; 31 weeks of performances)

| | |
|---|---|
| Playwright | Rachel Crothers |
| Directors | Rachel Crothers and Sam Forrest |
| Producer | Sam Harris |

### Cast

| | |
|---|---|
| Hallie Livingston | Tallulah Bankhead |
| Eileen Baxter-Jones | Katharine Cornell |
| Trevor Leeds | Edwin Hensley |
| Theodora Gloucester | Francine Larrimore |
| Oliver Comstock | Guy Milham |
| Scottie Wilbur | Hugh Huntley |
| Margaret Rainsford | Merle Maddern |
| Herbert Gloucester | Frederick Perry |
| Billy Wade | Robert Ames |
| Mr. Heyfer | Frederick Maynard |

### The Play's History

Rachel Crothers' latest comedy had its first New York performance at the new Klaw Theatre. Miss Crothers wrote *Nice People* as a commentary on the reaction of "every well-bred and reasonably observant woman of 40 or more" to the disreputable behavior of girls who came from the "best" families (B508). A popular playwright, Miss Crothers' work dealt mainly with women's position, especially in high society.

### Synopsis

After the death of his wife, millionaire Hubert Gloucester of Park Avenue gives his charming twenty-year-old daughter, Teddy, freedom to do as she pleases. It pleases her to smoke, drink, dress daringly and go to parties with her friends as all the society girls are doing.

Gloucester defends Teddy's friends as "nice" people from "smart" families until she defies him and meets her boyfriend, Scottie, and their crowd for a night on the town. Their fun extends through the next day and following night. Teddy and Scottie, who have stopped at the Gloucester's cottage on Long Island for a bite to eat, are detained by a severe storm and Scottie's inebriation. Finding them there the next morning, Teddy's father thinks the worst and demands that Teddy marry Scottie. When she refuses, he forbids her to return home.

Fortunately, there is one witness who can attest to Teddy's innocence. A young man, Billy Wade, who had also been driven by the storm to seek shelter at the Gloucester's cottage, had sat through the night with Scottie in his sottish slumber while Teddy slept upstairs.

When Teddy's friends abandon her, she finally agrees to  marry Scottie, but Billy Wade convinces her that she can take care of herself. In the end, she rejects her father's money and the "nice" people for life in the country with Billy.

## Reviews

*New York Times* (3/3/21)--Critic Alexander Woollcott found the conclusion disappointing in that it was "so painfully shopworn in the theatre," but thought the "play was well cast." He gave plaudits to Francine Larrimore, and special mention to Tallulah Bankhead and Guy Milham. Of the others, he said: "It would be easiest to sum up the rest of the company by the sweeping statement that every one does very, very nicely" (B508).

*Variety* (3/11/21)--The trade publication judged *Nice People* to be on a par with the best of the season. The principal fault was in the play which has entirely spent its theme by the end of the first scene of the second act. The result is "one of severe padding, of telling the story over again" in the second and third acts. The moral lesson for society would have been more effective if the heroine had been made to bear "the logical consequences of her acts." As for the acting, Miss Bankhead's portrayal of the "catty" Hallie Livingston rivaled Miss Larrimore's leading role. Katharine Cornell was complimented for her "deft handling" of her less prominent role. *Variety* reported that her talent was apparent and her "sympathetic touch" made Eileen Baxter-Jones stand out (B310).

## Commentary

Burns Mantle reported that the play was more successful with the public than with reviewers. The theme's timeliness and the open discussion of a modern debutante's manners and morals interested a large segment of the public (B141).

Critics considered it another typical comedy drama with a "forced and artificial" ending. They did, however, find it to be an "incisive" criticism of society and gave Crothers credit for writing one of the better plays of the season--at least the first two acts.

Eileen was Miss Cornell's first part under commercial management on Broadway. She got the role through the suggestion of Mrs. Wolcott, an influential Patroness-at-Large, and almost lost it because of a tonsillectomy, but a delay in the rehearsal schedule saved the part for her. It was a small role and one in which Kit admitted she made no "lasting" impression (B047, p. 38). According to Kit, Miss Crothers did most of the directing and coached her to get the sure-fire laughs that she believed she had written. Somehow Kit could not get the right twist, nor the laughs Miss Crothers insisted were there. Fortunately, the role of Eileen didn't call for the aggressiveness that Tallulah Bankhead as Hallie fit so well. Kit could only "assume the style of that decade" (B163, p. 130). At least she had broken into Broadway.

During the run of *Nice People* the McClintics read *A Bill of Divorcement* and Kit was intrigued with the part of Sydney Fairfield. It was her good fortune that Allan Pollock had the American rights to the play and had seen her as Jo in *Little Women*. Overriding the objections of casting director Fred Latham, who was not impressed with Miss Cornell, Pollock insisted on giving the role to her. She was hired, gave her notice to Miss Crothers in mid-August and played in *Nice People* for the last time on September 3. The play ran until September 30 (a total of 31 weeks) and then went on tour.

******

S23     A BILL OF DIVORCEMENT
        (Opened:  October 10, 1921, at the George M. Cohan Theatre, New York; 173
        performances)

<u>Credits</u>
Playwright                                          Clemence Dane
Director                                               Basil Dean
Casting                                               Fred Latham
Producer                                        Charles Dillingham

<u>Cast</u>
Margaret Fairfield                                   Janet Beecher
Hester Fairfield                                        Ada King
Sydney Fairfield                                Katharine Cornell
Bassett                                          Lillian Brennard
Gray Meredith                                   Charles Waldron
Kit Pumphrey                                        John Astley
Hilary Fairfield                                    Allan Pollock
Dr. Alliot                                           Arnold Lucy
The Rev. Christopher Pumphrey                         Fred Graham

<u>The Play's History</u>
        *A Bill of Divorcement*, written by Clemence Dane (pseudonym for actress
Winifred Ashton), had been a notable success with Meggie Albanesi in the role of
Sydney, in London's 1920-21 season.
        In the audience was Allan Pollock, an actor who had suffered shell-shock and
severe wounds in the war and had spent almost three years in the hospitals being "made
over by the war surgeons" (B142, p. 63).  Pollock identified with Dane's character, Hilary
Fairfield, who had also been a victim of war.
        Different stories surrounding Pollock's acquisition of the play have been told.
Burns Mantle reported that Pollock, having almost given up returning to the stage, was
fascinated by Hilary, understood him and knew he could play the role.  He convinced the
owners of his ability and bought the American rights to the play (B142).  In the Mosel
version of the circumstances, a group of Pollock's friends at the Players Club, who were
concerned about him, bought the American rights, gave them to Pollock and supplied the
backing.  They also approached Charles D. Dillingham, who was then in London
considering the extension of his production ventures to include dramatic plays (he had
heretofore limited himself to musical shows) in New York, and persuaded him to
undertake an American tour of *A Bill of Divorcement*.  He agreed.
        The play, set in the future, was written when discussion of a proposed divorce
bill that would change existing English laws was taking place.  The bill was aimed at
correcting current abuses, many of which had resulted from "war marriages" (B142, p.
64).  Dane was asking her audience to project themselves into 1933, when the divorce bill
would become law.
        The play was presented in New York against formidable competition on one
of the busiest weeks of the fall season.  There were five openings that night which
included Helen Hayes as the star in Booth Tarkington's play *The Wren* and the Theatre
Guild's presentation of Arthur Richman's *Ambush* with Florence Eldridge.

## Synopsis

Margaret Fairfield's husband has been institutionalized since the war from shell-shock that has left him deranged. She has obtained a divorce under the new law on the grounds of her husband's insanity.

Years have passed and Margaret's marriage to Gray Meredith is just a week away. Already suffering from a twinge of guilt, Margaret is troubled because her seventeen-year-old daughter Sydney is leaving school to marry, just as Margaret herself had done during the war. She is also troubled by Sydney's excitability; sometimes she is like her father.

Sydney is alone with Aunt Hestor, with whom she and her mother live, when her fiance Kit tells them that his father, the church rector, cannot perform the ceremony for Margaret because of her divorce. The sanitarium calls to inform them that Hilary, Sydney's father, has escaped before his scheduled release and will probably return to his home. Sydney learns from her aunt that her father's shell-shock had brought on the inherited family insanity, which accounts for the "nervy" behavior of all of them.

As expected, Hilary appears. When he learns of the divorce, his behavior confirms Sydney's fears about marrying and perpetuating the family illness. Not wanting her mother to give up her chance for happiness, Sydney breaks her engagement to Kit, convinces her mother that she wants a career and goes with her father.

## Reviews

*New York Globe* (10/11/21)--"Superb" was Kenneth Magowan's description of Katharine Cornell's acting. "It is a brilliant piece of work, sensitive with all the sensitiveness that must be suggested in this daughter of an insane man....Another of the outstanding actresses of the next ten years comes forward" (B410).

*New York Times* (10/16/21)--Woollcott lamented the fact that the British title of the play had been retained for the American production. It was misleading in several respects: it had no meaning in this country and the play was chiefly about hereditary insanity rather than divorce. He applauded Miss Dane's recognition of the honesty and courage of the younger generation. Of Katharine Cornell he said that she played "the central and significant role" giving "a performance of memorable understanding and beauty." Both she and Mr. Pollock hold "Miss Dane's work at a level the season will seldom reach" (B503).

*New Republic* (12/28/21)--Citing the weaknesses in the play, namely the author's attenuation of its dramatic force, Robert Morss Lovett found most of the acting admirable. The role of Sydney, he noted, was the most difficult. Miss Cornell was "convincing and moving" with Margaret and Hilary but overplayed her "flippant protest" and threw the audience's sympathy to Hester Fairfield (B137).

## Commentary

On the evening of October 10, rain dampened the dressy premiere of *A Bill of Divorcement* which, among the superstitious in the theater, was a sign of good luck. In the audience were Laura Elliot, Frances Wolcott and other friends of the McClintics. Because of other openings that evening, only three of the first-line critics appeared.

Reviews were neither unfavorable nor enthusiastic. Fortunately, music critic Carl Van Vechten had been in the audience and had reacted with enthusiasm as well as concern about the play's fate. Rushing to call Alexander Woollcott, who had reviewed

Helen Hayes that evening, Van Vechten urged him to see and save the play. Forthwith, Woollcott attended the matinee, rallied the other critics, wrote a splendid review for the Sunday edition and became a devotee of Katharine Cornell thereafter. On Friday the reviews by Burns Mantle and Kenneth Macgowan were "brilliant" and by the following week receipts were improving (B149, p. 220).

For several reasons the playgoing public responded slowly. The playwright was unknown and Pollock had not been seen by American audiences for some time. Furthermore, the title of the play had led the them to believe the play was either about war and therefore depressing, or light and entertaining. Woollcott suggested that, in America, shell-shock was less familiar than in Britain, and the play dealt only secondarily with divorce. The real focus was on hereditary insanity. In his review of October 16, he proclaimed the play to be "worth more than all of them (the other plays) put together" (B503).

In 1921, actors customarily took curtain calls at the end of each act, with the big ovation usually coming at the end of the second act. On opening night there were six curtain calls, one of which was for Kit alone. After the first week of languishment the playgoers suddenly began to buy tickets and demand a reason for the play's closing. *A Bill of Divorcement* was moved to the Cohan Theatre at Times Square where it ran as a hit.

The association with Dean, the director, was an uneasy one for Miss Cornell. Because he had wanted Meggie Albanesi, who had played the role in London, or at least someone like her, he was displeased and unsympathetic with Miss Cornell. Fortunately, he was too occupied with the problems of the actress playing Margaret to give attention to Miss Cornell until her part was set and then there was little comment he could make. It was also fortunate that Miss Cornell's concentration on developing Sydney kept her distracted from Dean's behavior.

The role of Sydney offered Miss Cornell an opportunity to contrast the rather brash, self-assured Sydney with the courageous, empathic young woman she revealed when she realized that she bore the taint of insanity. Miss Cornell rose to the challenge of her difficult role and was clearly on her way up in the theatrical world.

\*\*\*\*\*\*

## S24    WILL SHAKESPEARE
(Opened: January 1, 1923, at the National Theatre, New York; 80 performances)

### Credits
| | |
|---|---|
| Playwright | Clemence Dane |
| Settings | Norman Bel Geddes |
| Music | Deems Taylor |
| Producer | Winthrop Ames |

### Cast
| | |
|---|---|
| Anne Hathaway | Winifred Lenihan |
| Will Shakespeare | Otto Kruger |
| Mrs. Hathaway | Angela Ogden |

| | |
|---|---|
| Henslowe | John L. Shine |
| Queen Elizabeth | Haidee Wright |
| Mary Fitton | Katharine Cornell |
| Kit Marlowe | Allan Birmingham |
| Stage Doorkeeper | Wallace Jackson |
| Stage Hand | Herbert Clarke |
| A Boy | Lewis Shore |
| Landlord | Harry Barfoot |
| A Man | Samuel Godfrey |
| Another Man | William J. Kline |
| Maid of Honor | Cornelia Otis Skinner |
| Street Hawker | Anne Williamson |
| Secretary | William Worthington |
| A Seneschal | Charles Romane |

### The Play's History

This play was first performed in London by the Reandean Company at the Shaftsbury Theatre on November 17, 1921.

### Synopsis

Henslowe, sent by the Queen to find a promising playwright for England, persuades the young Will Shakespeare to come to London where he will find his fortune and a winsome woman. His wife Anne begs him to wait until the birth of their child which will be later than she had told him. Enraged by her deceit in getting him to marry her, he refuses to believe that she is expecting a child and leaves her.

Ten years later, in London, Will has written a play, *Romeo and Juliet*, which has been inspired by his love for Mary Fitton, the Dark Lady of the Sonnets. During the performance of the play, his wife's mother appears and begs him to see his dying son. Will promises, but Mary Fitton detains him and he does not go.

Soon tired of Will, Mary turns her affection to his friend, Christopher (Kit) Marlowe. Finding them together, the jealous, lovesick Will lunges at his friend and in the ensuing scuffle, Marlowe dies.

The Queen sends for Shakespeare, discharges Mary from her service and orders Will to take up his pen and "earn a world for England." Now realizing the pain he caused his wife, he hears Anne calling him to come back to her when he needs "a breast to die on."

### Reviews

*New York World* (1/2/23)--Heywood Broun commented that, in the tavern brawl scene, "Miss Cornell gives the most spirited and swaggeringly romantic performance we have known in seasons. It is an act lighted so superbly that great threatening shadows dance upon the walls like overtones. Miss Cornell seems to be a gusty wind before which these phantoms waver." He then cautioned her about her bouncing (B313).

*New York Daily News* (1/3/23)--Burns Mantle thought that a highlight of *Will Shakespeare* was Katharine Cornell, as Mary Fitton, when she was playing Juliet. The young Shakespeare was presenting his new play, *Romeo and Juliet*, for the Queen's approval. Mantle said that Cornell, well supported by Otto Kruger, played the role "beautifully and movingly" (B422).

*Variety* (1/5/23)--The major trade paper responded enthusiastically to *Will Shakespeare*. Miss Dane was praised for her brilliant writing of a play that had "great power and great interest." The four main parts, taken by Kruger, Wright, Lenihan, and Cornell, were played admirably. The reviewer wrote that Katharine Cornell's Mary Fitton had "...extraordinary beauty and power. Tender in lovemaking, fiery as the queen's maid, her selection was most fortunate." The scene between her and Kruger was "a brilliant bit of emotional playing, particularly on her part" (B311).

## Commentary

Except for the three women's parts (Anne, Queen Elizabeth, and Mary Fitton), the critics did not like the play. John Corbin and Heywood Broun gave the highest praise to Haidee Wright for her portrayal of the Queen. Broun commended Winifred Lenihan and Katharine Cornell for magnificent performances but cautioned Miss Cornell to learn to bounce upon the furniture more "shrewdly" or she would most surely break something (B313). The comment disturbed her enough to explain that "her bouncing would have been smoother" had she not been ill before the beginning of rehearsals (B163, p. 165).

What the critics disliked most about the play was the playwright's portrayal of Shakespeare as "a poor fish" (B176). John Corbin thought that the playwright, in three hours (the play, which had been extensively cut, did not end until 11:30), could have given an impression of some of Shakespeare's fine qualities admired by his friends. Instead, Corbin said, the author had drawn him as a "dupe" whose character has not "even the simplest of human emotions" (B338). Miss Cornell liked the play, found Mary Fitton an exciting part and could not understand why the play wasn't more successful. It closed at the end of 8 weeks, after 80 performances. The role did give her an opportunity to put her athletic abilities to use and, being so different from Sydney Fairfield, exemplified her versatility.

\*\*\*\*\*\*

## S25    THE ENCHANTED COTTAGE
(Opened: March 31, 1923, at the Ritz Theatre, New York; 8 weeks of performances)

### Credits
| | |
|---|---|
| Playwright | Sir Arthur Wing Pinero |
| Director | Jessie Bonstelle |
| Producers | Jessie Bonstelle and |
| | William A. Brady, Jr. |

### Cast
| | |
|---|---|
| Laura Pennington | Katharine Cornell |
| Mrs. Minnett | Clara Blandick |
| Major Murray Hillgrove | Gilbert Emery |

| | |
|---|---|
| Oliver Bashforth | Noel Tearle |
| Rev. Charles Corsellis | Harry Neville |
| Mrs. Corsellis | Ethel Wright |
| Mrs. Smallwood | Winifred Frazer |
| Rupert Smallwood | Herbert Bunston |
| Rigg | Seldon Bennett |

## Laura's Dream

| | |
|---|---|
| First Bridal Couple | Thomas Broderick |
| | Phyllis Jackson |
| Second Bridal Couple | Roland Hanson |
| | Gudrun Mantzius |
| Third Bridal Couple | Stanley Lindahl |
| | Grace Dougherty |
| Ethel | Gwyneth Gordon |
| Bridesmaids | Dorothy Revere |
| | Elizabeth Collins |
| First Witch | Clara Blandick |
| Second Witch | Helen Ryan |
| Third Witch | Cora Calkins |

## The Play's History

 *The Enchanted Cottage*, written as a fable, was produced in London at the Duke of York's Theatre on March 1, 1922. For Pinero, it was a new experiment, which critics believed to be reminiscent of, if not highly influenced by, J. M. Barrie.

 The New York production opened just 20 days after the closing of *Will Shakespeare*. The stage managing was poor with something going wrong at every performance. That and the fact that the critics did not like the play contributed to its failure.

## Synopsis

 Oliver Bashforth, late lieutenant, 8th Bengal Regiment, has returned from the war, shellshocked, broken and seeking refuge in a country cottage, the remnant of a legendary manor. Major Hillgrove pays a friendly visit to the embittered Bashforth whose only companion is his eccentric housekeeper, Mrs. Minnett, suspected of witchcraft. Blinded by the war himself, Hillgrove has been escorted to the cottage by Laura Pennington, a poor, unattractive, gentle young woman.

 To escape his mother's plan to put him in the care of the rector and his wife, Oliver insensitively suggests that Laura share the cottage with him; they will marry, of course. He hurts the girl deeply. Upset by his own ineptness, he implores her to see him again with the result that they fall in love and marry.

 Visibly to the audience, Laura becomes lovely and desirable and Oliver becomes straight and handsome. Laura's dream of a grand wedding is played out for the audience with ancestral couples who have honeymooned in the cottage, with witches, bridesmaids, imps, cherubs and children.

 Before Oliver's parents, the Smallwoods, arrive for a visit, Oliver and Laura explain their miracle to Hillgrove and ask him to prepare the parents for the change in them. When they arrive, the Smallwoods see the newlyweds just as they had been, a pathetic pair. Thinking them demented, the parents make a hasty departure. Oliver and

Laura learn from Mrs. Minnett that "a man and woman in love have a gift of sight that's not granted to other folk." Their lost illusion only deepens their love and happiness. Laura has another dream, this time of a beautiful child who comes to her.

## Reviews

*New York Times* (4/2/23)--In commenting on the acting of Miss Cornell and Mr. Tearle, John Corbin found them "admirable." He thought that the art by which both actors, "without sacrificing a jot of truth, indicate that love has brought some little measure of outward strength and beauty with its transformation of the spirit" is "especially noteworthy" (B339).

*New York Daily News* (4/23)--Burns Mantle commended Miss Cornell for her "sense of drama" and other "commanding assets" which enabled her to make "the spinster very real and human" (B414).

*New York Post* (4/23)--J. Rankin Towse thought the fable was a pretty one, but the "blend of the fanciful" with "the somewhat crudely conventional" was not a happy one. Moreover, the actual transformation of the neurotic cripple and ugly maiden into a handsome soldier and beautiful bride signified distrust of the ordinary audience's intelligence and weakened the moral the author was attempting to convey (B486).

## Commentary

Although critic John Corbin liked the acting of Cornell and Tearle he panned the play for its "sentimental phantasy," the "forced and tasteless" humor of the curate and his wife, and Pinero's failure to leave "enough to the imagination." He did, however, commend the playwright for this portrayal of the social conditions of men who were "hopelessly maimed" and the women who were "doomed" to spinsterhood (B339). J. Rankin Towse of the *New York Post* viewed the actual transformation of the couple into a beautiful bride and handsome groom as disastrous. On the other hand, he granted that the fable was "pretty," had "charm" and "truth" (B486).

Miss Cornell thought that Laura was "an exquisite person to play--sensitive, fragile, filled with light" (B047, p. 56). It was good contrast for the hoydenish Mary Fitton she had just played in *Will Shakespeare*. However, poor management created a good deal of frustration for all the actors, particularly Miss Cornell, who had her first attack of temperament with the stage manager because of the many problems with the lights. It was the last time that she acted under the direction of Miss Bonstelle who had given her encouragement and invaluable training.

******

S26     **CASANOVA**
(Opened: September 26, 1923 at the Empire Theatre, New York; 77 performances)

## Credits
Playwright                                                Lorenzo de Azertis
Translation                                               Sidney Howard

| | |
|---|---|
| Settings | Herman Rosse |
| Director of a Ballet | Michael Fokine |
| Co-Producer and Composer | Deems Taylor |
| Producers | A. H. Woods and |
| | Gilbert Miller |

## Cast

| | |
|---|---|
| Columbine | Beatrice Belreva |
| A Guitar Player | Doris |
| Pulcinella | George Royle |
| Battista, His Page | Herbert James |
| A Fat Man | Harry Fielding |
| A Gentleman in Black | Horace Healy |
| A Roman Soldier | George Blackmore |
| Alfani-Celli | Philip Wood |
| Manzoni | B. N. Lewin |
| A Waiter | Walter Soderling |
| A Gambler | William Marr |
| Giulietta | Dinarzade |
| Captain Michael Echedy | Mario Majeroni |
| Henriette | Katharine Cornell |
| Giacomo Casanova, Chevalier de Seingalt | Lowell Sherman |
| A Lieutenant | Ralph Belmont |
| Innkeeper | Edward Le Hay |
| First Archer | J. C. Wallace |
| Second Archer | Edward F. Snow |
| Leduc | Ernest Cossart |
| A Banker in Cesena | Harold Hartsell |
| A Gambler | Harry Redding |
| Monsieur Dubois | Victor Benoit |
| The Abbe Bernis | Horace Braham |
| Innkeeper | A. G. Andrews |
| Monsieur Antoine | David Glassford |
| First Postillion | James Powers |
| Second Postillion | Jacob Kingsberry |
| Third Postillion | Frank Newcomb |
| Fourth Postillion | Charles Vincent |
| The Beautiful Governess | Gypsy O'Brien |
| The Dancer from Milan | Mary Ellis |
| The Courtesan | Judith Vosselli |
| Rose | Shelia Hayes |
| Manon | Nellie Burt |

## The Play's History

This was the first production of *Casanova*, which was considered a poor translation of the Spanish play. The young dancer featured in the Fokine ballet was to become known as Valentina, the designer who would later create beautiful clothes for Miss Cornell (B163, p. 170).

## Synopsis

Set in 1755, the play opens with a carnival ballet, then turns to a scene at an inn in Cesena, Italy, where Casanova is seated at a gaming table. A beautifully dressed masked lady, who has fled from France and her unbearable husband, enters with an elderly, courtly Captain who has promised her transportation to Parma. Henriette's beauty, of course, captures Casanova's attention.

When the police come (at the innkeeper's request) to search Henriette's room for a marriage license (even though she and the Captain have separate rooms), Casanova defends her. He then entreats her to join him for ninety days of a golden feast and passion.

Ninety days later at Lake Geneva, the feast is over and they are in love. Casanova is deeply in debt. Henriette will stay if he says, but he must promise it will be forever. When he asks her for an hour to regain his fortune at the gaming table without making the promise, she leaves to return to France. Finding her gone, Casanova discovers a baby cap in her embroidery work.

While he is lamenting his loss, the French Ambassador arrives to offer him a handsome income to take over the finances of France. He accepts and immediately sends four postillions to bring her back but her carriage has crossed the border before she can be overtaken. Casanova is grief-stricken.

Twenty years later in the Cesena Inn where they had met, he has been very ill. His servant has absconded with everything and he is again in debt to the innkeeper who has given him refuge. A beautiful young woman, who looks like Henriette, comes to see if he is feeling better before she leaves. After she has gone to her carriage, he sinks slowly to kiss the floor where his daughter had stood and dies.

## Reviews

*Variety* (10/4/23)--The trade paper reported that *Casanova* was something of a surprise, in that many of the critics gave Katharine Cornell more personal honors than Lowell Sherman. Most of the critics lauded the costly production which they thought was "picturesquely romantic." The play itself did not meet the high expectations, although it was making from $12,000 to 13,000 weekly (B472).

*New Republic* (10/10/23)--Critic Stark Young observed that the play "does not really speak our language," and requires "a peculiar Latin irony and sophistication" which the actors and production lacked. Furthermore, he said that the whole theme took its meaning from Casanova and "Mr. Sherman has no imagination, style, wit, speed or variety" (B245).

## Commentary

Because the part of Henriette is so small (with only eighteen sides), one wonders why Miss Cornell chose to play her. She was eager to do so, she said in her autobiography, for several reasons. "Perhaps it was the lure of those white DuBarry wigs and the lovely clothes," she wrote, but "she was the only really defined part in the script." Furthermore, the dual characterization and the contrast between the mistress and the daughter presented her an interesting opportunity (B047, p. 61).

The critics were kind to Miss Cornell, but not to Sherman. Percy Hammond, in the *New York Tribune*, thought he resembled "a beautiful butterfly in agony" in the scene where he awaited Henriette's return (B376). Of Miss Cornell, *The New York Times* reviewer reported that she "suffused her scenes with the lure of feminine sensibility and courageous adventure" (B446). Despite the lavish costumes, the extensive cast and the "theatric expertness," the play did not have appeal for Broadway audiences.

******

## S27    THE WAY THINGS HAPPEN
(Opened: January 28, 1924, at the Lyceum Theatre, New York; 24 performances)

### Credits

| | |
|---|---|
| Playwright | Clemence Dane |
| Settings | Franklin Abbott & J.P. Carey Co. |
| Costumes | O'Kane, Conwell & Elsie, Ltd. |
| Producer | Guthrie McClintic |

### Cast

| | |
|---|---|
| Mrs. Farren | Zeffie Tilbury |
| Shirley Pride | Katharine Cornell |
| Martin Farren | Tom Nesbitt |
| Harness | Augusta Haviland |
| Muriel Hanbury | Helen Robbins |
| Chussie Hare | Reginald Sheffield |
| Bennett Lomax | Ivan Simpson |
| Mrs. Simpson | Lillian Brennard |
| Dr. Rodson | T. Wygney Percyval |
| A Porter | Orlando Smith |

### The Play's History

After the failure of *Will Shakespeare*, Clemence Dane wrote *The Way Things Happen*. Although she had not seen Katherine Cornell in the roles of Sydney Fairfield or Mary Fitton, Miss Dane had confidence that she could play Shirley Pride. The play was produced in America before it appeared in London. It was the first play with Miss Cornell that McClintic had produced and directed, so it was a bold step for them (B163, p. 171). The tryout in Philadelphia was a great success.

### Synopsis

Living with Mrs. Farren and her son Martin is mousy twenty-year-old Shirley Pride, who Mrs. Farren saved from an orphanage when the girl's mother died. Shirley is in love with Martin who has become engaged to Muriel Hanbury, a possessive, demanding flirt. To keep Muriel's affection Martin has bought expensive gifts he can ill afford and confides to Shirley that he has lost an important piece of paper which he must find or throw himself under the nearest train.

Lomax, who pretends to be Martin's friend, tells Shirley that Martin, who has been gambling, has "borrowed" some bearer bonds and that he, Lomax, has stolen Martin's receipt for the bonds. He blackmails Shirley into submitting to him in return for the receipt.

Unfortunately, Martin learns of the seduction, berates Shirley for her sacrifice, confesses his theft and goes to prison. While he is away, Shirley dutifully cares for the failing Mrs. Farren who lives for her son's return, but dies before he arrives. When Martin does come home he is still unrelenting, until he suddenly realizes that he and Shirley were made for each other.

## Reviews

*New York Times* (1/29/24)--John Corbin judged the action in the play to be "so far from being humanly inevitable as to be thoroughly avoidable--in fact quite unnecessary." The part played by Miss Cornell, "though desperately unwise, does not seem quite impossible" as she played it, but the two men "strain credulity" (B341).

*Variety* (1/31/24)--Explaining that few women should attempt to write domestic plays, *Variety* conceded that the British are able to handle some of the pitfalls and come up with something that is seldom less than good. Although she never achieves greatness, stated the reviewer, Miss Dane contrives to give "poignancy, heart interest and sustained substance" to a plot that "wouldn't pass the third assistant reader for a second-rate New York producer." Finding Miss Cornell to be "the outstanding figure," the reviewer thought she "has the playing power of distinct technical talent in addition to a luminous and sympathetic personality. She can sneer and weep and smile, and she can fight and yield and suffer--these are about all that a young actress need do well" (B438).

*Theatre Magazine* (4/24)--The impression editor Arthur Hornblow had formed from seeing Miss Cornell in previous parts was confirmed by her portrayal of Shirley Pride. He predicted there would be "no limitations to the roles she will be playing--practically everything in the range of drama." Highly complimentary of her "physical as well as spiritual beauty," her "cultivated, appealing voice" and "vast reserve of emotional power," he stated that he "should like to see her in the classic roles...in this interesting, sad-eyed, young actress we may have an American Duse of future years" (B097).

## Commentary

The press in Philadelphia received *The Way Things Happen* as Dane's best play; for 3 weeks it played to packed houses. Consequently, the company had high hopes for its New York opening. However, neither the New York critics nor the audiences liked the play. Critics thought it was a poor play but they did commend Miss Cornell. Burns Mantle of the *New York News* saw her as a "gifted youngster" with "more of the Duse quality than any of the other younger women of the stage." She "feels character sensitively and beautifully," he wrote, and "has the gift of projection" (B421). Arthur B. Waters of the *Philadelphia Ledger* compared her to Mrs. Fiske but with having "a depth of womanly sympathy" that was sometimes lacking in Mrs. Fiske (B490).

The gripping scene in which Martin wrenches from Shirley the confession that she submitted to Lomax to save him from prison was an exhausting scene for which Miss Cornell drew 21 curtain calls in New York. According to Miss Cornell, however, "the women in the audience didn't understand the girl, and the men in the audience hated the man" (B163, p. 170). The play ran for only 24 performances.

It was the first role of this kind that Miss Cornell had played, and she loved it. She also learned a technique for playing with tremendous intensity without burning herself out. Before the play closed she was asked to play Lalage in *The Outsider*.

\*\*\*\*\*\*

**S28    THE OUTSIDER**
(Opened: March 3, 1924, at the Forty-Ninth Street Theatre, New York; 13 weeks of performances)

## Credits

| | |
|---|---|
| Playwright | Dorothy Brandon |
| Director | Robert Milton |
| Settings | Livingston Platt |
| Producer | William Harris, Jr. |

## Cast

| | |
|---|---|
| Mr. Frederick Ladd, F.R.C.S. | Whitford Kane |
| Sir Montagu Tollemache, F.R.C.S. | T. Wygney Percyval |
| Mr. Vincent Helmore, F.R.C.S. | Kenneth Hunter |
| Sir Nathan Israel, F.R.C.S. | John Blair |
| Mr. Jasper Sturdee, M.S. | Lester Lonergan |
| Lalage Sturdee | Katharine Cornell |
| Madame Klost | Fernanda Eliscu |
| Anton Ragatzy | Lionel Atwill |
| Pritchard | Florence Edney |
| Basil Owen | Pat Somerset |

## The Play's History

The play, which Leon M. Lion produced and presented with Frank Curzon at the St. James's Theatre in London, opened June 1, 1923. The leads were played by Leslie Faber in the role of Ragatzy and Isobel Elsom as Lalage.

Harris had originally asked Miss Cornell to take the part in the American production, but she was already playing in *The Way Things Happen*. *The Outsider* had opened in Baltimore and, when *The Way Things Happen* closed suddenly, Miss Cornell was asked to replace Ann Davis who, by request, left the show. After seeing *The Outsider* in Baltimore, Miss Cornell agreed to accept the challenge. During the 6 days of rehearsal and one out-of-town rehearsal and run-through, the third act was revised a number of times and finally returned to its original state. Understandably, Miss Cornell felt very nervous about the opening in New York.

After a slow start the play became a hit. While business was still excellent, every show in town was closed by the Actors' Equity in May. *The Outsider* was, when closed, the most financially successful of the plays in which Miss Cornell had appeared.

## Synopsis

Dr. Ladd has appealed to the high council in the Royal College of Surgeons to consider admitting Ragatzy, a practitioner with no medical credentials, into their circle. By using his invention, "the rack," Ragatzy has cured crippled clients for whom the surgeons could do nothing. Except for Ladd, who has sent patients to Ragatzy, all of the surgeons oppose the outsider's admission. The strongest opponent is the highly respected Dr. Sturdee whose own daughter's hopeless crippled condition resulted from treatment by an incompetent "quack."

Upon learning that Sturdee has a crippled daughter, Ragatzy connives to get entrance to see the beautiful Lalage, an accomplished musician. He perceives at once that Lalage is in love with Basil, a librettist, who would be seriously interested in her if only she could "do things" with him.   Ragatzy exploits her yearning to win Basil and persuades her that he can cure her.

After lying strapped to "the rack" for a year, Lalage is to demonstrate her cure before the surgeons and Basil.  When the great moment arrives for her to walk, she rises, takes a step forward and collapses at Basil's feet.  Although Basil says he will still marry her, Lalage sends him away.  Sturdee acknowledges that what Ragatzy has done is the first step toward Lalage's recovery.  He, Dr. Sturdee, has spent the year learning how to complete the process surgically.  He invites Ragatzy to get his physician's degree and join him.  Lalage, realizing that it is Ragatzy she loves, unconsciously rises and walks into his arms, thus demonstrating the power of love.

## Reviews

*New York Times* (3/4/24)--The critic found fault with the first act and the sometimes false characterization of Ragatzy.  He stated that, without question, Katharine Cornell could be credited for much of the play's effectiveness and saw this as "the best of her several fine performances here."  She and Miss Brandon, being crippled herself, had made the role of Lalage "authentic," "moving" and "thrilling" as well (B449).

*Variety* (3/5/24)--The trade paper reported that *The Outsider* was "gripping" and Miss Cornell's performance "thrilling."  Describing her apparel, the reviewer said she was most attractive in the first act.  In the second act she wore "an orange chiffon lace overskirt, long wing sleeves, a girdle of pastel shades of roses."  She shared a lengthy applause with Lionel Atwill.  In the same issue of *Variety*, comments from critics in other newspapers were quoted: it was one of the "most notable" plays of the season, it was "absorbing and stimulating" and had a "stirring emotional character" (B463).

## Commentary

When Miss Cornell saw the play in Baltimore and consented to take the part, she did not agree with the directions for Lalage.  She felt it was illogical for the crippled girl to move a great deal and thus draw attention to her condition.  With permission to play the role as she interpreted it, she portrayed Lalage in a way that conveyed the insight and feeling with which the author had written it.  Arthur Hornblow in *Theatre Magazine* stated that she made "the young crippled girl a very human, appealing figure."  Her acting, he said, "was marked with fine sincerity and naturalness" (B099, p. 15).  Burns Mantle thought the performance was "beautiful" and "technically finished" (B416).

Alexander Woollcott disliked the contrived scene at the end which required "all the principal characters to behave as if they were not quite bright."  However, he had high praise for  Katharine Cornell who had alleviated "the distresses of an otherwise disturbing evening in the theatre."  She had played the part with the insight and sensitivity that moved her audiences and made an unbelievable situation believable (B505).

\*\*\*\*\*\*

**S29**    **TIGER CATS**
(Opened: October 21, 1924, at the Belasco Theatre, New York;  48 performances)

## Credits
| | |
|---|---|
| Playwright | Mme. Karen Bramson |
| Adapted from "Les Félines" | Michael Orme |
| Director | David Belasco |
| Producer | David Belasco |

## Cast
| | |
|---|---|
| André Chaumont | Robert Loraine |
| Susanne | Katharine Cornell |
| Count Vernard de Vauzelle | Reginald Mason |
| Yvonne | Mary Servoss |
| Jacqueline | Ruth Dayton |
| Clement | Ben Johnson |
| Marianne | Sydney Thompson |
| Jules | Henry Carvill |
| Henriette | Rea Martin |
| A Clerk to Clement | William Boag |

### The Play's History
The play had been produced in London with Edith Evans and Robert Loraine in the leading roles. Belasco had engaged Loraine to take the same part opposite Miss Cornell in the New York production.

### Synopsis
André Chaumont, an eminent neurologist, has the misfortune of marrying a woman who cannot tolerate his devotion to his work or the admiring lady listeners who surround him at his lectures. His wife's jealousy, extravagance, egotism and possessiveness result in his neglect and loathing of her. His rejection infuriates her and she takes a lover. Her boasting of the affair drives André into such a frenzy that he shoots her. She lives, and thus, wins her point. In the end he loses his work-- everything--and has nothing left but her.

### Reviews
*New York Times* (10/22/24)--Stark Young found the play lacking in "intellectual substance" and "theatrical interest," but thought Belasco could not have chosen a better cast. He complimented Loraine for the dignity and restraint that he brought to his role, and Katherine [sic] Cornell for her "remarkable playing." He thought her portrayal was not always "palatable" but she had proven herself to be sincere as an artist and to have promise in the theatre (B511).

*Herald Tribune* (10/23/24)--In Percy Hammond's review he called *Tiger Cats* a "despondent sex tragedy." He found the play to be, to say the least, "monotonous at times" (B378).

*Judge* (11/15/24)--George Jean Nathan reported that the character is "so exaggerated that one momentarily expects a German or an Irish comedian to come on stage and squirt seltzer at it. The whole play has a hard time avoiding burlesque" (B437).

## Commentary

At David Belasco's urging, Miss Cornell had taken the part in *Tiger Cats* because she thought it would be "good discipline and a complete change" (B047, p. 67). As it turned out, the experience was unpleasant. The play itself was disagreeable and Suzanne Chaumont was "a horrible woman." Miss Cornell's greatest difficulty was with the leading man and the playwright. Edith Evans had played Suzanne in London with Loraine who insisted Cornell play the part as Evans had--loud and shrieking. It was not Cornell's style and, consequently, she was having a terrible time with the role, which appalled Mme. Bramson.

Miss Cornell clearly was not getting along with Loraine and, to make matters worse, in rehearsal he accidently gave her a badly burned arm when he held the pistol too close to her. Both the burn and Loraine gave her so much trouble that she secretly prayed she would lose her arm and be unable to continue in the part (B163, p. 177).

Finally, she approached Mme. Bramson, who also preferred Evan's style, and explained that she believed she could do the part effectively in a quietly vicious way. Belasco upheld Miss Cornell's wishes, and after an outburst of temper, she played Suzanne her way. The result was powerful. Even Mme. Bramson was pleased with the good notices. The tension between Loraine and Cornell was probably intensified by critic Young's comment that "he was eclipsed by the remarkable playing of Katharine Cornell" (B511). On the other hand, Alan Dale's remark in the *New York American* that Loraine "had developed into an actor of genuinely remarkable 'attack'" may have assuaged Loraine's animosity somewhat (B355).

******

**S30**     **CANDIDA**
(Opened: December 12, 1924, at the Forty-Eighth Street Theatre, New York; 5 months of performances)

## Credits

| | |
|---|---|
| Playwright | G. Bernard Shaw |
| Director | Dudley Digges |
| Settings | Woodman Thompson |
| Producer | Actors' Theatre |

## Cast

| | |
|---|---|
| Miss Prosperine Garnett | Clare Eames |
| Rev. James Mavor Morell | Pedro de Cordoba |
| Rev. Alexander Mill | Gerald Hamer |
| Mr. Burgess | Ernest Cossart |
| Candida | Katharine Cornell |
| Eugene Marchbanks | Richard Bird |

## The Play's History

Actors' Theatre had been founded after the strike of 1919, with the idea of giving actors an opportunity to play their favorite roles for two weeks at special matinees without remuneration. In 1924, it became an organization by which actors could take part in a play without billing or star treatment. Because *Candida* had no starring role, it was a good selection for the Actors' Theatre. When Miss Cornell was chosen to play Candida, there was considerable grumbling from other actors. Some felt her portrayals of maladjusted women made her an unlikly choice for the serene Candida.

Written by Shaw in 1895, *Candida* was first played in 1897, by a repertory company touring the English provinces. It was seen in London in 1900. Prior to its first professional production by Arnold Daly, in 1903, the play was performed in private for a little theater group in Chicago in 1899. In his first production Arnold Daly played Marchbanks with Dorothy Donnelly as Candida. Thereafter, he revived it in repertory with Chrystal Herne as Candida in 1905, Margaret Wycherly in 1907, and Hilda Spong in 1915.

Miss Cornell's portrayal made Candida a star role. When she left the show to begin rehearsals in *The Green Hat*, Peggy Wood took over the role. Burns Mantle reported that Miss Wood did very well in following Miss Cornell's outstanding portrayal of Candida (B415).

## Synopsis

The Reverend James Mavor Morell, a Christian Socialist clergyman of the Church of England, oversees St. Dominic's parish in a middle-class northeast district of London. The Reverend is a popular and accomplished orator in constant demand as a lecturer. On a sunshiny morning in October, 1984, he turns down an invitation to speak before the Hoxton Group of Freedom. His refusal is prompted by his secretary Prossie's disapproval of what she calls a group of Communist Anarchists.

James is expecting his wife Candida to arrive home for a brief visit. She is spending several weeks south of London while their children recuperate from an illness. Distracted by the unexpected visit of Candida's father Burgess, Morell misses his wife's train. To his consternation, she arrives by cab accompanied by Marchbanks, a shy, homeless eighteen-year-old poet whom James had brought into their home.

When the two men are alone, Marchbanks confesses his love for Candida and accuses James of being selfish and demanding of her. James orders him out of the house but retracts when Candida insists that Marchbanks join them for lunch; Marchbanks accepts.

Later that day James' dejection increases when Candida tells him that, although he doesn't know it, Marchbanks is in love with her just as James is unaware that Prossie and other women are in love with him. She urges him to speak before the Hoxton group and offers to accompany him, but he insists she stay home with Marchbanks.

That evening, while the others are at the lecture, Marchbanks reads poetry to Candida. James returns early to confront her about her "choice." Unaware of Marchbank's confession to James, Candida realizes the situation after James and Marchbanks engage in an impassioned argument. Reminding the young poet that when he is thirty she will be forty-five, she chooses her husband James, "the weaker of the two."

## Reviews

*Boston Transcript* (12/24)--H. T. Parker reviewed the play, saying "Candida was Miss Katharine Cornell, who achieved the part by mental and spiritual sensibility....Beyond Mr. Shaw was it transfigured" (B452).

*Wall Street Journal* (12/15/24)--Enthusiastic about Miss Cornell's Candida, James S. Metcalfe stated that she "brought out the sensitive and spiritual nature of the clergyman's wife in a way to show why there was no resistance to her control of others" (B428).

*The Argonaut* (3/1/25)--Gertrude Furman wrote that Miss Cornell's emphasis on Candida's "spiritual quality" was perhaps her "most important contribution to the acting history in this lustrous part" (B363).

## Commentary

Because of her appearances as rather trashy, maladjusted females, the other actors in the Actors' Theatre were not happy about the casting of Miss Cornell in the kind of role for which she had no experience. She was then playing in *Tiger Cats* which overlapped the *Candida* production by a week. Moreover, the play was opening to the keen competition of the Lunts in *The Guardsman*, Helen Hayes and Lionel Atwill in *Caesar and Cleopatra* and other top shows. Much to the surprise of the doubters, after 3 weeks, a special matinee ticket demand became so great the Actors' Theatre decided to try a commercial run at the Forty-Eighth Street Theatre. The play opened on December 12, 1924, and ran for 5 months, 10 performances more than its first American run.

As Stark Young explained in *The New York Times*, all of the roles were excellent parts and the play offered "fine motivations," "fine humor," and rich dramatic contrast as well as "charming dialogue." Of Miss Cornell, he said that her "playing of all the last act was a thing so delicate and translucent and moving as we rarely see...it was gentle and wise and beautiful" (B509). A week later, he praised her for the understanding she brought to the role "that makes it wide and exquisite with life" (B510). Miss Cornell had imbued Candida with the dignity, love and compassion that reflected her own qualities.

A. Conger Goodyear, head of the Albright Museum in Buffalo, was so excited with *Candida* that he commissioned Eugene Speicher to do a portrait of Miss Cornell in the red dress she wore as Candida. Goodyear later bought the painting from the Albright Museum and gave it to Miss Cornell.

******

S31    **THE GREEN HAT**
(Opened: September 15, 1925, at the Broadhurst Theatre, New York; 29 weeks of performances)

## Credits

| | |
|---|---|
| Playwright | Michael Arlen |
| Director | Guthrie McClintic |
| Costumes | Mrs. Brock Pemberton |
| Producer | A. H. Woods |

## Cast

| | |
|---|---|
| A Lady's Maid | Antoinette Parr |

| | |
|---|---|
| An English Reporter | John Buckler |
| Manager of the Hotel Vendome | Gustave Rolland |
| Dr. Conrad Masters | A. P. Kaye |
| Gerald Haveleur March | Paul Guilfoyle |
| Napier Harpenden | Leslie Howard |
| Major General Sir Maurice Harpenden, Bart. | Eugene Powers |
| Hilary Townsend | Gordon Ash |
| Iris Fenwick, née March | Katharine Cornell |
| Venice Pollen | Margalo Gillmore |
| Lord De Travest | John Redmond |
| Turner | Harry Lilford |
| Sister Virginia | Gwyneth Gordon |
| Sister Clothilde | Anne Tonetti |
| Madelaine, a Nun | Florence Foster |
| Truble | Harry Barfoot |

### The Play's History

In 1924, Michael Arlen (pseudonym for Armenian Dikran Kouyoumdjian), a popular British novelist of the twenties and thirties, wrote a best seller, *The Green Hat*, from which the play was adapted. The New York production, which was to be a world premiere, was given to A. H. Woods. Tallulah Bankhead was to have opened in London after the New York production but, because of the prolonged run in Chicago, the London show's opening came first. Already an established hit on its trial run, which began in Detroit on March 29, 1925, the play had a 29-week run in New York before it was taken to Boston for 8 weeks. It then went on tour for 24 months, until the summer of 1927.

In 1926, Ruth Chatteron starred in the west coast production and Greta Garbo played the film version entitled *A Woman of Affairs* in 1928. Later, another film version, called *Outcast Lady*, featured Constance Bennett.

### Synopsis

When they were young Iris March and Napier Harpenden had fallen in love but were separated by Napier's father because he thought the Marches were "rotten" stock. Iris sought the consolation of many lovers, none of whom were adequate substitutes for her Napier.

Eventually she married Boy Fenwick who, on their wedding night, jumped from the hotel window to his death. To do "one decent thing in life" Iris had let everyone believe that it was her impurity that had driven him to suicide when, in truth, he had syphilis.

After ten years, just before Napier's wedding to Venice, Iris and Napier meet again. Still in love, they succumb to their passion as Iris tosses aside her green hat and turns out the light. Iris leaves and Napier's wedding to Venice takes place as planned.

Nine months later Iris, near death, is in a convent nursing home where she has given birth to a stillborn baby. Napier's willingness to leave Venice and run away with her revives Iris. Wishing to clear her name with his father, Napier discloses the truth about Boy's death. Humiliated, Iris says, "You have taken from me the only generous thing I have ever done in my life." Telling him that Venice is pregnant, she sends Napier back to his wife and drives to her death.

**Reviews**

*New York Times* (9/16/25)--The reviewer judged Miss Cornell to be "perfectly cast in the part" and thought the sympathy which the audience had for Iris was a "tribute chiefly to her acting" and the supporting cast (B434).

*Arts and Decoration* (11/25)--Although George Jean Nathan had nothing good to say about the play in his review in the *Morning Telegraph*, he reiterated his praise of Miss Cornell in this article: "...Here is one of the few young women of our American theatre who has in her an understanding of the art of acting" (B166).

*Theatre Magazine* (11/25)--Critic Arthur Hornblow thought Miss Cornell failed in *Tiger Cats* but had portrayed Iris very well. He had not thought her suited for the "sensuous, unscrupulous woman," but after seeing her, declared she "plays it well" (B098).

**Commentary**

Woods' first choice for Iris was Jeanne Eagels but she had become unreliable so Woods, with some reservation, offered the part to Katharine Cornell who was then appearing in *Candida*. Miss Cornell was intrigued by the role even though she was not Iris's type and Arlen's overheated dramatic prose was a challenge. Furthermore, McClintic disliked the play, thought it was claptrap, and not a part for her. However, she was determined and accepted the part. McClintic agreed to direct it, perhaps to keep her from failing too badly.

The trial opening was given in Detroit on March 29, 1925, with Jeanne Eagels in the audience, hoping to take over the part. The opening went so well that Eagels made a hasty departure and Miss Cornell was asked to play Iris in New York. McClintic made some changes in the script, and after 2 weeks in Detroit, they went to Chicago where tickets were in such demand that the show ran for 14 weeks, thus delaying the New York opening.

Miss Cornell's approach to the role of Iris was quite different from that of Tallulah Bankhead who was a natural for the part. Cornell didn't do anything that was expected of Iris--she didn't smoke, drink or behave seductively. Her Iris was quiet, subtle, understated and very effective (B119, p. 72). Dubious about Miss Cornell's ability to play the role before he saw the play, critic Ashton Stevens wrote in the *Chicago Herald-Examiner* that Miss Cornell rang "tiny bells up and down my unpurchasable vertebrae" (B478).

The advance publicity had piqued public interest and the demand for tickets in New York was so great that amounts in excess of $100 were being offered for a seat. After 29 weeks and 231 performances the play went to Boston for 8 weeks. It closed for the summer and opened again in the fall at the Majestic in Brooklyn before going on tour for 24 months.

The critics' reception of the play was lukewarm but they received Miss Cornell's acting enthusiastically, giving her excellent reviews. In fact, her performance catapulted her to stardom, she saw her name in lights for the first time and more than 200,000 green hats were sold to her female admirers (B512, p. 40). The play ran for over 2 years and toured as far west as Kansas City. It gave her a public.

******

S32    THE LETTER
(Opened: September 26, 1927 at the Morosco Theatre, New York; 13 weeks of performances)

## Credits

| | |
|---|---|
| Playwright | Somerset Maugham |
| Director | Guthrie McClintic |
| Settings | Raymond Sovey |
| Producer | Messmore Kendall |

## Cast

| | |
|---|---|
| Leslie Crosbie | Katharine Cornell |
| Geoffrey Hammond | Burton McEvily |
| Head Boy | M. Wada |
| John Withers | Allan Jeayes |
| Ong Chi Seng | James Vincent |
| A Sikh Sergeant of Police | B. Landon |
| Mrs. Parker | Mary Scott Seton |
| Chung Hi | Sam Kim |
| Chinese Woman | Lady Chong Goe |
| Mrs. Joyce | Eva Leonard-Boyne |
| Chinese Boys, Malay Servants: | K. Tanaka, Yong Mung, Ho Poi Kee, Lo Sing, Lum Hee, Tong See |

## The Play's History

*The Letter* was first produced by Gladys Cooper in London, on February 24, 1927, at the Playhouse. The three main characters were played by Leslie Faber, Nigel Bruce and Gladys Cooper. The play was shown at the Royal Alexandra Theatre in Toronto on September 12, 1927, before opening in New York. It was also taken on tour.

## Synopsis

The curtain opens as a shot is heard in the Crosbies' bungalow on a plantation in the Malay Peninsula. As Geoffrey Hammond staggers toward the veranda and falls, Leslie Crosbie fires bullets into his body. Calmly she sends for the Assistant District Officer and her husband Robert who is in Singapore. She claims that Hammond had tried to rape her and she killed him to save her honor. Leslie is arrested and taken to Singapore where she has not been allowed bail.

Leslie's story is reasonable except for the fact that she shot Hammond six times which indicates "uncontrollable fury." However, it looks like a tight case because Hammond's character is sullied by his living with a Chinese woman; then new evidence comes to the attention of Joyce, her husband's attorney.

A letter demanding that Hammond come to see her was sent by Leslie on the evening of the murder. When Joyce confronts Leslie about the letter she denies having written it, then invents another lie. Because of his friendship with Robert Crosbie, Joyce compromises his professional ethics and agrees to buy the original letter which is in the possession of the Chinese woman. Without understanding the importance of the letter or asking the price, Crosbie gives Joyce permission to make the purchase. Leslie is acquitted and is being welcomed home by the Joyces, when Crosbie discloses his plan to buy a company and move away where they can start a new life. Leslie and Joyce protest, but Crosbie's determination forces Joyce to tell him that the payment for the letter had depleted his savings. Demanding to see the letter, Crosbie asks Leslie what it means. She confesses that she and Geoffrey were lovers and that she killed him out of insane jealousy of the Chinese woman.

Her retribution? She will spend the rest of her life still loving the man she killed but trying to make amends to Crosbie, the man who loves her, "notwithstanding everything."

## Reviews

*New York Times* (9/27/27)--Brooks Atkinson thought Miss Cornell played "superbly" and "with incandescent intensity" but that "the part is at best a well-oiled vehicle suited to a noisy ride along Broadway." Despite his reaction, that excellent talent had been "squandered" on "pretty meretricious stuff," he expected that theatregoers would see *The Letter* (B278).

*New Republic* (10/12/27)--As she moves "toward her prime as a woman," she is becoming "more effective as a brilliant theatrical presence" able to convey "feeling and excitement," wrote Stark Young. He went on to suggest that she needs to take a risk for "richer dramatic substance" (B251).

## Commentary

Miss Cornell had not really wanted to do *The Letter* but Messmore Kendall had been persistent and she preferred it to the alternative, Eugene O'Neill's *Strange Interlude*. H. T. Parker of the *Boston Transcript* liked both the play and Miss Cornell whose voice, he wrote, "is rich in darkling colors, darting, choking as by an instant compulsion" (B453). John Sargent Bailey of the *Independent* was disappointed in Maugham but thought Miss Cornell was "superb" (B012). *Vogue's* editor, David Carb, agreed with Bailey and commented that the radiance emanating from her might save the play if it could be saved (B033). On the other hand, Gilbert Seldes of *The Dial* stated that "her performance adds nothing to her repute; it was a satisfaction to see that she remained for the most part unsullied by the tawdriness of her play" (B203).

Audiences flocked to see Miss Cornell. In fact, people who came to the play on opening night packed the sidewalk and alleyway to get a glimpse of her after the show. Even with the unfavorable press, they kept the show open for 13 weeks.

******

## S33 THE AGE OF INNOCENCE

(Opened: November 27, 1928, at the Empire Theatre, New York; 26 weeks of performances)

## Credits

| | |
|---|---|
| Playwright | Margaret Ayer Barnes |
| Dramatized from Novel of | Edith Wharton |
| Director | Guthrie McClintic |
| Settings and Costumes | Gertrude Newell |
| Producer | Gilbert Miller |

## Cast

| | |
|---|---|
| Alice Fordyce | Margaret Barker |
| Tom Hamilton | Henry Richard |
| Lucy Duane | Jean Howard |
| Harry Delaney | Stanley Gilkey |
| Sillerton Jackson | William Podmore |
| Jessie Lefferts | Nora Stirling |
| Mrs. Henry van der Luyden | Isabel Irving |
| Mrs. Manson Mingott | Katherine Stewart |
| Mr. Henry van der Luyden | Frazer Coulter |
| Julius Beaufort | Arnold Korff |
| May van der Luyden | Eden Gray |
| Newland Archer | Rollo Peters |
| Ellen Olenska | Katharine Cornell |
| The Duke of St. Austrey | Peter Spencer |
| Anastasia | Giannina Gatti |
| Stephen Letterblair | Albert Tavernier |
| Carlos Saramonte | Edouard La Roche |
| Jean | Pierre Soupault |
| Newland Archer, Jr. | Franchot Tone |

## The Play's History

Edward Sheldon, a childhood friend of Margaret Ayer Barnes, encouraged Miss Barnes to do a dramatization of Edith Wharton's novel and helped her with her first writing endeavor, a gesture for which he claimed no credit. Miss Wharton was somewhat displeased by the dramatization but the difficulties were resolved. She was delighted by the play's success.

*The Age of Innocence* opened in Albany on November 8, 1928, and was taken to Pittsburgh for a week before opening in New York. It closed in June, 1929. In the fall a 9-week tour of the play began in Washington, D.C. at the Poli Theatre and ended at the Shubert Teck Theatre in Buffalo.

## Synopsis

The play opens in New York in the 1870s on Astor Place at the debut of the van der Luyden's daughter May. Among the guests is a cousin of May's, Ellen Olenska, who has returned to New York after a disastrous marriage to Polish Count Olenska, a charming but cruel man who has caused her mental anguish and financial ruin.

Ellen's beauty, her elegant European gowns, and the way men flock around her is the gossip among the matronly guests. At first sight of her the heart of Newland Archer is captured, just before his engagement to cousin May is announced at the party.

During the engagement period May asks Newland to drop out of politics. When he objects, she breaks off the engagement. Feeling free to declare his love for Ellen, Newland does so, only to receive a letter from May that their wedding date is set. Ellen, who has not disclosed her feelings for him, persuades him that he must go ahead with the wedding, which he does.

Some time later Ellen begins proceedings to divorce the Count who responds by coming to America to take her back to Europe. Meanwhile, Newland has decided to divorce May so that he and Ellen may marry. Unknown to him, May visits Ellen to tell her she is bearing Newland's child. Without explanation to Newland, Ellen announces her reconciliation with the Count.  At a farewell party Newland learns the truth from Ellen and also learns he is to be a father.

Years later, after both the Count and May have died, Newland and his son call on Ellen in Paris.  While they are waiting for her to appear, Newland decides he cannot bear to spoil the remembrance of her beauty or for her to see him as he has aged. Insisting that his son stay and become friends with her, he leaves.  Ellen is heard calling her maid for her cane and the curtain closes just as she is about to enter.

## Reviews

*New York World* (11/28)--As other critics extolled Miss Cornell's beauty and acting so did St. John Ervine.  He proclaimed her a great actress who "magnificently portrays the period of this play, not only by the clothes she so richly adorns but by her attitude and manner" (B359).

*New Republic* (12/12/28)--Stark Young could hardly say enough about what Miss Cornell brings to the stage.  He described it as "the essence of theatricality; it has beauty and manners, a great gift for slipping easily into the right emotional intensity, and, most of all, something penetrating, quivering, absorbed in its own moment that cannot be described."  He compared her to the great Italian actress, Duse.  As for the play, he didn't think too much of it (B252).

*American-Mercury* (2/29)--George Jean Nathan thought the play was "undeniably poor."  In his view, it had failed to capture the mood or spirit of the novel (B168).

## Commentary

Many critics were highly enthusiastic about *The Age of Innocence*.  The only fault they found was in the partial failure of Miss Barnes to make the literary style conversational, this being a common peril in dramatizing novels.  The stilted talk, however, did not dampen their praise of Miss Cornell, the other actors and McClintic's skillful direction.  Critics extolled Miss Cornell's beauty which was enhanced by the elegant period costumes made in Paris with furs, velvets, bustles and trains.  Although Miss Cornell thought Ellen Olenska to be "an endearing person--charming and warm," she was nervous about the role (B047, p. 85).

Having become a full-fledged star, she suffered more than her customary stage fright, resulting in an accident on the day of her out-of-town opening in Albany.  She fractured her rib when she fell against a chair and a few hours later burned her arm on a hot pipe, but that did not stop the show.  As if a cracked rib and burned arm were not enough, when she was on her way to the theatre in Cleveland the limousine door was slammed on her finger.  The physician who was called diagnosed a crushed joint. Insisting that she had to go on, she persuaded the doctor to give her a shot of Novocain to numb the excruciating pain.  Incorporating the chiffon scarf which she wrapped around the swollen finger into her gestures, she played so convincingly that the audience was unaware of her discomfort.  The incident exemplified her sense of responsibility toward her audience and her company.

******

S34     **DISHONORED LADY**
        (Opened: February 4, 1930, at the Empire Theatre, New York; 16 weeks of
        performances)

### Credits

| | |
|---|---|
| Playwrights | Margaret Ayer Barnes |
| | and Edward Sheldon |
| Director | Guthrie McClintic |
| Producers | Gilbert Miller with |
| | Guthrie McClintic |

### Cast

| | |
|---|---|
| Madeleine Cary | Katharine Cornell |
| The Marquess of Farnborough | Francis Lister |
| Lawrence Brennan | Paul Harvey |
| Jose Moreno | Fortunio Bonanova |
| Rosie | Ruth Fallows |
| Richard Wadsworth | Harvey Stephens |
| Rufus Cary | Fred L. Tilden |
| Ella | Brenda Dahlen |
| Sims | Lewis A. Sealy |
| Riley | Edwin Morse |
| Albert | Jimmy Daniels |

### The Play's History

            After Miss Barnes had dramatized *The Age of Innocence*, she had collaborated
on a comedy with Edward Sheldon for Jane Cowl. That was successful and Sheldon
suggested they write a melodrama based on the famous case of Madeleine Smith who, in
1850, poisoned her lover to marry a man of her own station. While Ethel Barrymore, for
whom the play was intended, was being indecisive, McClintic bought it for Miss Cornell
at the time that she was still performing in *The Age of Innocence*.
            The tryouts took place in Buffalo and in Rochester, with the first performance
being at the Lyceum Theatre, January 26, 1930, in Rochester. Following the New York
run, a tour of the play ran through the fall. It marked Miss Cornell's first appearance on
the Pacific coast.

### Synopsis

            Socialite Madeleine Cary follows the pattern of her mother's faithlessness to
her father. Men are attracted to her and she to them; her latest torrid affair is with Joe
Moreno, a cabaret dancer she met in Paris.
            One of her father's married friends, Brennan, who is in love with her and has
been lavishing money and clothes on her, queries her about marriage to Farnsborough,
an eligible bachelor. She decides she will accept Farnsborough's proposal. Although she
confesses her follies to him, Farnsborough is ecstatic about her acceptance.
            When Joe Moreno reads the engagement announcement, he appears at her
home, becomes hysterical and threatens her. Madeleine knows what she must do.
            Appearing at Joe's apartment in the early morning hours, she succumbs once
more to his advances and then slips strychnine into his coffee. Before he dies, Joe

manages to call the police.  The evidence is clearly against Madeleine; she is arrested and held in jail.

Several months later, after the trial, Madeleine is free, saved by Brennan's testimony that she had been with him.  Her father, who is leaving, advises her to marry Farnsborough who still wants her.  Knowing that she would eventually hurt him by cheating on him, Madeleine sends Farnsborough away--perhaps the one decent thing she has done.

## Reviews

*New York Times* (2/5/30)--Brooks Atkinson thought that Miss Cornell treated the play as a "work of art" and was placing "very little value on her art."  He believed she "had too much instinctive magnificence" for this sort of play and counseled her to be "fastidious" about the kind drama she selects (B270).

*New York Evening Post* (2/5/30)--It's "a trashy chronicle of murder," wrote John Mason Brown.  He considered it "a waste, a wicked waste, of Miss Cornell's time and talents" (B320).

*Los Angeles Herald* (9/9/30)-- After seeing the play at the Biltmore, critic Harrison Carroll wrote of Madeleine, "Her one fine gesture is when she completely disillusions the man she loves, and sends him away.  As the curtain falls, she sits alone in the room, staring at nothing.  'Ah, well,' she sighs" (B325).

## Commentary

Despite the lurid story and the unpleasant woman in *Dishonored Lady*, audiences packed the theatre to see Cornell, "an exotic woman with a supple body and vibrant voice" (B039, p. 37).  Critics called it a "cheap melodrama" but critic Walter Winchell found Miss Cornell to be "electrifying," "spellbinding" and "enchanting."  One scene in which her leading man hit her on the jaw irritated Winchell so much that he wanted to give the actor a piece of his mind.  "Never in the history of the theatre has an actress of such distinction permitted such an exciting scene," he claimed (B501).

Richard Dana Skinner of *The Commonweal* had quite another  view of the play.  In his scathing review he condemned it as being poorly written, unfair to the theatre and certainly to Miss Cornell.  In his opinion, this was the worst "sentimentalized version of a degenerate" that she had played in either *The Green Hat* or *The Letter*.  The mystery was why she permitted "her fine talents to be exploited in such fifth-rate claptrap" (B212, p. 453).  What disturbed critics like Skinner, said Mosel, was that she played a role that did not measure up to their image of her, and "did it so well" (B163, p. 240).

******

THE ACTRESS-MANAGER YEARS (1931-1961)

S35    THE BARRETTS OF WIMPOLE STREET
(Opened: February 9, 1931, at the Empire Theatre, New York; 370
performances)

## Credits

| | |
|---|---|
| Playwright | Rudolf Besier |
| Director | Guthrie McClintic |
| Settings and Costumes | Jo Mielziner |
| Producer | Katharine Cornell |

## Cast

| | |
|---|---|
| Dr. Chambers | George Riddell |
| Elizabeth Barrett Moulton-Barrett | Katharine Cornell |
| Wilson | Brenda Forbes |
| Henrietta Moulton-Barrett | Margaret Barker |
| Arabel Moulton-Barrett | Joyce Carey |
| Octavius Moulton-Barrett | John Halloran |
| Septimus Moulton-Barrett | William Whitehead |
| Alfred Moulton-Barrett | Vernon Downing |
| Charles Moulton-Barrett | Frederick Voight |
| Henry Moulton-Barrett | Basil Harvey |
| George Moulton-Barrett | Leslie Denisson |
| Edward Moulton-Barrett | Charles Waldron |
| Bella Hedley | Dorothy Mathews |
| Henry Bevan | John D. Seymour |
| Robert Browning | Brian Aherne |
| Dr. Ford-Waterlow | Oswald Marshall |
| Captain Surtees Cook | John Buckler |
| Flush | Himself |

## The Play's History

Two producers had refused to undertake *The Barretts of Wimpole Street* before
Sir Barry Jackson decided to present it at the Malvern Festival in England on August 18,
1930. Before the script was offered to Miss Cornell, 27 producers in New York (in *Me
and Kit*, McClintic said there were 28) had already rejected it on the basis that it was a
Victorian costume play about the love story of two poets in whom the public would have
little interest.

At the time she decided to do *The Barretts* it had not yet been produced in
London where audience reaction would have been tested. The McClintics were taking
a large risk, particularly when it was to be Miss Cornell's first production as
actress-manager. Furthermore, Al Woods, her manager in *The Green Hat*, did not think
the public would accept her in the role of an invalid. The difficulty in casting also
reflected the doubts of actors about the play. Lionel Barrymore turned down the offer to
play Moulton-Barrett; several actors refused the role of Browning because his appearances
on stage were few and brief. Even Brian Aherne, who finally accepted the role, needed
to be persuaded.

While McClintic was in London signing Brian Aherne for Browning, he was able to see *The Barretts* which had opened a few weeks earlier, with much acclaim.  He was also able to visit Wimpole Street to make drawings for an exact replica of Elizabeth's room.

The first time that *The Barretts* was given in the United States was the opening of the tryout at Hanna Theater in Cleveland on January 29, 1931.  After a disastrous dress rehearsal, Miss Cornell insisted that the opening be delayed.  However, all seats for 4 performances were already sold so the show opened as scheduled.  Of the 3 reviews that appeared the next day only one was favorable; it was a rave.  Her hometown audience reacted pessimistically but the New York opening proved them wrong.  *The Barretts* made enough money to pay off the mortgage on the McClintics' Beekman Street home.

### Synopsis

Elizabeth Barrett spends her life as an invalid in the airless bed-sitting room of 50 Wimpole Street where she is virtually the prisoner of a tyrannical father who terrorizes her and her siblings.  Barrett's domination of Elizabeth suggests an incestuous impulse.  Her strength ebbs away and she has all but lost her will to live.  Miraculously, her will returns when Robert Browning, fellow poet with whom she has been corresponding, steps into her room and her life.  They fall in love at once and Browning manages to call weekly without encountering Barrett although he fully realizes the morbid effect of his presence.

As Elizabeth regains strength, Barrett cruelly rejects the doctor's recommendation that she spend a winter in Italy for her health.  Barrett's sensual response to his flirtatious niece and his inhuman treatment of his daughter Henrietta, who is in love with Captain Cook, makes life even more intolerable.  The final blow is Barrett's announcement that they will move to the country where they will be too isolated for callers and worldly temptation.

Meanwhile, Browning is determined to remove her from these gloomy premises.  He persuades her to marry him secretly, then return home for a few days awaiting the propitious moment for them to depart for Italy.  As Elizabeth is leaving letters for her family and preparing for her escape to Italy, Barrett returns home unexpectedly.  His impassioned confession, that Elizabeth's love is all that he has, removes all doubt.  When he has gone, she leaves quickly with Wilson and Flush to join Browning and to live in Italy.

An hour or two later her siblings find the letters and Henrietta, handing Barrett his letter, begs him to forgive Elizabeth.  After a few moments of silent fury, he orders Octavius to fetch her dog to be destroyed.  When he learns that Flush has gone with Elizabeth, he tears her letter into little pieces, letting them drop to his feet.

### Reviews

*Variety* (2/18/31)--"B'way Grosses Slightly Lower But 'Barretts' Exceeds Expectations" was the headline of this review about the group of new plays that had opened.  The reception of *The Barretts* was more cordial than anticipated, making it one of the top five non-musicals.  It drew over $21,000 the first week.  *Variety* had not thought it would do well but gave it an enthusiastic endorsement (B291).

*New York Times* (2/22/31)--In Brooks Atkinson's second review of the play he predicted that Miss Cornell "will be not only a great actress but a great force in the theatre" if she continues to apply her unusual talent as she does in the role of Elizabeth.

He described her as "a studious actress," who has "design" and "stir" in her acting. Her beautiful voice "can lick at the dialogue like a flame" and she uses it "like a musical instrument." He commended the other players and McClintic's direction which had given the play a wide range of life's emotions. Finally, he said that Miss Cornell's "Elizabeth gives you a feeling of exaltation..." (B271).

## Commentary

For the first production of the C. & M. C. Productions "Katharine Cornell Presents--" shone on the marquee. On February 9, 1931, *The Barretts of Wimpole Street* opened at the Empire Theatre on the same evening of the premiere of a new opera across the street at the Metropolitan Opera in a teeming rain which resulted in an impossible traffic tie-up. Even with a delayed curtain only 52 people were seated on the first floor when it opened, and during the first act, the actors' voices were often drowned out by the banging seats as over 800 soggy latecomers found their places. Despite this, at the end of the first act, the curtain closed to thunderous applause and the house was filled when the second act began. The audience loved the play but there were still skeptics. Among them was Stanton Griffis, one of the financial backers. The play's fate was in the hands of the critics.

While the McClintics and several friends talked over the play at their Beekman Place house, Woollcott came to assure them that "the reviews will be splendid" and that it was probably Miss Cornell's "finest performance" (B163, p. 273).

Woollcott was right. When the reviews came, the critics were overwhelmingly favorable. In the *New York News* Burns Mantle reported that Miss Cornell "is going forward rapidly with the job of turning a fine actress into a great actress" (B147). Benjamin De Casseres stated in *Arts and Decoration* that "Elizabeth Barrett is the finest role Miss Cornell has given us yet" (B055).

For 16 weeks *The Barretts of Wimpole Street* played to houses filled to capacity. By the end of 2 months, the production was able to repay Griffis and Goodyear who had backed the show. It played on Broadway a year and a week, with a 6-week layoff for Miss Cornell's illness.

In midsummer of 1931, the summer heat became oppressive, and she developed a pressure and lump at the base of her skull along with a persistent vibration inside her head. There was no air conditioning and during the first act, she spent 45 minutes on the sofa with shawls draped around her shoulders and a heavy afghan covering the lower half of her body. Doctors could find nothing physically wrong but the show was closed for 6 weeks to give her rest. She recovered sufficiently to resume on schedule.

Despite the predictions that the show would not survive the temporary closing, long lines of playgoers waited to buy tickets and the box office was flooded with mail orders. Fortunately, Ray Henderson had been hired soon after *The Barretts* was opened. It was his job to promote Miss Cornell and her company. However, her love of privacy, her discipline and dedication to her work did not make for exciting or titillating press stories, but Henderson sensed that the public admired her as a lady. When qualities of good breeding and old values were eroding, they were delighted with her Elizabeth. Henderson's press releases about the thoughts, plans, honors, activities and audiences of Miss Cornell kept her before the public who eagerly awaited her return. Moreover, his consistent reference to her as "Miss Cornell" not only reinforced her image, but it was also adopted by the press (B163, p. 291).

Two months after the play was resumed Miss Cornell's symptoms had returned and her anxieties grew. It was decided to close the show and take it on tour on a week-to-week basis. Her love of the road revived her enthusiasm.

William Lyon Phelps went to see *The Barretts* the last week of its New York engagement. Hundreds were being turned away at the box office and he commented in *Scribner's Magazine* that the spectators "made such a wall of humanity in the 'Standing Room Only' space," that he could hardly get to the aisle. After the show he talked with Miss Cornell about her upcoming tour. Impressed that she did not do "the customary thing" by sending a second or third "road company" but took it herself, he said she was giving American people a rare opportunity. In his opinion, seeing *The Barretts of Wimpole Street* "enriched one's intellectual and spiritual existence" (B186; B187).

The show was closed on February 13, 1932, to a full house and 3 rows of standees who applauded, cheered and cried. After 370 performances it had established a record at the Empire. It opened two nights later in Boston and was taken on tour.

\*\*\*\*\*\*

## S36      LUCRECE
(Opened: December 20, 1932, at the Belasco Theatre, New York; 31 performances)

### Credits

| | |
|---|---|
| Playwright | André Obey |
| Translation | Thornton Wilder |
| Director | Guthrie McClintic |
| Settings and Costumes | Robert Edmond Jones |
| Music | Deems Taylor |
| Producer | Katharine Cornell |

### Cast

| | |
|---|---|
| First Soldier | William J. Tannen |
| Second Soldier | George Macready |
| Tarquin | Brian Aherne |
| Collatine | Pedro de Cordoba |
| Brutus | Charles Waldron |
| First Narrator | Blanche Yurka |
| Lucrece | Katharine Cornell |
| Julia | Kathleen Chase |
| Emilia | Joyce Carey |
| Sidonia | Harriet Ingersoll |
| Marina | Brenda Forbes |
| Second Narrator | Robert Loraine |
| Valerius | George Macready |
| First Servant | Francis Moran |
| Second Servant | Barry Mahool |
| Third Servant | Charles Thorne |
| Citizens, Soldiers, Servants | |

## The Play's History

Le Viol de Lucrece had been successfully produced in Paris in 1931 by La Compagnie des Quinze and then in London where Conger Goodyear saw it with Clemence Dane and Mrs. Patrick Campbell. They thought it was a good play for Miss Cornell, and after reading it, she shared their reaction. Goodyear was sent to Paris to negotiate for rights to produce it and it was decided that *Lucrece* would follow *The Barretts of Wimpole Street* when it closed.

Thornton Wilder, who had a knowledge of French, did the translation. Guthrie thought the Cornell production should have magnificence which was in contrast to the poetic simplicity of the Paris production. Robert Edmond Jones created a spacious Roman colonnade against a gray backdrop and designed the costumes in the rich warm colors of the Renaissance. Mosel described the tableau of Lucrece and her handmaidens in the first act as having the "effect of a magnificent renaissance tapestry come to life" (B163, p. 308). The actors wore dull gold half-masks and bronze green draped robes, giving the play a classic tone.

The tryout opened in Cleveland at the Hanna Theatre, Nov. 29, 1932, and in New York at the Belasco on December 20, 1932. After 31 performances the play closed. It was one of her few clear failures and one of the two productions, prior to World War II, that did not show a profit.

## Synopsis

Inside a Roman army tent The Lt. Collatine and his dinner guests are listening and laughing as Brutus relates the events of their surprise raid on their homes in Rome the previous night to settle a wager as to whose wife is most dutiful in her husband's absence. Collatine was declared to be the most fortunate husband for his wife Lucrece was found in her home spinning with her maids; the others wives were caught in unseemly behavior. Throughout the remainder of the play the action is interspersed with explanations and foretelling of woeful events by two narrators.

Inflamed by Collatine's boasting, the King's son Tarquin leaves the tent to hide until the others have departed and Collatine has retired. He rides directly to Collatine's home, stopping on the pretense of the need for rest. Demonstrating the hospitality befitting a king's son, Lucrece bids her servants to prepare him a room.

When all the household is asleep, Tarquin enters Lucrece's bedroom, threatens to slay her and her servant, rapes her and rides back to camp. The next morning her servants are alarmed by Tarquin's departure and the unhappy state of their mistress.

Lucrece sends a message requesting Collatine to return home and orders her servants to burn her bed. Rumors spread through Rome and crowds gather around Collatine's house. Accompanied by Brutus, Collatine arrives to be greeted by his wife who is dressed in black. With the aid of Valerius she tells of Tarquin's visit and his violation of her, then sinks to the ground, dead from the knife she has thrust into her breast. Brutus swears vengeance on Tarquin.

## Reviews

*Variety* (11/30/32)--Enthusiasiatic applause rang through the Playhouse Square Theatre in Cleveland at the premiere of *Lucrece*. The reviewer stated that the audience "responded appreciatively" to Deems Taylor's overture and music. Both he and translator Thornton Wilder were present. No other reaction to the play was expressed (B390).

*New York Times* (12/21/32)--In Brooks Atkinson's opinion, the acting is "of rare excellence." Miss Cornell gives to the few scenes in which she appears "the glowing fires of greatness." Speaking of the narrators, he wrote, "If it were poetry and beauty that came from these burnished, high-nosed masks, it would unhinge the mind and crack the theatre" (B278).

*Variety* (12/27/32)-- Although there was "high interest" in the premiere of *Lucrece*, the trade paper reported that the chances for the show's success looked doubtful despite its gross of $14,000 in the first 7 performances. The presence of composer Deems Taylor and translator Thornton Wilder appeared to be of more interest than the play (B483).

## Commentary

The comments of Brooks Atkinson in *The New York Times* and John Anderson in the *New York Journal* were representative of reactions to the play. Atkinson had much praise for the production and thought it could have been "a memorable experience" had the "literary qualities" been "a match" for the acting and the "regal surroundings" (B278). John Anderson was more critical, calling the play "stilted, too conscious of its own art, and quietly, but firmly tiresome." He disliked the use of narrators who "manage to make a nuisance of themselves" and the "artistic whim-whams." On the other hand, he found the acting of Miss Cornell and Mr. Aherne in the rape scene to be "played with such power and brilliance that the scene becomes fairly incandescent." Her performance, he reported, "reaches a mute eloquence that is incredibly sensitive and lovely" (B257). Miss Cornell herself did not feel the rape scene went well and would have been more effective if done with dancers as it had been in Paris.

Many theatregoers liked the play. An ovation lasting over twenty minutes was accorded her on the last night of its performance. Upholding Miss Cornell's production, H. T. Parker of the *Boston Transcript* said her detractors "didn't know anything about classical drama" (B047, p. 121). Despite the play's failure, Miss Cornell would have liked to try it again. A great deal of enthusiasm had gone into its production and she believed "too much love" had killed it (B047, p. 117). The experience did give her the impetus to try Shakespeare, which would prove to be one of her great accomplishments.

\*\*\*\*\*\*

S37    **ALIEN CORN**
       (Opened February 20, 1933, at the Belasco Theatre, New York; 12 weeks of performances)

## Credits
Playwright                               Sidney Howard
Director                                 Guthrie McClintic
Settings                                 Cleon Throckmorton
Producer                                 Katharine Cornell

## Cast
Ottokar Brandt                           Siegfried Rumann

| | |
|---|---|
| Piano Tuner | Ludwig Steiner |
| Mrs. Skeats | Jessie Busley |
| Stockton | E. J. Ballantine |
| Watkins | Richard Sterling |
| Elsa Brandt | Katharine Cornell |
| Phipps | Charles D. Brown |
| Julian Vardaman | Luther Adler |
| Skeats | Charles Waldron |
| Harry Conway | James Rennie |
| A Chauffeur | James Vincent |
| Muriel Conway | Lily Cahill |
| A Policeman | Francis Moran |

## The Play's History

The title of Sidney Howard's play had been taken from the lines in Keats' *Ode to a Nightingale* in which he refers to "...Ruth when, sick for home...stood in tears amid the alien corn..." (B418; B047, p.82). When Miss Cornell read it one evening, she liked it immediately and contracted the next morning for the rights to produce it. However, before it could go into production, she had to fulfill the public's demand for *The Barretts of Wimpole Street* and wait for the actors to become available for *Alien Corn*. She particularly wanted Siegfried Rumann, who was engaged elsewhere, to play Elsa's father, so while waiting, she produced *Lucrece*. It was almost two years before she could undertake *Alien Corn*.

The play's tryout took place in Baltimore on February 13, 1933, before the New York opening on February 20. After a 12-week run, it was taken on tour to Boston, Philadelphia and the midwest. Although the show was running during the worst of the Great Depression and there was a lack of enthusiasm for the play, it prospered. When the "Bank Holiday" was declared, Griffis told Miss Cornell to close *Alien Corn* (Gert Macy, Ray Henderson and McClintic were all out of town). Instead, she kept it open and instructed the box office to accept any kind of payment for tickets. Every IOU was paid, confirming her faith in people. The production, which had cost just over $7,665 to produce, made a profit of over $33,700 (B512, p. 117).

## Synopsis

Elsa Brandt, a talented young woman aspiring to be a concert pianist, was brought by her musical parents from Vienna to America when she was four years old. During the Great War they were interned in a camp in Georgia where her mother had died of pneumonia and her father's attempt at suicide had left him partially paralyzed. Now, 15 years later, Elsa is teaching, which she loathes, at Conway College for Women in order to provide a living for her father and herself.

Elsa yearns to go to Vienna to study music. Her hopes for a scholarship are dashed when she is disqualified by her foreign birthplace.

Harry Conway, an influential alumnus, is attracted to Elsa, and wants to help her but his wife discovers that he and Elsa are in love. She thwarts Elsa's efforts to give recitals and prevails upon the trustees to request Elsa's resignation from the College.

Julian, a teacher who is also in love with her, offers her the solution: she will marry him and he will take care of her and her father. When he learns that she loves Harry Conway, Julian shoots himself and Elsa rejects the man she loves to pursue her dream of being a concert pianist in Vienna.

**Reviews**

*New York Tribune* (2/33)--Describing her as "beautifully dark and rhythmic," Percy Hammond stated that "any play in which Miss Cornell appears is interesting. Her acting always is so true that it makes a dramatist's counterfeits seem real" (B375).

*New York Times* (2/26/33)--Brooks Atkinson found the acting to be uniformly excellent. He complimented the McClintics for demonstrating their ability to create an artistic, organic whole. He also had fine things to say about Miss Cornell's voice as well as her "glow," and "sense of the theatre." He concluded by commenting on our good fortune to have someone with "a genius of acting who takes pride in her craft" (B283).

*Los Angeles Herald* (10/28/33)--Reviewer W. E. Oliver stated that *Alien Corn* was written for a star. For that reason he thought the "script suffers from all the defects and phoney theatricalism that star-slanting usually inflicts on the best of playwrights" (B447).

**Commentary**

As usual, the McClintics selected a fine cast, all of whom drew favorable comments from some of the critics. Although W. E. Oliver thought the focus was on the "star," Brooks Atkinson reported that the play "had moments of matchless beauty," and Miss Cornell had given "realistic integrity" to the part of Elsa (B283).

Miss Cornell liked Elsa and thought it was one of best roles she had played. The convincing portrayal of the part demonstrated her masterful control of her body. First, Elsa frequently reverted to speaking German. Although Miss Cornell was proficient in French, she had only a limited use of German which she had acquired during her visits in Garmisch. However, her "sense of the language" and "feeling for its nuances" gave "validity" to her portrayal (B163, p. 304). In addition, the role demanded that she play like a concert pianist. Her childhood exposure to piano lessons had suffered the diversion of other interests, but her love of music and her self-discipline enabled her to match her fingering so well to the offstage piano that friends were incredulous. To make it appear authentic, it took long hours of practice with a dummy keyboard as well as the McClintic's ingenious arrangement of the pianos. In order that the sound emanate from the stage, the movement of an offstage piano had been fitted into the one onstage, which was hollowed out to join the two. This also made it possible for Miss Cornell to see Miss Madden, who was actually playing. On one occasion, when Miss Madden fainted during an excessive hot spell, Miss Cornell covered the sudden interruption by saying "Oh, I'm tired. I don't think I'll practice any more today" (B047, p. 120).

Mosel and Macy contended that Miss Cornell strongly identified with the demon that drives Elsa and leaves her no peace. Miss Cornell had expressed her own sense of being driven by her acting as "a necessity that's wished upon you" (B163, p. 317).

******

**S38      THE BARRETTS OF WIMPOLE STREET**
(Transcontinental Repertory Tour: November 5, 1933- June 20, 1934. Opened: November, 1933, in Buffalo, New York; 144 performances during tour)

## Credits

| | |
|---|---|
| Playwright | Rudolf Besier |
| Director | Guthrie McClintic |
| Setting and Costumes | Jo Mielziner |
| Producer | Katharine Cornell |

## Cast

| | |
|---|---|
| Doctor Chambers | David Glassford |
| Elizabeth Barrett Moulton-Barrett | Katharine Cornell |
| Wilson | Brenda Forbes |
| Henrietta Moulton-Barrett | Helen Walpole |
| Arabel Moulton-Barrett | Pamela Simpson |
| Octavius Moulton-Barrett | Orson Welles |
| Septimus Moulton-Barrett | Irving Morrow |
| Alfred Moulton-Barrett | Charles Brokaw |
| Charles Moulton-Barrett | Lathrop Mitchell |
| Henry Moulton-Barrett | Reynolds Evans |
| George Moulton-Barrett | George Macready |
| Edward Moulton-Barrett | Charles Waldron |
| Bella Hedley | Margot Stevenson |
| Henry Bevan | John Hoysradt |
| Robert Browning | Basil Rathbone |
| Doctor Ford-Waterlow | A. P. Kaye |
| Captain Surtees Cook | Francis Moran |
| Flush | Himself |

## The Play's History

Miss Cornell had already toured with *The Barretts* immediately following her New York closing on February 13, 1932. This was her first repertory tour, which included *Candida* and *Romeo and Juliet* as well as *The Barretts*, and the most publicized of her tours. It is significant because it provided audiences throughout the country with an opportunity to see live theatre. It also gave Miss Cornell a following of fans who remained loyal to the end of her career. In addition, it inspired other tours. She proved that people in the outreaches of America were hungry for good theatre.

The tour encompassed 75 towns and cities, took 29 weeks and extended from November 22, 1933, to June 20, 1934. Miss Cornell believed in taking the theatre to the people. Ray Henderson suggested that a repertory tour would give her a larger audience and the opportunity to develop her role of Juliet before taking it to New York. Knowing that audiences did not patronize a Shakespearean play until they heard that it was "good," Henderson planned the repertory so that *The Barretts* and *Candida*, which were sure to draw large audiences, could pay the expenses. The tour began in Buffalo where Miss Cornell wanted her tryout opening of *Romeo and Juliet*.

At that time the once popular road tours had become rare. Consequently, performances were scheduled in old filthy, cobwebby, rat-infested, dilapidated opera houses, tents, community halls or high school auditoriums. Movie house owners, threatened by the competition, refused to rent their facilities to the live theatre, which was the reason for making few stops between Buffalo and Seattle.

In Amarillo the actors competed with a sandstorm, in Oakland with a basketball game separated from their stage by a thin partition. While the company members were enduring the inadequate facilities and forces of nature, audiences across the country were driving miles to see them. The tour played to 500,000 people with *The Barretts* drawing the largest audiences. In Des Moines, Iowa, they played to their largest audience of 4,251. The tour grossed about $650,000 and the repertory played to 500,000 people (B512, pp. 138,142).

## Synopsis
See *The Barretts of Wimpole Street*, 1931 (S35).

## Review
*Variety* (12/5/33)--The trade publication reported a complete sellout and standing room only for the Saturday night performance of *The Barretts* in Buffalo. This began the long transcontinental repertory tour. (B301).

## Commentary
The most memorable event of that tour occurred on Christmas night in Seattle, Washington, where *The Barretts* was scheduled for an evening performance, beginning a week's engagement in Seattle. They had left Duluth on Saturday morning, December 23, and were to arrive in Seattle, McClintic's hometown, early Christmas morning. The troupe was enjoying the Christmas party Miss Cornell had arranged while the management was becoming uneasy because of telegraphed reports warning of trouble ahead. Washouts resulting from 23 days of persistent rain were making travel through Washington perilous and uncertain. As the train pulled out of Spokane, it became apparent that they would not arrive in Seattle on schedule. After stopping for the hasty construction of a new trestle, they finally drew into the King Street Station at 11:15 p.m., three hours after curtain time. As a tired, unhappy troupe stepped down to the platform they were greeted with the unbelievable message that 1200 ticket-holders, the entire house, were still waiting at the theatre to see them. Trucks and limousines were lined up at the station to transport them to the Metropolitan Theatre where both Guthrie McClintic's and Miss Cornell's names shone on the marquee.

The monumental task of transporting equipment, stagehands and actors to the theatre was accomplished in 15 minutes and the audience began filling the seats. McClintic suggested the curtain be raised to allow the audience to watch the stage being set while he explained what was going on as the electricians and stagehands performed a miracle. Reminiscing and filling in with anecdotes, McClintic held the audience enthralled. For additional entertainment Flush was trotted out numerous times and the stage manager posed on the sofa for Miss Cornell while lighting was being set. At one o'clock the curtain was lowered. Five minutes later the play began.

The cast gave an "intoxicating" performance, thus reciprocating the great compliment the audience had paid them. When the final curtain came down, the audience, in no hurry to leave, overwhelmed the actors with curtain calls. It was an experience none of them would forget (B244, p. 72).

******

**S39**    **ROMEO AND JULIET**
Transcontinental Repertory Tour, November 5, 1933-June 20, 1934. (Opened: November 29, 1933, at the Erlanger Theatre, Buffalo, New York; 39 performances during tour)

Credits

| | |
|---|---|
| Playwright | William Shakespeare |
| Director | Guthrie McClintic |
| Settings and Costumes | Woodman Thompson |
| Producer | Katharine Cornell |

Cast

| | |
|---|---|
| Escalus, Prince of Verona | Reynolds Evans |
| Paris, kinsman to the prince | George Macready |
| Montague | A. P. Kaye |
| Capulet | David Glassford |
| An Old Man of Capulet Family | Arthur Chatterton |
| Romeo, son of Montague | Basil Rathbone |
| Mercutio, kinsman to the prince | Orson Welles |
| Benvolio, nephew to Montague | Charles Brokaw |
| Tybalt, nephew to Lady Capulet | Francis Moran |
| Friar Laurence, a Franciscan | Charles Waldron |
| Friar John of the same order | Lathrop Mitchell |
| Balthasar, servant to Romeo | Irving Morrow |
| Sampson | Robert Champlain |
| Peter, servant to Capulet | John Hoysradt |
| Gregory, servant | R. Birrell Rawls |
| Abraham, servant to Montague | Lathrop Mitchell |
| An Apothecary | John Hoysradt |
| Officer | Robert Champlain |
| Watchman | Julian Edwards |
| Lady Montague | Brenda Forbes |
| Lady Capulet | Merle Maddern |
| Juliet, daughter to Capulet | Katharine Cornell |
| Nurse to Juliet | Alice Johns |
| Chorus | Orson Welles |

Citizens of Verona, Kinsfolk of both houses, Maskers, Guards, Watchmen and Attendants

The Play's History
See *Romeo and Juliet*, 1934 (S41).

Synopsis
See *Romeo and Juliet*, 1934 (S41)

Reviews
*New York Times* (11/30/33)--The reviewer reported that the Buffalo opening was the beginning of a long repertory tour and makes no comment about the reception of the play. The critic merely stated that the Buffalo audience "commented as much on

the pace of the play as on Miss Cornell's acting." One theatregoer had remarked "that its modern handling 'should help keep Shakespeare alive'" (B429).

*Variety* (12/5/33)--The public was apathetic over the premiere and 3 performances of *Romeo and Juliet*, *Variety* reported. Word "trickling in from the west toward which the Cornell repertoire is headed" indicates that the same kind of reaction to the play can be expected. The reviewer speculated that for some members of the audience the ghosts of former Juliets, Modjeska and Marlowe, will flutter in the wings. Many scenes were "vocally and verbally incoherent, one of the worst offenders being Orson Welles. Charles Waldron as Friar Laurence stole the show and Alice Johns' Nurse was a "delight" (B448).

## Commentary

The tour opened with *Romeo and Juliet* in Buffalo on November 29, 1933. Almost everything seemed to go wrong in the dress rehearsal. The critics were tactfully kind but two fans, who had grown up in Buffalo and knew the Cornell family, thought Miss Cornell was almost "limp," and certainly not a convincing teenager in love.

Chicago and Milwaukee critics who saw the play several days later, called the production bad. As the tour progressed it improved, even jumping to first place in San Francisco. In Los Angeles, Miss Cornell pleased her severest critic, her Aunt Florence Stribling, who had never reconciled herself to having a niece in the theater. After seeing her as Juliet, she conceded that her niece could be an actress and a lady as well (B047, p. 135).

However, McClintic knew this production wasn't his best directorial effort. A remark he overheard while sitting behind two ladies at a matinee gave him a clue. One lady had said, "I knew it! When the curtain went up on this show I knew it would have a bad end" (B149, p. 289). The comment sent him to the nearest bookstore to get a new copy of the play which he read with fresh insight. The sets that he had ordered to be beautiful and somber he now visualized as ablaze with the warmth and gaiety of hot-blooded young love (B065). When the tour reached Cincinnati the original set was given away and he began with a new approach to the New York production.

******

S40     **CANDIDA**
(Transcontinental Repertory Tour, November 5, 1933-June 20, 1934. Opened: December, 1933, at the Metropolitan Theatre, Seattle, Washington; 42 performances during tour)

## Credits
| | |
|---|---|
| Playwright | G. Bernard Shaw |
| Director | Guthrie McClintic |
| Setting and Costumes | Woodman Thompson |
| Producer | Katharine Cornell |

## Cast
| | |
|---|---|
| James Mavor Morell | Basil Rathbone |
| Miss Prosperine Garnett | Brenda Forbes |

| | |
|---|---|
| Alexander Mill | John Hoysradt |
| Mr. Burgess | A. P. Kaye |
| Candida | Katharine Cornell |
| Eugene Marchbanks | Orson Welles |

**The Play's History**
See *Candida*, 1924 (S30).

**Synopsis**
See *Candida*, 1924 (S30).

**Review**
*Variety* (6/12/34)--The trade paper described Miss Cornell's 1933-34 repertory tour as "the most outstanding dramatic accomplishment in recent years" (B348).

**Commentary**
The same sets designed for the 1924 production of *Candida* were used. As Henderson predicted, both *Candida* and *The Barretts* brought in the best box-office receipts, with *Candida* running second. The total production cost of the tour was $42,833 with a net profit of $73,206 (B512, p. 188). No particularly significant incidents with *Candida* during the long tour were reported.

******

**S41  ROMEO AND JULIET**
(Opened: December 20, 1934, at the Martin Beck Theatre, New York; 9 weeks of performances)

**Credits**

| | |
|---|---|
| Playwright | William Shakespeare |
| Director | Guthrie McClintic |
| Settings | Jo Mielziner |
| Music | Paul Nordoff |
| Director of Dances | Martha Graham |
| Producer | Katharine Cornell |

**Cast**

| | |
|---|---|
| Escalus | Reynolds Evans |
| Paris | George Macready |
| Montague | John Miltern |
| Capulet | Moroni Olsen |
| An Old Man | Arthur Chatterton |
| Romeo | Basil Rathbone |
| Mercutio | Brian Aherne |
| Benvolio | John Emery |
| Tybalt | Orson Welles |
| Friar Laurence | Charles Waldron |

| | |
|---|---|
| Friar John | Paul Julian |
| Balthasar | Franklyn Gray |
| Sampson | Joseph Holland |
| Peter | David Vivian |
| Gregory | Robert Champlain |
| Abraham | Irving Morrow |
| An Apothecary | Arthur Chatterton |
| Officer | Irving Morrow |
| Guards | Angus Duncan |
| | Ralph Nelson |
| Lady Montague | Brenda Forbes |
| Lady Capulet | Irby Marshal |
| Juliet | Katharine Cornell |
| Nurse | Edith Evans |
| A Street Singer | Edith Allaire |
| Chorus | Orson Welles |

Citizens of Verona, Kinsfolk of both houses, Maskers, Watchmen, Attendants: Margaret Craven, Jacqueline De Witt, Lois Jameson, Agnete Johansen, Ruth March, Pamela Simpson, Gilmore Bush, John Gordon-Gage, William Hopper, Albert McCleery, Charles Thorne

## The Play's History

There is evidence that Shakespeare wrote *Romeo and Juliet* about 1591 and revised it about 1596, at a time when he was more interested in writing poetry than plays (B095). The story, derived from the English poem *The Tragicall Historye of Romeus and Juliet* which was written in 1562, is a tragedy of fate which portrays "the simple passion and heartbreak of youth" (B170, p. 975). According to some critics, it is not a well-written play and one of his lesser ones (B095, p. 84). Despite its flaws, the lyric vitality fits the youthful passion, and the emotional intensity makes it genuinely moving for audiences, particularly when played well (B170, p. 975). As Norman Holland, Shakespearean scholar, unkindly noted, the play has appeal for "older actresses who seem to have an irresistible urge to play the fourteen-year-old Juliet opposite a handsome young lover" (B095, p. 84).

Well known is the fact, that in Shakespeare's day, no women were allowed on stage and the great women's parts were played by young boys. Actors were not intended to imitate people; their method was that of declamation (B084, p. 39).

Preceding Miss Cornell, there had been many Juliets on the American stage including Julia Marlowe, Maude Adams, Helen Modjeska, Eva Le Gallienne and Jane Cowl. Miss Cornell had worked on the role of Juliet during her countrywide repertory tour of 1933-34. Because the McClintics were not satisfied with that production, they gave all of their costumes and sets to a theatre in Cincinnati while on tour and began anew with their interpretation and production of the play.

After a tryout run in Buffalo and Detroit, *Romeo and Juliet* opened December 20, 1934, an entirely new production with some of the same cast (Rathbone, Forbes, and Waldron). In the middle of the New York run, Edith Evans' husband died and Brenda Forbes played the nurse until Blanche Yurka was prepared to take it.

## Synopsis

In the hope that his beautiful daughter Juliet may become betrothed to the rich

Count Paris, Capulet, head of a noble house in Verona, Italy, invites friends to a masque in Juliet's honor. An uninvited guest in disguise is Romeo, of the house of Montague, with whom the Capulets have carried on an ancient feud that has long provoked brawls and violence in the city streets. At the moment, Romeo is pining for Rosaline, but when he and Juliet set eyes on one another, they fall hopelessly in love.

On the day that they are secretly wed by the Friar, Romeo is provoked into killing a Capulet. For his deed he is banished from the city and Juliet's father commands Juliet to prepare for marriage to Count Paris. Juliet seeks the help of the Friar who gives her a potion that will put her into a deathlike trance while he sends for Romeo to come and take her away. Hearing that she is dead, Romeo enters her tomb to find her on her bier. In despair, he ends his own life. When Juliet awakens from her trance and discovers the tragic consequences of her plan, she seizes Romeo's dagger and dies upon his body. The Friar arrives too late; the long feud between the Montagues and Capulets has ended in the sacrifice of their beloved children.

## Reviews

*Variety* (12/11/34)--Reviewing Romeo and Juliet after its tryout opening in Detroit, *Variety* predicted that Broadway "will sit up and take notice of this artistic production." The reviewer stated that "Miss Cornell proves her ability to enact the classics, lending Juliet a youthful and naive quality unlike any Juliet since Marlowe." *Variety* speculated that the show would probably lose money because of the expensive production, which has resulted in "the most finished Shakespearean offering in years....There are many nice things to say about the production. It is lavish and yet in good taste; it has exceptionally fine acting, and it is colorful." (B456).

*New York Times* (12/21/34)--Brooks Atkinson proclaimed the play to be "on the high plane of modern magnificence" in which Miss Cornell had "hung another jewel on the cheek of the theatre's nights." He commended her respect for drama and for surrounding herself with superior actors although he was a little disappointed in Rathbone and Aherne. Add to this McClintic's direction and Mielziner's settings, he said, "and you have a 'Romeo and Juliet' that will endure in the memory of our theatre" (B284).

*Commonweal* (1/4/35)--"We have gradually become aware," wrote Grenville Vernon, "that perhaps alone among American actresses Katharine Cornell has been touched by the wand of genius." He was particularly impressed by her youthfulness in "the things of the spirit" and her "exquisitely musical voice." He believed that "no Juliet of this generation has equaled her" (B229).

*Literary Digest* (1/5/35)--The critic reported that Miss Cornell's "conception of the role, her understanding of the character of Juliet, and, finally, her alluring costumes all combined to make a portrait which lit up her mobile features, gave magic grace to her expressive hands and accented her lovely voice" (B006).

## Commentary

When McClintic realized that the first production of *Romeo and Juliet* which they had taken on the repertory tour needed revision (the comments of two ladies in the audience had given him a clue to the problem), he took a new approach. Where the first sets had been beautiful but muted and somewhat sombre, he now visualized the play "ablaze with warm, vital colors, Juliet in a red dress." The action reflected the "breathless" and "headstrong" passion of youth; the tragedy evolved from "youth's fervor," "recklessness" and "its refusal to turn back" (B065; 149, p. 290). Except for one obsolete comedy scene, the text was kept intact and the scenes were a continuity of action broken into only two acts.

Miss Cornell went to Garmisch to work again on Juliet's role. She said it had taken her "a whole winter and all the next summer to feel she could even touch Juliet" (B047, p. 127). She had not been one of the "older actresses," to whom Holland referred, who had an irresistible desire to play Juliet. In fact, she undertook the part only at the insistence of her advisers and friends. Forty years old (secretly 45), she knew that if she were ever to do the play, it had to be soon. Her one condition was that she could take her time to grasp the role before it was taken to New York. Her preparation was well rewarded.

The enthusiastic reception of the audience moved Miss Cornell to tears--the only time she cried at an opening. With few exceptions, the critics were extravagant in their praise. Edith J. R. Isaacs wrote that "of the whole performance there is no more to say than it is the East and Juliet is the sun!" (B109, p. 94). Although obviously more than fourteen, she was "by all odds the most lovely and enchanting Juliet our present-day theatre has seen," said John Mason Brown in the *New York Post* (B321). In an article "...And Juliet is the Sun," *Literary Digest* reported that she played an impulsive, "bright and girlish Juliet" who, in her burning ardor, "all but fell over the parapet into Romeo's waiting arms in her unchecked eagerness to come closer to her beloved" (B006).

Some unfavorable notices cited the occasional lack of speech clarity which was sacrificed in keeping the swift moving pace. The most unkind criticism came from Robert Garland who described Miss Cornell's Juliet as "overwrought" and possessed of "neurasthenia" (B372).

The new production, which had cost $43,000, sold out at every performance with as many as 100 standees, even at matinees. The play was to have run for 6 weeks but Guthrie extended it another three. It had run for 9 weeks and 77 performances and was still playing to capacity when it closed on February 26, 1935. It had earned approximately $55,000 (B512, p. 91). The closing was a relief to Miss Cornell who had developed a cough which was plaguing her, particularly in the tomb scene. Two nights later the season was resumed with a revival of *The Barretts*.

Juliet was one of her supreme accomplishments. As Stark Young claimed, the characters in the play "are moved by real emotion," and Miss Cornell's performance "makes you believe in love" (B248). For her performance as Juliet she was awarded the Drama League's Medal in 1935.

******

S42    **THE BARRETTS OF WIMPOLE STREET  (1935 Revival)**
       (Opened: February 23, 1935, at the Martin Beck Theatre, New York; 3 weeks of performances)

**Credits**

| | |
|---|---|
| Playwright | Rudolf Besier |
| Director | Guthrie McClintic |
| Settings and Costumes | Jo Mielziner |

Producer                                                            Katharine Cornell

**Cast**
Dr. Chambers                                                         Moroni Olsen
Elizabeth Barrett Moulton-Barrett                          Katharine Cornell
Wilson                                                                   Brenda Forbes
Henrietta Moulton-Barrett                                  Margalo Gillmore
Arabel Moulton-Barrett                                            Joyce Carey
Octavius Moulton-Barrett                                   Burgess Meredith
Septimus Moulton-Barrett                                       David Vivian
Alfred Moulton-Barrett                                      Robert Champlain
Charles Moulton-Barrett                                    John Gordon-Gage
Henry Moulton-Barrett                                           Gilmore Bush
George Moulton-Barrett                                         Irving Morrow
Edward Moulton-Barrett                                      Charles Waldron
Bella Hedley                                                      Margot Stevenson
Henry Bevan                                                         John Hoysradt
Robert Browning                                                     Brian Aherne
Doctor Ford-Waterlow                                         Reynolds Evans
Captain Surtees Cook                                             John Emery
Flush                                                                         Himself

## The Play's History
This was a revival of *The Barretts* for which Miss Cornell had received acclaim in her initial record-breaking run in New York and the tour that followed it. The memorable Christmas night performance in Seattle had occurred on the long transcontinental repertory tour in 1933-34.

## Synopsis
See *The Barretts*, 1931 (S35).

## Review
*New York Times* (2/26/35)--Atkinson reported that, by consensus, the show in 1935 was better than in 1931. In short, he said, *The Barretts of Wimpole Street* "simply remains one of the events of any theatrical season" (B274).

## Commentary
Two nights after the closing of *Romeo and Juliet* Miss Cornell revived *The Barretts* on February 23, 1935, with the intention of running it for only 4 weeks. The cast was a mixture of the original company with Brian Aherne as Browning and one newcomer, Burgess Meredith, as Occy and Margalo Gillmore as Henrietta.
Reviews were excellent; critics thought the show had "grown richer and more satisfactory" (B163, p. 359; B512, p. 80). Audiences, however, did not respond to the critics' warm reception and the show was closed on March 16, 1935, after only 24 performances.

******

**S43    FLOWERS OF THE FOREST**

(Opened: April 10, 1935, at the Martin Beck Theatre, New York; 40 performances)

<u>Credits</u>

| | |
|---|---|
| Playwright | John van Druten |
| Director | Auriol Lee |
| Settings | Jo Mielziner |
| Produced under supervision of | Guthrie McClintic |
| Presented by | Katharine Cornell |

<u>Cast</u>

| | |
|---|---|
| Beryl Hodgson | Brenda Forbes |
| Naomi Jacklin | Katharine Cornell |
| Lewis Jacklin | Moffat Johnston |
| Matheson | Arthur Chatterton |
| Mercia Huntbach | Margalo Gillmore |
| Leonard Dobie | Burgess Meredith |
| Mrs. Huntbach | Leslie Bingham |
| Thomas Lindsay | John Emery |
| Richard Newton-Clare | Hugh Williams |
| Rev. Percy Huntbach | Charles Waldron |
| Mrs. Ettles | Alice Belmore Cliffe |

**The Play's History**

Written by John van Druten, the theme was taken from lines of "A Lament for Flodden" by Jane Elliott, poetess and pacifist of the eighteenth century:

"The Flowers of the Forest, that fought aye the foremost,
The prime of our land, lie cauld in the clay" (B047, p.306).

**Synopsis**

The play is about the glory and horrors of war, death, honor and the meaning of life. The opening scene is in the present (1934) at the home of Lewis and Naomi Jacklin who approach life with little enthusiasm. Naomi's spinster sister Mercia brings a box of letters written to Naomi by her fiance Richard, who died of wounds in the war in 1917.

At the Jacklin's invitation, Beryl, secretary to Mr. Jacklin, brings her boyfriend Leonard, who is outspokenly anti-war, to meet them. Leonard takes from the shelves a book of war poems which happen to have been written by Naomi's fiance. In a flashback to the vicarage in Sussex during the war years both Naomi and Mercia are in love with young men who are going off to the war. Their parents extol the glories of war and, because Mercia's fiance Tommy views fighting as a duty rather than a privilege, Mercia refuses to marry him. On the other hand, Naomi's fiance Richard believes war is an honor, even though he has a fear of dying without having a son.

Two years later, in 1916, Tommy has been killed, but Mercia insists that she did the only thing she could do by sending him away. The relationship between Richard and Naomi is strained when he comes home to recuperate from wounds. Unknown to him, Naomi is carrying his child and is crushed by his vehement declaration that it is insane to bring a child into the world. Convinced that he does not love her, she aborts the child. Richard, too, dies of war wounds before Naomi can reach him.

The final act is again in the present. Beryl and Leonard have stopped by the Jacklin's and, while there, Leonard is stricken with excruciating head pains, the onset of telepathic powers. In his seeming delirium, Leonard brings a message from the dying Richard to Naomi. It removes her doubts about Richard's love and convinces her there is still richness in life.

## Reviews

*New York Times* (4/9/35)--Brooks Atkinson wrote that the play was promising in the first act but that the playwright had not driven his theme through the evening. In his opinion, the ending of the play was "trivial" and its expression "maudlin." As for Miss Cornell, he said that she played with her usual competence and beauty but at times seemed to be "almost detached" (B273).

*New York Post* (4/9/35)--John Mason Brown reported that the play "failed to project itself across the footlights." He did commend Miss Cornell for bringing to it "all of her beauty, grace, her memorability, her presence, her generosity, her vibrant intelligence and her natural instincts..." (B318).

*Nation* (4/24/35)--Commenting on several of van Druten's earlier successful plays, Joseph Wood Krutch points out the playwright's strengths in writing drawing room plays and his limitations in attempting serious drama. His range of emotional feeling, says Krutch, runs the gamut "from A to B." *Flowers of the Forest* raises "its voice with disastrous results." Miss Cornell plays the leading role "for all its worth" but is unable to make the "big" scenes genuine or moving (B125).

## Commentary

The play opened in New York to an audience that was more impressed with it than English audiences had been. Miss Cornell had wanted to do the play because of its anti-war theme, but the play was disappointing. As Atkinson noted, the author had not given "coherent shape" to the actors' emotions (B273). John Anderson, in his review in the *New York Evening Journal*, thought Mr. van Druten had written "an aimless meditation" on war and Miss Cornell "emerges with far more dramatic value than she deserves" (B259). On the other hand, Nelson Bell of the *Washington Post* commented favorably about Miss Cornell's "finished artistry" (B306). Robert Garland of the *World Telegram* thought her portrait of Naomi was "rich and radiant" (B370).

From the beginning the play had trouble. McClintic did not like it and Auriol Lee, who had the production rights, insisted on directing. Because Miss Cornell did not feel that she could work without her husband, a compromise was made and McClintic supervised. However, rehearsals were nightmarish, largely as a result of Miss Lee's tendency to doze off and McClintic's intolerance. It was learned later that the unfortunate woman was suffering the symptoms of early encephalitis.

Mosel suggests that an incident which occurred at the New York opening may have had an effect on the play's reception there. Shortly after the play began, a woman having an epileptic attack had to be carried from the theatre. To distract the audience Miss Cornell improvised by cajoling Burgess Meredith, who was playing Dobie, into having a temporary "spell." By the time the woman had been removed, Meredith had recovered, leading the audience to wonder if the whole incident was part of the play

(B163, p. 364). At any rate, *Flowers of the Forest* failed with the critics and the boxoffice. It closed after 40 performances.

\*\*\*\*\*\*

## S44    ROMEO AND JULIET
(Opened: December 23, 1935, at the Martin Beck Theatre, New York; 2 weeks of performances)

### Credits

| | |
|---|---|
| Play | William Shakespeare |
| Director | Guthrie McClintic |
| Settings & Costumes | Jo Mielziner |
| Music | Paul Nordoff |
| Producer | Katharine Cornell |

### Cast

| | |
|---|---|
| Escalus | Reynolds Evans |
| Paris | John Cromwell |
| Montague | Arthur Chatterton |
| Capulet | Charles Dalton |
| An Old Man | Joseph Roeder |
| Romeo | Maurice Evans |
| Mercutio | Ralph Richardson |
| Benvolio | Tyrone Power, Jr. |
| Tybalt | Irving Morrow |
| Friar Laurence | Charles Waldron |
| Friar John | David Orrick |
| Balthasar | William Roehrick |
| Sampson | David Orrick |
| Peter | David Vivian |
| Gregory | Robert Champlain |
| Abraham | Grant Gordon |
| An Apothecary | Joseph Roeder |
| Officer | Carl Allan |
| Lady Montague | Lois Jameson |
| Lady Capulet | Alice Johns |
| Juliet | Katharine Cornell |
| Nurse | Florence Reed |
| Chorus | Ralph Richardson |

Citizens of Verona, Kinsfolk of both houses
Maskers, watchmen, attendants and guards: Evelyn Abbott, Charlott Fitch, Anne Froelick, Ruth March, Harriott Marshall, Gabrielle Morgan, Albert Allen, John Cornell, Richard Graham, Hudson Shotwell, Kurt Steinbart and Fred Thompson

### The Play's History
For early history see *Romeo and Juliet*, December 20, 1934, the opening date

of her first Broadway presentation of the play. Her first production of *Romeo and Juliet* was taken on tour in repertory with *Candida* and *The Barretts of Wimpole Street*, in 1934-35, and discontinued before the tour ended. Except for some of the actors, the 1934 opening in New York was an entirely new production.

In the fall of 1935, Miss Cornell toured the eastern seaboard and the midwest with her production of *Romeo and Juliet*: Chicago, Des Moines, Omaha, Wichita, Tulsa, Oklahoma City, Memphis, Nashville, Louisville, Indianapolis. Toledo, Fort Wayne and Rochester. At the end of ten and one-half weeks the production ended at the Martin Beck Theatre in New York for a 2-week run through the Christmas holiday. Major changes had been made in the cast. Basil Rathbone was replaced by Maurice Evans. Other newcomers were Florence Reed who was playing the nurse; Ralph Richardson was Mercutio, Tyrone Power, Jr. was Benvolio, and Irving Morrow was cast in the role of Tybalt.

## Synopsis
See *Romeo and Juliet*, 1934 (S41).

## Reviews
*New York Post* (12/24/35)--In the opinion of John Mason Brown, Miss Cornell "is incontestably the foremost American Juliet of her generation," and he doubted that her "equal has been seen anywhere in our time." He claimed that her *Romeo and Juliet*, is "the most distinguished and compelling revival of a Shakespearean tragedy that has been made in this country in our time." Her Juliet is at present "deeper, more vibrant and more memorable than it ever was." He also thought that the actors in the original company had grown in the roles and time had perfected the production which, a year earlier, had been admirable (B321).

*New York Herald Tribune* (12/35)--"Maurice Evans: Miss Katharine Cornell's New Romeo" was the headline of a review by Lucius Beebe. Beebe thought the production of *Romeo and Juliet* had been influenced by Granville-Barker who, in his opinion, ranked as the finest Shakespearean scholar (B305).

## Commentary
Maurice Evans was physically too small to play opposite Miss Cornell so compensation for the new Romeo's lack of height was made by elevating his shoes. Some thought Basil Rathbone's portrayal had been arctic, lacking in emotional range and speech clarity. This had not escaped comment from critics who thought Evans was more likeable and persuasive. Audiences gave him vigorous applause for the balcony scene, the real test of his talent. The critics also received Florence Reed, Ralph Richardson and Irving Morrow favorably. Edith J. R. Isaacs found Miss Cornell's performance of Juliet to be richer than it had been the previous year. *The New York Times* reviewer Lewis Nichols declared that "The evening, of course, is still Miss Cornell's: 'Romeo and Juliet' remains her party" (B443).

******

**S45**    **SAINT JOAN**
(Opened: March 9, 1936, at the Martin Beck Theatre, New York; 11 weeks of performances).

Credits

| | |
|---|---|
| Playwright | G. Bernard Shaw |
| Director | Guthrie McClintic |
| Settings | Jo Mielziner |
| Music | Paul Nordoff |
| Producer | Katharine Cornell |

Cast

| | |
|---|---|
| Captain Robert de Boudricourt | Joseph Holland |
| His Steward | Arthur Chatterton |
| Joan | Katharine Cornell |
| Bertrand de Poulengey | Tyrone Power, Jr. |
| Monseigneur de la Tremouille | Charles Dalton |
| The Archbishop of Rheims | Charles Waldron |
| Page to the Dauphin | Robert Champlain |
| Giles de Raise | David Vivian |
| Captain la Hire | Barry Kelly |
| The Dauphin | Maurice Evans |
| Duchess de la Tremouille | Ruth March |
| Dunois | Kent Smith |
| Page to Dunois | Edward Ryan, Jr. |
| Richard de Beauchamp | Brian Aherne |
| Master John de Stogumber | George Coulouris |
| Page to Warwick | Walter Marquis |
| Peter Cauchon | Edwardo Ciannelli |
| Brother John Lemaitre | Arthur Byron |
| Canon John d'Estivet | Joseph Holland |
| Canon de Courcelles | Irving Morrow |
| Brother Martin Ladvenu | John Cromwell |
| The Executioner | Barry Kelly |
| An English Soldier | Charles Dalton |
| A Gentleman of 1920 | Arthur Chatterton |
| Court Ladies: | Hilde Albers, Anne Froelick |
| Courtiers and Soldiers: | Richard Graham, David Orrick |
| | William Roehrick, Hudson Shotwell |
| | Kurt Steinbart, Fred Thompson |

The Play's History

The play is based on the story of Joan of Arc who was born about 1412. The daughter of a working farmer, she was a pious Catholic and, according to Shaw, one of the first Protestant martyrs. Living, dressing and fighting like a man, she was, Shaw said, "one of the queerest fish among the eccentric worthies of the Middle Ages". In 1431, she was burned at the stake for heresy, witchcraft and sorcery and for her "unwomanly and insufferable presumption" (B207, p. 747). She humiliated men by being right. Had she learned how to handle them, Shaw believed her life would have been longer, but she was a naive and capable country girl who was "a born boss". Even those who professed to be her friend were unwilling to lift a hand to save her (B207, p. 766).

History has judged her to be a genius and a saint. In 1456, the charges against her were annulled. Nearly six centuries later she was declared venerable (1904) and Blessed (1908). In 1920, her canonization was accomplished.

In 1921, Margaret Anglin played *The Trial of Joan of Arc* at the Shubert. Woollcott reported that there was "magic" in the way she became "the wide-eyed mystical girl of the play (B504). The first performance of *Saint Joan* was done by the Theatre Guild in New York City on December 28, 1923. Winifred Lenihan was in the title role which Miss Cornell had turned down because of her commitment to *Casanova*. A year later, on March 26, 1924, its first performance in London took place in the New Theatre on St. Martin's Lane. Sybil Thorndike played Joan in the London debut and again when it was revived in 1931.

In 1924, the play was also produced in Berlin with Elisabeth Bergner, whose performance gave her an international reputation and, later, landed her the film role. When she came to New York to make her American debut in *Escape Me Never*, which she had played with great success in London, she saw Miss Cornell in *Romeo and Juliet*, urged her to do *Saint Joan* and offered to delay the release of her film version until after Miss Cornell had produced it. Brian Aherne, who wanted to play Warwick, gave Miss Cornell further encouragement.

## Synopsis

When "voices" give her God's instructions to take the fate of France into her own hands, Joan seeks an audience with Captain Robert de Boudricourt to request a horse, armor and men to lead a siege against the English at Orleans. He sends her to the Dauphin, heir to the throne. Joan promises to crown the Dauphin in Rheims Cathedral if he will give her command of the army to carry out God's will for France. He grants her the authority to do with his dispirited army as she will.

After leading the victorious siege against the English at Orleans, she leads France to victory again and again, thus incurring the wrath of the English. By taking her orders directly from God, rather than the Church officials, she also arouses the animosity of the Church prelates whose authority she supersedes. Both her countrymen and the enemy see her as a rebel against the Church, God and Nature (the latter because she wears man's clothes). They agree she must perish.

She is brought to trial for heresy, sorcery, idolatry and blasphemy. To save herself from death she signs a form of recantation, then realizes that she will be kept in perpetual imprisonment. She chooses the alternative, to be burned at the stake.

In the Epilogue the Dauphin has a dream in which Joan and those involved in her death reappear to tell what has befallen them since her burning. Joan learns that her charges have been annulled and she may be canonized as a saint. Dunois asks that she forgive them.

Left alone, a radiant light descends on her as she speaks her final lines: "O God that madest this beautiful earth, when will it be ready to receive Thy saints? How long, O Lord, how long?"

## Reviews

*New York Times* (3/15/36)--Critic Brooks Atkinson stated that Shaw's *Saint Joan* was the one play of Shaw's that "approaches greatness." He cited the passion-laden passages, the integrity and eminence of the characters, the wit, Shaw's shrewd knowledge of the hypocritical political talk of the time, and the lyricism of some of his lines.

Atkinson criticized Shaw for his heartless egotism and the deep resentment he had engendered by his lack of humility and intellectual snobbery. Then, Atkinson generously credited him for beginning to become a part of the human race and for "borrowing the tongue of an angel for the best speeches in the play" (B285).

*Nation* (3/25/36)--Joseph Wood Krutch pronounced that *Saint Joan* was "one of very few classics of the modern theater." In his opinion, McClintic had staged it with "great skill" and it was one of the "finest performances" in Miss Cornell's career (B127).

*New Republic* (3/25/36)--"Miss Cornell understands the role with all her luminous absorption" stated Stark Young. The most impressive thing is the "power she has of bringing on to the stage a kind of trance in which she moves, strangely alone among the players and yet gentle--a trance and seeming restatement of herself, all inner voice" (B250).

*New York Sunday News* (3/22/36)--Burns Mantle found the three hours of *Saint Joan* to be "a bit of a strain" but found the sacrifice worthwhile. "The Cornell beauty that worries the pressmen" he explained, "is a spiritual rather than physical beauty. It illumined *Lucrece* and added a glow of glorified courage to the invalided Elizabeth Barrett....It hovers over and about the staged story of *Saint Joan* like an enveloping halo and settles finally upon it as a benediction" (B420).

## Commentary

Having decided that *Saint Joan* would be their next production, the McClintics planned to open the fall season (1935) with a tour of *Romeo and Juliet* for ten and a half weeks. Cast replacements were necessary because Rathbone and Aherne were both in Hollywood, and the casting for *Saint Joan* had to be done. Having heard that Maurice Evans' Dauphin in the Old Vic-Sadler Wells production was outstanding, McClintic engaged Evans for the roles of Romeo and the Dauphin. The entire cast for *Saint Joan* was made up of Cornell's equals, an outstanding cast who did justice to the play.

This was the only time Miss Cornell had ever had to postpone an opening because of illness. On the tryout tour she had caught the flu in Buffalo and the doctor told her she had to go to bed. The delay was psychologically devastating to her. Not only was she keyed up for the opening but she also felt a deep responsibility to her fellow actors and her audiences. She knew she had to conserve her vitality and practice strict discipline to avoid illness. In other words, she had to save herself for the theatre.

Shaw had been attacked for the lengthiness of the play (three and a half hours), a matter which he defends in a similarly lengthy preface. The long speeches which Shaw believed vital to the understanding of the "tedious matters" of the Church, the feudal system and other forces of the times, could certainly have been less wordy. In his typical arrogance Shaw asks, "What do its discomforts matter when the play makes us forget them?" (B207, p. 800).

Critics have also disputed the lengthy Epilogue which, in Burns Mantle's view, "robs the play of its tragic purge." He grants that, in Cornell's production, it had worked well and had given Saint Joan the glorious ending that Shaw felt she deserved. Mantle concluded that "Joan was one of the authentic triumphs of Miss Cornell's career" (B413).

Despite her demoralizing delay in opening *Saint Joan*, it was one of the productions of which she was most proud. She decided to close the play at the end of an 11-week run in New York in order to take it on a 7-week tour to Boston, Philadelphia, Chicago, Los Angeles and San Francisco. It was still doing excellent business ($21,000 per week) and was one of the 3 top shows in New York (the other two were *Victoria Regina* with Helen Hayes and *Idiot's Delight* with Alfred Lunt and Lynn Fontanne).

For both Shaw and Miss Cornell *Saint Joan* was their zenith. Mosel observed that "Joan seems to have been the one great stage role she was fated to play from the beginning" (B163, p. 374).

******

## S46    THE WINGLESS VICTORY
(Opened: December 23, 1936, at the Empire Theatre, New York; 15 and one-half weeks of performances)

### Credits

| | |
|---|---|
| Playwright | Maxwell Anderson |
| Director | Guthrie McClintic |
| Settings | Jo Mielziner |
| Producer | Katharine Cornell |

### Cast

| | |
|---|---|
| A Girl | Mary Michael |
| Reverend Phineas McQueston | Kent Smith |
| Jared Mungo, Church Elder | Arthur Chatterton |
| Winston Urquhart, Church Elder | John Winthrop |
| Mrs. McQueston | Effie Shannon |
| Ruel McQueston | Myron McCormick |
| Venture, Wife of Phineas | Lois Jameson |
| Faith Ingalls | Ruth Matteson |
| Happy Penny, a seaman | Barry Kelly |
| Letty, a maid | Theodora Pleadwell |
| Nathaniel McQueston | Walter Abel |
| Oparre | Katharine Cornell |
| Toala | Helen Zelinskaya |
| Durian | Claire Howard |
| Harry, a Bailiff | John Winthrop |
| Van Zandt, a Sailor | Victor Colton |
| Longshoreman | Franklin Davis |

### The Play's History

*The Wingless Victory* was first performed in the National Theatre, Washington, D.C., on November 24, 1936, where it began a 4-week tryout. It opened in New York to capacity audiences for the first week and a half, and then receipts dropped. After 11 weeks, *The Wingless Victory* played in repertory with *Candida*. Because *Candida* drew larger audiences, *The Wingless Victory* was closed after the 15th week.

**Synopsis**

The setting is in the early winter in 1800 in Salem, Massachusetts. When the prodigal son, Nathaniel, comes home after seven years as a vagabond sailor to the house where his brother, The Reverend Phineas McQueston, and his wife live with his mother, he is greeted with hostility. Expecting to be welcomed, he has brought his beautiful wife Oparre, a Christian Malay princess, their two children and a nurse. Despite Oparre's efforts to win them, the bigoted, self-righteous McQuestons and townspeople treat the dark-skinned beauty and her children with contempt. Only Ruel, Nathaniel's younger brother, treats her kindly.

Nathaniel's wealth cannot buy the friendship or compassion of townsmen who refuse to repay the money they borrow from him. Their vengeance is aided by the discovery that Nathaniel's ship may not be *The Queen of Celebes* but the stolen Dutch ship, *The Wingless Victory*. His brother Phineas, the church elders and townspeople force Nathaniel to send his family away or lose all that he has. Realizing that there will never be a home for them, Nathaniel bids his wife to leave.

Oparre takes the children and Toala, their nurse, to the ship where Toala brings out a phial of hemlock she had carried from the Celebes. Repenting too late, Nathaniel comes to beg forgiveness and to go with Oparre. The nurse and children have already fallen into eternal sleep and Oparre dies in his arms. Accompanied by Ruel, he sails away from the intolerance and persecution of their Puritan town.

**Reviews**

*Variety* (12\23\36)--Detroit's reception of *Wingless Victory* at the Cass Theatre was enthusiastic. For 8 performances the theatre was filled at $3.30 top prices. At $2800 it eclipsed the previous year's *Saint Joan* and set a record of many years' standing. Because Miss Cornell got her start with Bonstelle in Detroit, "it goes completely goofy over her any time she appears here regardless of the vehicle," the reviewer stated. Seats were sold out in advance for almost every performance (B345).

*Variety* (12/30/36)--After the New York opening *Variety* predicted that *Wingless Victory* would not miss despite some first-night differences in opinion, and even though it lacked the lure of some of Miss Cornell's earlier appearances. The reviewer commented on Maxwell Anderson's flair for writing blank verse, the form used in this play, and thought the play excellent theatre. *Variety* reported that it holds the audience even with the long speeches. As for the acting, "Miss Cornell is everything that stardom means. She can be alluring as Oparre....Walter Abel, Effie Shannon and Ruth Matteson are 'standouts in support'" (B502).

*New Republic* (2/3/37)--Critical of Anderson's play, Stark Young wrote that "to it's service Miss Cornell brought the translucence and instrumental qualities of herself as acting medium." Young quoted a long passage of verse from the play to illustrate, for those who were not familiar with it, the "tired rhythmic patterns, superfluous images and lyric cliches." He called the play "semi-tosh from start to finish" (B246).

**Commentary**

Oparre in *The Wingless Victory* was the only Oriental role that Miss Cornell played and one of her most physically tiring roles. Not only did the body makeup that she used take hours to apply and remove, but it also confined her to the theatre between matinees and evening performances and made her skin very sensitive. In addition, the emotional scene at the end of the second act, the infanticide of her children and her suicide were enervating. To add to the strain when on tour, she carried a thirty-five year old midget, who weighed twice as much as the child she replaced, up the curving staircase. (Child labor laws in most states prohibited the use of children under the age of twelve as actors).

The critical response to *The Wingless Victory* was mixed. Some reviewers judged it to be the best drama of the season; others found it to be poorly written and wordy. In Brooks Atkinson's opinion, Maxwell Anderson did not develop the situation or convey a real understanding of the Oriental mind and body. Moreover, he thought the playwright could have put some of the offstage events into acting. Atkinson commented that Mr. Anderson could write in language that is "sinewy, pungent, glowing and biting," but his words in *The Wingless Victory* had lost their "magic" and become "an impediment of theatrical speech" (B289).

Although reviewers were critical of Anderson's drama, they had plaudits for Miss Cornell. In the role of Oparre, Gilbert Gabriel of the *New York American* said she was "most beautiful to see, most thrilling to hear, most memorable to meet in angry passion, in eloquent death" (B366). Richard Watts, Jr. found her to be never "more heroic, more noble in her spirit and her playing" (B498).

At the end of the New York run and a short tour, Miss Cornell decided to rest for a year. She had worked for 20 years without stopping and it was time to take stock of her career.

******

**S47    CANDIDA (Second Revival)**
(Opened: March 10, 1937, at the Empire Theatre, New York; 50 performances)

**Credits**

| | |
|---|---|
| Playwright | G. Bernard Shaw |
| Director | Guthrie McClintic |
| Settings | Woodman Thompson |
| Producer | Katharine Cornell |

**Cast**

| | |
|---|---|
| Miss Proserpine Garnett | Mildred Natwick |
| James Mavor Morell | Kent Smith |
| Alexander Mill | Morgan Farley |
| Mr. Burgess | A. P. Kaye |
| Candida | Katharine Cornell |
| Eugene Marchbanks | Robert Harris |

**The Play's History**

Miss Cornell had played Candida with great success in 1924. In 1933-34 she had also taken it on tour in repertory with *The Barretts of Wimpole Street* and *Romeo and Juliet* while she was absorbing the role of Juliet. During that tour of 29 weeks she had performed in *Candida* 42 times. The play was taken to Brooklyn, where the tour closed. It did not go to Broadway.

## Synopsis
See *Candida*, 1924 (S30).

## Reviews
*New York Sun* (3/37)--Richard Lockridge praised the play and found Miss Cornell's performance difficult to describe. She had made the closing scene in which Candida chooses between her husband and Marchbanks "one of the most moving scenes in the contemporary theatre," he wrote. "If it does not bring a lump to your throat, you have been boiled too long" (B404).

*Chicago News* (5/21/37)--Lloyd Lewis reported that, in his showgoing experience, Miss Cornell does what no one else ever did before, "she takes Shaw out of his plays and puts his characters in his place." In his opinion, the show was "undated," had acquired "a new lucidity" and "the mood and tone" had been preserved "when Miss Cornell was not on stage" (B403).

## Commentary
Her second revival of *Candida* on Broadway played 50 performances for Wednesday matinees and Monday and Saturday nights in repertory with *The Wingless Victory*.

The intervening years since her first Broadway appearance in the role of Candida had added depth and the lustre of old polished silver to her portrayal. Brooks Atkinson found her performance to be "immeasurably finer" than in the earlier production and credited the play with being "a little masterpiece of human serenity" (B263). Although critics thought that Marchbanks had seemed somewhat cowardly at first, they applauded the performances of the other players.

\*\*\*\*\*\*

**S48    HEROD AND MARIAMNE**
(Opened: October 26, 1938, at the Nixon Theatre in Pittsburgh; 4 weeks of performances)

## Credits
| | |
|---|---|
| Playwright | Clemence Dane |
| Adapted from the German Classic by | Friedrich Hebbel |
| Director | Guthrie McClintic |
| Settings | Harry Horner |
| Costumes | Valentina |
| Music | Karol Rathaus |
| Producer | Katharine Cornell |

## Cast
| | |
|---|---|
| Herod | Fritz Kortner |

| | |
|---|---|
| Joseph, Herod's Brother-in-law | Peter Capell |
| Judah, a Jewish Commander | Lawrence Fletcher |
| Serubabel | Arthur Chatterton |
| Philo, his son | Richard Ellington |
| Secretary to Herod | Robert C. Currier |
| A Slave | James Welch |
| Titus, a Roman Commander | Kent Smith |
| Lamech, a Pharisee | Joseph Holland |
| A Courtier | Philip Carr |
| Three Prisoners | Vincent J. Donehue |
| | Norman Stuart |
| | David Savage |
| Two Soldiers | Vincent Copeland |
| | John Kerr |
| Joab | Robert H. Harris |
| Alexandra, the Queen's mother | Florence Reed |
| Mayor of the Palace | Edgar Kent |
| Mariamne | Katharine Cornell |
| An Attendant to Mariamne | Ruth March |
| Mute Slave | Philip Gordon |
| Attendant to Alexandra | Lois Jameson |
| Alexandra's Slave | Mildred Dunnock |
| Reader Slave | David Savage |
| Perfume Seller | Robert C. Currier |
| Sohemus, Governor of Galilee | McKay Morris |
| Selima, wife of Joseph | Dorothy Patten |
| A Roman Soldier | Norman Stuart |
| Caspar, an Indian King | Byron McGrath |
| Melchior, a Mongol King | A. Winfield Hoeny |
| Balthazar, a Negro King | R. Earl Jones |
| The Chief Judge | Edgar Kent |
| A Soldier | Frank Swann |

## The Play's History

The play was adapted from the German classic, *Herodes and Mariamne*, by Friedrich Hebbel, one of the great German poets and dramatists of the 19th century. He viewed society in terms of Hegel's theory of the "categorical imperative," that a force determines an individual's destiny. He also conceptualized "dramatic conflicts as historical or historically determined processes." A struggle exists in most of his historical plays between the old and the new orders. In his tragedies he departed from the idealism of the Goethe era to the "realism, determinism and psychological drama of Ibsen, Strindberg and Shaw" (B128, p. 394). Miss Cornell produced the American premiere of Clemence Dane's adaptation of Hebbel's classic.

## Synopsis

King Herod of Jerusalem orders the deaths of those who he believes are his enemies, one of whom is Aristobulus, the brother of his wife Mariamne. When Herod receives a call to meet with Antony, he fears that Antony may kill him. Fiercely jealous of his beautiful wife, Herod attempts to exact her promise that she will follow him in

death if he is killed.  Believing he should trust her, she makes no promise.  Herod secretly orders his Viceroy, his sister's husband Joseph, to kill Mariamne should he die.
When rumor of Herod's death reaches Jerusalem, Joseph  suggests to Mariamne that he will spare her life so that they may share the bed and throne.  Offended by his proposal, she assures him that she will take her own life.
Herod returns to prepare for war as Antony's ally against Octavius and Rome and accuses his wife of seducing Joseph.  Herod sends Joseph to death and returns to battle unreconciled with Mariamne but having arranged with his new Viceroy to kill her in the event of his death.
Again, rumor that Herod has been killed comes to Mariamne and she plans a feast to demonstrate her defiance of his distrust.  Herod returns in the midst of the feast and sends her to prison.  By remaining silent at her trial, Mariamne chooses to die rather than to live with the psychopathic jealousy of the man she loves.

## Reviews

*Cleveland Plain Dealer* (10/38)--"You see what draws authors and actors to this theme.  Here is a page from history and legend that is thick with brilliant pageantry, with strong color, naked hates and dim horrors," reported W. F. McDermott.  However, he thought that "distracting detail" cluttered the play, taking the attention away from the relationship of Herod and Mariamne.  He described the last scene of the play as "reminiscent of the trial episode in Saint Joan," judging it to be "as fine as anything that Miss Cornell has ever done."  McDermott captured the essence of the play's failure in his concluding comment: "But the play does not come alive.  It never takes wings" (B426).

*Detroit Free Press* (11/1/38)--Len G. Shaw thought the show made amends for its slow start with steadily mounting interest in the succeeding scenes.  The playwright was too broad in the statement she attempted to make, Shaw stated.  However, largely through the efforts of Miss Cornell and the "superior support" she had, the play was successful.  For Miss Cornell, it was a triumph, "pictorially" and "histrionically" (B466).

*Washington Post* (11/14/38)--The headline for Wilella Waldorf's review announced that Katharine Cornell was abandoning *Herod and Mariamne*.  As Waldorf explained, reviews have not been "exactly cheerful news" and although business has not been "appreciably affected," the McClintics have decided against taking the show to New York.  Waldorf noted that other stars, such as Ina Claire who had closed *Yankee Fable*, were also having trouble finding suitable plays (B489).

## Commentary

According to Mosel the play was a colossal failure, which the McClintics did not want to admit until Gert Macy confronted them with the unhappy reactions of the audiences (B163, p. 422).  In fact, the argument that ensued resulted in Gert being dismissed by Miss Cornell, who on the following morning, morosely confessed that Gert was right and begged her to stay with the company, which she did.  Mosel and Macy could not understand why the McClintics had selected the play except for Miss Cornell's loyalty to Clemence Dane and her inability to say no.
Shaw of the *Detroit Free Press* commended Miss Cornell for her "appealing qualities" and the musical, meaningful reading of her lines.  He also tactfully referred to

the declamatory delivery of her leading man Fritz Kortner, who gave little regard to what others were saying, as "a vibrant reading." Shaw thought the performance was a triumph for Miss Cornell (B465).

The McClintics were unable to cancel their engagement in Washington, D.C., but they did not take the play on to New York. An expensive production, it grossed $72,000 in the 4 weeks that it ran, but did not make enough to repay production costs (B512, p. 126).

******

## S49    NO TIME FOR COMEDY
(Opened: April 17, 1939, at the Ethel Barrymore Theatre, New York; 24 weeks of performances)

### Credits

| | |
|---|---|
| Playwright | Samuel N. Behrman |
| Director | Guthrie McClintic |
| Settings | Jo Mielziner |
| Costumes | Valentina |
| Producers | Katharine Cornell and Playwrights' Company |

### Cast

| | |
|---|---|
| Clementine | Gee Gee James |
| Linda Esterbrook (known onstage as Linda Paige) | Katharine Cornell |
| Philo Smith | John Williams |
| Gaylord Esterbrook, called "Gay" | Laurence Olivier |
| Amanda Smith | Margalo Gillmore |
| Robert | Peter Robinson |
| Makepeace Lovell | Robert Flemyng |

### The Play's History

Behrman's *No Time for Comedy,* was a comedy of manners. As William Klink, who did a critical analysis of it, said, "Behrman attempts to generate humor from a play in a chaotic time and he nearly succeeds" (B120, p. 168).

### Synopsis

Waiting for an idea for a new play in the winter of 1938, Gay Esterbrook is very depressed that he has nothing of cosmic significance to say. Linda Paige, his actress-wife, suggests that humor, at which he is talented, is important in "the jungle of life." She is waiting for a suitable play and urges him to write another of his brilliant and charming comedies for her. However, Gay has fallen under the spell of Amanda Smith, who specializes in bringing out the latent potential in unsuspecting men. She exploits Gay's dilemma by convincing him that he should write about the Spanish war, death and immortality.

Having been warned by Amanda's husband, Philo, of the danger Gay is in, Linda confronts Amanda at her home where Gay is writing. Gay denounces Linda for her "superiority" and announces his intention of marrying Amanda. Meanwhile, Philo Smith has fallen in love with Linda and proposes marriage to her.

Gay, convinced that his new "profound" play is no good, sends Linda the script for her confirmation of his fears. She gives him an idea for a play, and offers to help him. As he packs his things to take Amanda to Spain, Linda's idea for a play suddenly grips him; he will call it "No Time for Comedy!" He realizes he loves Linda, who is only too happy to tell Philo she can't marry him, and the curtain falls as Gay agonizingly attempts to explain his change of heart to Amanda.

## Reviews

*New York Times* (4/18/39)--Brooks Atkinson found that Miss Cornell was playing "with effortless skill and personal sincerity." She seemed at ease and "thoroughly relaxed" in comedy. He stated that her performance wins friends for her as well as the play (B280).

*Variety* (4/19/39)--With a strong favorable reaction to *No Time For Comedy*, the legitimate theatre season in Baltimore was winding up well. *Variety* reported $23,500 weekly with most performances having standing room only at the Maryland Theatre where the play was having its tryout run (B344).

*Variety* (4/26/39)--As expected in New York, *No Time For Comedy* opened at the Barrymore to bring in over $21,000 for its first week. After the debut there were standees only at all performances. The show rated close to the top show, *The Philadelphia Story*, and exceeded *The Little Foxes* and *Abe Lincoln*. Because of the Easter slump and the World's Fair, *Variety* predicted there would be no upturn until June when vacations begin (B292).

## Commentary

When Robert Sherwood first asked Miss Cornell to join the Playwrights' Company and play *No Time for Comedy*, her immediate reaction was negative. Comedy frightened her. However, McClintic urged her to do it and, according to Mosel, Behrman would probably have taken the play away from the Playwrights' Company had she not acquiesced (B163, p. 427).

At the suggestion of Behrman's agent, Harold Freedman, the McClintics cast Laurence Olivier as Gaylord, which was his first appearance in the United States. The other leading men, Williams and Flemying, were also English and excellent in comedy.

Even with these seasoned male leads who helped her, Miss Cornell had a dreadful time delivering her lines for their comic effects and was so discouraged after the out-of-town opening that everyone feared she would withdraw from the show (B163, p. 428). They didn't know her tenacity.

What could have been a psychological hurdle for her was the disparity in her age and Olivier's (he was 32 and she was 46), although it was not apparent. Typical of her, she gave credit to Olivier for saving the play while she was overcoming her nervousness. Miss Cornell's beauty, grace and sincerity complemented Olivier's charm and engaging good looks to make *No Time for Comedy* "one of her great authentic hits" (B163, p. 431).

When Olivier had to leave the show to return to London, Francis Lederer took the role of Gay, an unfortunate substitute for which Gert Macy took responsibility. Lederer was not an easy person with whom to work and the play did not run as smoothly as it had. By that time, however, Miss Cornell had gained confidence and skill and was able to fill in with her wit where Lederer lacked it. She also saw to it that the company members got along well.

Of the eighteen reviews of *No Time for Comedy* that Lynda Towle Moss evaluated, seven were rated as "favorable" and five as "favorable to mixed" (B512, p. 199). The others were "mixed" to "unfavorable." Brooks Atkinson's review was overwhelmingly favorable. He judged *No Time for Comedy* to be "the most thoroughly comic" of Behrman's plays and spoke glowingly of Miss Cornell (B280). Other critics disagreed with him. They not only thought the play was weak but they were also divided in their appraisal of Miss Cornell's acting. In his critique of the play, William Klink's appraisal was that the "suave" dialogue is "monotonous and unilluminating" and characterization development is flawed. He pointed out that the leading man does not convey the qualities that would give credibility to his being a "good" playwright (B120, p. 168).

The ultimate proof of *No Time for Comedy*'s success was its long run and box office receipts. Bringing in over a million dollars, it had the third largest gross of the C. & M. C. Productions. The profit was almost $117,000 (B512, p. 176).

******

## S50    THE DOCTOR'S DILEMMA
(Opened: March 11, 1941, at the Shubert Theatre, New York; 15 weeks of performances)

### Credits

| | |
|---|---|
| Playwright | G. Bernard Shaw |
| Director | Guthrie McClintic |
| Settings | Donald Oenslager |
| Costumes | Motley of London |
| Producer | Katharine Cornell |

(Motley is the firm name for Elizabeth Montgomery and Peggy Harris)

### Cast

| | |
|---|---|
| Redpenny | Stanley Bell |
| Emmy | Alice Belmore Cliffe |
| Sir Colenso Ridgeon | Raymond Massey |
| Dr. Schutzmacher | Clarence Derwent |
| Sir Patrick Cullen | Whitford Kane |
| Mr. Cutler Walpole | Ralph Forbes |
| Sir Ralph Bonington | Cecil Humphreys |
| Dr. Blenkinsop | Colin Keith-Johnston |
| Jennifer Dubedat | Katharine Cornell |
| Louis Dubedat | Bramwell Fletcher |
| Minnie Tinwell | Margaret Curtis |

The Newspaper Man                                                                    Leslie Barrie
A Secretary                                                                          David Orrick

### The Play's History

       *The Doctor's Dilemma: a Tragedy* was published in 1906.  In his usual fashion, Shaw prefaced his lampoon with a long treatise on doctors and, in the play, denounces their profession for quackery and numerous other offenses.  In 1927, Alfred Lunt and Lynn Fontanne had played the Dubedats in The Theatre Guild's production in which Lunt had played the death scene with high "flourish" and deep "tragedy."  The McClintics staged it with less "glitter" (B260).

       Because Jennifer Dubedat was neither a starring role nor the kind of woman that Shaw liked, he was surprised that Miss Cornell wanted to do the part.  In fact, he suggested that, if she took it on tour, she double as Jennifer and Minnie Tinwell, which he regarded as a far more interesting role.

       The play was opened in New York after a 3-week tryout tour in Detroit, Columbus, Cincinnati, and Cleveland.  The 15-week run set a record for the Shaw play--its longest run in the United States and also the most profitable.  The Actors' Equity sponsored a matinee to interest high school students in the theatre.  Between 13,000 and 14,000 students paid five cents each to attend.

       Following the New York closing the show toured the west coast for 14 weeks.  When Pearl Harbor was bombed, *The Doctor's Dilemma* was in San Francisco at the Curran Theatre, to begin its second week on December 8, 1941.  Boxoffice receipts dropped by half.  The play, along with *Rose Burke*, was taken on a cross-country tour.  It had a total of 121 performances.

### Synopsis

       On June 15, 1903, the knighting of Dr. Ridgeon for his  discoveries in the treatment of tuberculosis brings together a group of his colleagues to congratulate him.  While they discuss "scientific matters," Ridgeon ignores a lady in his waiting room.  Finally, to be rid of her, he agrees to see her.  One glance at the beautiful Mrs. Dubedat hardens his resolve to refuse her tubercular husband as a patient.  He explains that he can treat only a limited number of cases who are selected for their worthiness to be saved.

       As evidence of her husband's qualifications Mrs. Dubedat displays his art work.  Intrigued by her husband's drawing of her (Ridgeon is a bachelor, very susceptible to feminine beauty), he invites the Dubedats to a dinner party so that he may determine Louis Dubedat's worthiness.  At the party Louis, unknown to Jennifer Dubedat, reveals himself as a scoundrel, albeit a talented and charming one.

       Blenkinsop, a colleague, creates a dilemma by disclosing that he, too, has tuberculosis.  Confident that Jennifer is interested in him, Ridgeon declines to treat Louis in the event that he should die, thus making Ridgeon open to criticism.  Much to Jennifer's distress, Sir Bonington is elected to treat Louis.  The treatment fails and Louis dies.

       Some time later Ridgeon appears at a showing of Louis's art work.  Jennifer, looking happy, prosperous and beautifully dressed, reproaches him for his mistake with Louis.  Ridgeon confesses that, because of his love for her, he had let Sir Bonington treat Louis.  Shocked, she dispels Ridgeon's fantasy that she was interested in him and accuses him of murder.  Insisting that he is her best friend for saving her from a scoundrel, he realizes that he has "committed a purely disinterested murder," when she informs him that she has remarried.

## Reviews
*New York Post* (2/12/41)--Finding it "immensely satisfying," John Mason Brown thought that Miss Cornell's revival of Shaw's tragi-comedy had come as a "delight." She "proves her wisdom and skill" as an actress as well as a manageress, and it's one of Mr. McClintic's best jobs of directing (B315).

*New York Newspaper "PM"* (3/12/41)--Louis Kronenberger, whose review was unenthusiastic, found the satire to be outworn and the whole thing "a much too protracted joke." Moreover, in his opinion, the play had "enough ideas, themes and theses for several plays." As for Miss Cornell, he explained that he had "never been able to go into ecstasies" over her acting, but granted that "last night she seemed as charming as she looked" (B401).

## Commentary
Even though Shaw thought Jennifer was an ordinary part easily filled by a dozen women, Miss Cornell's characterization earned glowing reviews. According to critic John Anderson, Miss Cornell played Jennifer Dubedat "eloquently and beautifully." He paid her tribute for refusing "to distort the play" by putting undue emphasis on the role of Jennifer (B260). Also applauding her, Richard Lockridge judged her to be "in full flower," and described her acting as "warm and glowing" with moments of her "electrifying quality" (B407). Critic Sidney Whipple, noted that her "exceptional restraint" suggested a great "reservoir of power" in Mrs. Dubedat's character (B499). Furthermore, in Brooks Atkinson's words, her magnetic genuineness pulls together Mr. Shaw's "capricious gabble" and holds the attention of the audience (B267).

Inasmuch as the play itself was aging, wordy and somewhat encumbered by the lingering remembrance of the Lunt's performance in the minds of some, reviewers were highly complimentary. Atkinson said that McClintic had chosen a cast of stars who highlighted Shaw's wit and made the play "sparkle" (B267). Sidney Whipple thought Oenslager's settings were "perfect" and John Anderson praised Motley's costumes as being "enough to knock your eyes out" (B499; B260).

******

## S51 ROSE BURKE
(Opened: January 19, 1942, at the Curran Theatre, San Francisco; 2 weeks of performances)

### Credits
| | |
|---|---|
| Playwright | Henri Bernstein |
| Director | Guthrie McClintic |
| Settings | Donald Oenslager |
| Costumes | Main Bocher |
| Producer | Katharine Cornell |

### Cast
| | |
|---|---|
| Marcel Dutrey | Jean Pierre Aumont |
| Rose Burke | Katharine Cornell |

| | |
|---|---|
| Barbara, Duchess of Rockwell | Doris Dudley |
| James Forman | Philip Merivale |
| Judy Sheldon-Shepherd | Catharine Doucet |
| Maximilian Elgart | Clarence Derwent |

## The Play's History

After seeing Miss Cornell as Elizabeth in *The Barretts*, Henri Bernstein, a French playwright, vowed he would write a play for her. According to Mosel, from that time until he finally appeared with an unfinished play he was writing for her, Bernstein "sent pressing love letters" as well as "flowers, pronouncements, and promises" to Miss Cornell. Excitable and dramatic, "a boulevardier with wild ideas," he had just escaped from the Nazis in France when he came to New York. Miss Cornell was playing in *The Doctor's Dilemma*. He pursued and persuaded her to do *Rose Burke* (B163, p. 443).

The play was to go into rehearsal at the end of the tour of *The Doctor's Dilemma*, which had just completed its first week in San Francisco when Pearl Harbor was bombed. Involvement in war resulted in a dramatic drop in boxoffice receipts.

The McClintics decided to go into the rehearsal of *Rose Burke* in San Francisco, open there on January 19, 1942, for a 2-week run and tour with it and *The Doctor's Dilemma* to New York. They went to Portland, Seattle, and across to Minneapolis, St. Paul, Milwaukee, Detroit and Toronto, where the tour was discontinued.

## Synopsis

Rose Burke, a stunning widow and famous sculptress, is working on the head of Barbara, Duchess of Rockwell, which she transforms into a figure representing Britannia. Rose is in love with Jim Forman, a well-known economist whose work requires him to be away for long periods of time. She finally reveals her feelings, suggesting marriage to him just before he departs on another extended trip. Jim reciprocates, at least in declaring his love for her, but she does not hear from him.

After considerable time has passed, she consents to marry Marcel, a young Frenchman, despite the difference in their ages. She has given up her apartment and is leaving to visit her parents before her wedding when Jim Forman appears to tell her how much he loves her and to explain his inability to make a commitment of marriage until now. It is too late. Rose lets him go without a word of her deep hurt.

When he has gone she vents her frustration by destroying the figure of Britannia which has complicated her life. The decisive act is followed by another. She sends her maid to call Jim back as she writes a note of regret to Marcel.

## Reviews

*New York Times* (1/25/42)--Lawrence Davies made no comment about his reaction to the play but explained Bernstein's use of the drama "to defend the French and express faith in the ultimate defeat of the Axis." Through the character of Dutry, he said the French had not really surrendered; their leaders had "duped" them (B357).

*Variety* (1/28/42)--The demand to see the world premiere was so heavy that the theatre asked pass-holders to come the next night so their seats could be sold. Because of poor communication, business fell off. The show made $18,000. Next stop was scheduled for Portland; then onto Seattle, Minneapolis, St. Paul, Milwaukee and Detroit (B342).

*Variety* (2/4/42)--Miss Cornell played a 3-show engagement of Rose Burke in Portland where she is always a favorite. Monday night house was well packed. The show grossed about $10,000 in 1,300 seater at $3.00 top ticket price (B346).

## Commentary

San Francisco playgoers, delighted to be the scene of a premiere, packed the Curran Theatre. They were drawn to the play because it was written especially for Miss Cornell by a French playwright for whom the Nazis had declared a death sentence. Moreover, it was the American debut of a favorite French movie and stage star, Jean Pierre Aumont. The fashionably dressed women in the audience were enthralled with Main Bocher's creations for Miss Cornell, who was on stage for all but a few moments of the play. (There had been complaints that she had appeared too little in *The Doctor's Dilemma.*)

Stunned by being plunged into a war, neither critics nor audiences were in the mood for the "boulevard drama." Possibly, they also became impatient with Bernstein's secondary theme, the world situation and his defense of France.

Even though it was making money as they crossed the country, Miss Cornell decided the play did not meet the audiences' expectations of her. Her loyal fans in New York probably would have flocked to see her, but she would not abuse their loyalty by disappointing them. *Rose Burke* was closed in Toronto, the second of the three plays during her career that she did not bring to New York.

\*\*\*\*\*\*

## S52    CANDIDA (Fourth Version)
(Opened: April 27, 1942, Shubert Theatre, New York; 5 weeks of performances)

## Credits

| | |
|---|---|
| Playwright | G. Bernard Shaw |
| Director | Guthrie McClintic |
| Setting and Costumes | Woodman Thompson |
| Sponsored by | American Theatre Wing War Services |
| Stage Manager | Edward P. Dimond |
| Producer | Katharine Cornell |

## Cast

| | |
|---|---|
| Miss Proserpine Garnett | Mildred Natwick |
| James Mavor Morell | Raymond Massey |
| Alexander Mill | Stanley Bell |
| Mr. Burgess | Dudley Digges |
| Candida | Katharine Cornell |
| Eugene Marchbanks | Burgess Meredith |

## The Play's History

See *Candida* (1925, S30) for history of the play prior to Miss Cornell's first production. See also The Transcontinental Tour of *Candida* (1934-35, S40) and *Candida*

(1937, S47) for the first three of the five versions which Miss Cornell was to present during her career.

For this revival Raymond Massey, Burgess Meredith and Mildred Natwick recreated their roles from earlier performances. The United States Army gave a special leave to Meredith and Warner Brothers Pictures loaned Massey for the production.

### Synopsis

See *Candida* (1925, S30).

### Reviews

*New York World-Telegram* (4/28/42)--In John Mason Brown's opinion, Shaw's comedy "came into a new and completely glorious life." Praising the actors and director McClintic, who were giving so abundantly of their services and "extraordinary gifts," he said that "not since the war began has it been possible to forget it so entirely in the theatre. Or to remember with such certainty...that the values represented by this *Candida* are the very civilized values for which any sacrifice should be gladly made." He went on to commend Miss Cornell for her most beautiful portrayal of Candida and her "rich" and "liquid" voice that "lingers long in the ears after her final choice has been made. She is radiant, mysterious, compelling, all-mothering; sage with the sagacity of her sex as Shaw intended her to be; and yet simple as only a truly great artist can be." The other actors were equally outstanding, Brown reported. Burgess Meredith was, in his view, "brilliant," making Marchbanks "a happily believable person." He described Natwick's Prossy as "superlative," Digges' Burgess as "magnificent" and Bell's young curate as "delightful" (B319).

*New York Times* (5/3/42)--Brooks Atkinson found that, in this version, *Candida* was finer than in earlier productions. He observed that Miss Cornell's technique had resulted in an effortless and richer portrayal. The audience is only aware of a "rare person" to whom her husband and a young poet are devoted, he stated (B265).

### Commentary

With the country deeply involved in the war effort, Miss Cornell volunteered her services by reviving *Candida* under the auspices of The American Theatre Wing War Services, Inc. for the benefit of the Army Emergency Fund and the Navy Relief Society. Support of the war effort was apparent in the overwhelming contributions of time and money. The actors donated their services, the Shuberts gave the theatre without charge, the stagehands' unions relinquished their compensation and Shaw claimed no royalties.

The play was to run for four matinees and one Sunday evening performance, but the demand for tickets was so great that 3 more weeks were added. Even after that, 12 additional performances were given before the play was taken to the National Theatre in Washington, D.C. for a week.

In every respect, this fourth version of the McClintic's *Candida* was considered to be definitive. The acting of the star-studded cast was near perfect and this was the most popular of Miss Cornell's productions. The play was not only a financial success (it made $36,817 each for the Army Emergency Fund and the Navy Relief Society, and almost $10,000 for The American Theatre Wing), but it also delighted the critics. The creative cast brought deeper insight and richer characterizations than had the previous casts, fine as they were.

It was a particular triumph for Burgess Meredith whose Marchbanks was outstanding in a role he nearly missed playing. After Miss Cornell's death in 1974, he told the story to *The New York Times* (B151). He was a draftee at the Santa Ana Air Force Base in California when Miss Cornell and Gert Macy called him and asked him to play the part. He said, "I'd love to but I'm cleaning latrines at the moment." Miss Cornell told him to sit tight, and within a couple of hours he was summoned to the headquarters of his commanding officer who was staring incredulously at a telegram. "He said, 'Private Meredith, I'm ordered to have you flown at once to New York to act in some goddam play!...Some goddam war--eh, Private Meredith?'" "Yes sir," was Meredith's reply.

Of course, at the end of the show he went back to duty, cleaning latrines. He said, "All during the war, I kept with me the picture of the two of us doing that fireplace scene together." In the view of Brooks Atkinson, Burgess Meredith had been the best Marchbanks in a quarter of a century. Miss Cornell had generously extended herself to give him that opportunity.

******

## S53    THE THREE SISTERS
(Opened: December 21, 1942, at the Ethel Barrymore Theatre, New York; 15 weeks of performances)

**Credits**

| | |
|---|---|
| Playwright | Anton Chekhov |
| English text by | Alexander Koiransky |
| | and Guthrie McClintic |
| Director | Guthrie McClintic |
| Settings and Costumes | Motley of London |
| Producer | Katharine Cornell |

**Cast**

| | |
|---|---|
| Olga | Judith Anderson |
| Masha | Katharine Cornell |
| Irina | Gertrude Musgrove |
| A Maid | Patricia Calvert |
| Tuzenbach | Alexander Knox |
| Solyony | McKay Morris |
| Chebutykin | Edmund Gwenn |
| Anfisa | Alice Belmore Cliffe |
| Ferapont | Arthur Chatterton |
| An Orderly | Kirk Douglas |
| Vershinin | Dennis King |
| Andrey Prozorov | Eric Dressler |
| Kuligin | Tom Powers |
| Natasha | Ruth Gordon |
| Fedotik | Stanley Bell |
| Roddey | Tom McDermott |
| Another Lieutenant | Walter Craig |
| A Maid | Marie Paxton |

## The Play's History

*The Three Sisters*, completed late in 1900 when Chekhov was recuperating from tuberculosis, was one of his last four plays. Although there is controversy about the importance of *The Three Sisters,* scholar Brustein judged it to be "the most stunning example of his (Chekhov's) dramatic approach" (B030, p. 372). The stylistic innovations that Chekhov made in his last years were to become trendsetters for modern drama.

Before the Cornell revival, the play had been presented twenty years earlier in New York with Mme. Chekhov and Maria Ouspenskaya. Miss Cornell's tryout took place in Washington, D.C., where every seat for a week's engagement had been sold a week in advance. The audience and press were enthusiastic. On the way to New York they gave a Sunday performance to GIs at Camp Meade. Despite the severe cold in an unheated improvised theater, the soldiers cheered. After three weeks on the road, the play opened in New York. During that engagement, a benefit performance was given for the Stage Relief Fund and another for the Red Cross. The play ran for 122 performances before going on tour. When it closed after a total of 230 performances, it had achieved the longest run *The Three Sisters* had ever had anywhere and exceeded the run of any Chekhov play in the United States.

## Synopsis

The lives of the cultured upper middle-class Prozorov family (Masha, Olga, Irina and their brother Andrey) seem to have stopped with the death of their father. For lack of money and the impetus to act, they are trapped in a provincial garrison town in Russia at the turn of the century. They want desperately to escape the boredom of this dull, decadent town by moving back to their former home, Moscow, which represents purpose and life to them. However, their last hope is gone when their brother Andrey marries the vulgar, ambitious bourgeois, Natasha. He gives up his aspirations to be a scientist, turns to gambling and secretly mortgages their house to pay his debts.

Except for the visits with the officers of the military battalion and the army doctor, Chebutykin, life is spent in humdrum routine. Through their own inertia and the oppression of the environment, the Prozorov sisters gradually succumb to their dispossession maneuvered by the malevolent Natasha. She steadily confines them to smaller spaces in the house, squelches their efforts to find enjoyment or to be charitable to the victims of a fire and pushes their faithful servant into a government flat.

Masha, the most unhappy of the sisters, married to a pompous teacher, falls in love with Vershinin, a married colonel. Olga, perpetually tired, is a teacher who has lost her interest in teaching. Irina hates her work in the telegraph office and decides to marry a man she does not love for a chance to get back to Moscow.

When the military leave town, Masha's affair with Vershinin is ended. The fiance of Irina is killed in a duel and she moves to an apartment; Olga is installed as headmistress of the high school, a position she hates; Andrey has fallen into mediocrity. For all but Natasha, their dreams have faded and hope is gone. Natasha has swept the house clear of them all and will order the destruction of the "avenue of fir trees" and "the maple."

## Reviews

*New York Herald Tribune* (12/22/42)--Howard Barnes, who viewed the presentation as a rare experience in theatre, considered *The Three Sisters* to be one of Chekhov's minor classics which was "still badly out of key with the tempo of the contemporary theater." He gave credit to the acting, which "does much to conceal the deficiencies of the subject matter," and to the principals, who "contrive to make their plight absorbing." He still found the play "somewhat wanting" (B297).

*New York Daily News* (12/22/42)--Burns Mantle said, "more power to her," as he credited Miss Cornell with "not only reviving the theatre's modern classics" but also the "modern theatre itself." In his opinion, the performances were the best since the Moscow Art Players had presented *The Three Sisters* 20 years earlier. The Cornell production is a "fine reading of the Chekhov masterpiece of frustration," Mantle wrote. "Here is the human loneliness that can be suffered and sustained by hemmed-in minds confined to a hemmed-in community brilliantly realized." Mantle suspected that audience awards would go to Ruth Gordon and Edmund Gwenn "who have the best opportunities to stir interest." All other members of the cast made much of their moments in the spotlight in a "handsome" setting, under the "fluid and interesting" direction of Guthrie McClintic (B419).

## Commentary

Considering the subtlety of meaning and gloominess of tone, the success of *The Three Sisters* was a credit to the insight, professionalism, and artistry of the McClintics. If not well done, the play can bore the audience. Chekhov's structure results in vagueness, lack of form and action. As Lewis Nichols of *The New York Times* aptly described the play, "It is a tight-rope walk, with carnage awaiting those actors who fall off" (B444).

Using indirect-action, Chekhov buries his plot, putting violent acts, such as a fire and duel, and the emotional climaxes, such as the Masha-Vershinin affair, offstage or between acts. Furthermore, his characters are not conventional hero-victims. The triviality of their daily routine and the brooding of the unhappy characters disguises the development and crisis, and as Howard Barnes commented, "tends to communicate that boredom to the audience" (B297). While the action that is going on offstage is reported, the actors must convey the tension. In Lewis Nichols' words, *The Three Sisters* requires everything it can get from a cast" (B444).

The cast was a selection of the best stars available who, in the opinion of Louis Kronenberger of the *New York Newspaper PM*, acted in the spirit that he felt sure Chekhov intended. He commended them for avoiding "the sombre and lachrymose," and for letting the comedy as well as the pathos spring from their characterizations (B397).

It was somewhat ironic that Ruth Gordon, who had urged McClintic to do the play so that she could play Masha, should receive the most praise from critics for her portrayal of Natasha. Perhaps because their parts had more dramatic potential, she and Edmund Gwenn got the highest honors from several reviewers. Critic Richard Lockridge said that Miss Cornell played Masha "beautifully" and John Anderson stated that she had added "greatly to her stature as an actress-manager" (B405; B258). Kronenberger noted that, through teamwork, the all-star cast avoided the star effect (B397). McClintic's skillful direction and Miss Cornell's willingness to subjugate herself to the performances of her equals accounted for the success of *The Three Sisters*.

\*\*\*\*\*\*

## S54    LOVERS AND FRIENDS
(Opened: November 29, 1943, at the Plymouth Theatre, New York; 21 weeks of performances)

### Credits

| | |
|---|---|
| Playwright | Dodie Smith |
| Director | Guthrie McClintic |
| Settings and Costumes | Motley of London |
| Producers | Katharine Cornell and John C. Wilson |

### Cast

| | |
|---|---|
| Rodney Boswell | Raymond Massey |
| Stella | Katharine Cornell |
| Agnes | Katherine Hynes |
| Lennie Lorrimer | Carol Goodner |
| Martha Jones | Anne Burr |
| Edmund Alexander | Henry Daniell |

### The Play's History

This production of *Lovers and Friends*, produced with John C. Wilson at the Plymouth Theatre in New York, was its premiere. Averaging over $19,000 in receipts per week, it played to near capacity houses for 21 weeks in New York. It averaged even larger receipts during a 6-week tour of 4 eastern cities. The total profit was almost $74,000, despite the fact that most critics did not consider it to be up to Miss Cornell's standards or abilities. After the New York run, *Lovers and Friends* was taken on a 6-week tour of eastern cities. With 4 weeks of the tryout tour the total number of performance weeks was 31 (B512).

### Synopsis

On the evening of a late spring day in 1918, Stella Pryor meets Rodney Boswell in Regent's Park to tell him that her actress friend Lennie is breaking her date with him for a fellow they describe as a "cad." Although he's supposedly in love with Lennie, Rodney is immediately attracted to Stella and she to him.

Twelve years later, Rodney is a successful lawyer living happily with Stella and their twin sons, away at boarding school. Before Stella suspects anything, Rodney announces that he is in love with Martha Jones, secretary to Edmund Alexander, a novelist-playwright, and wants a divorce. Approaching the situation sensibly, Stella asks him to wait until he is "sure," and suggests to Martha that she test her love for Rodney by living with him before the divorce is finalized. The suggestion insults Martha's idealism.

Meanwhile, Stella has accepted a part in Edmund's play, and is beginning to enjoy herself. Just when she is convinced that her marriage is finished, Rodney announces that Martha is a fraud and he is through with her. Now in love with Edmund, Stella reneges on her promise to marry him.

In 1942, Stella and Rodney, who have found contentment together, visit in Regent's Park where they see Lennie off to meet her husband, Edmund. Stella learns that Rodney knew all along about her feelings for Edmund, a secret she thought she had kept, and has been waiting for her to tell him that it's all over. It is. She recalls the moment she fell back in love with Rodney and wonders how, in spite of war, one can sometimes feel so happy.

## Reviews
*New York Daily News* (11/30/43)--One of the most negative voices among the critics, John Chapman found the play to be "a whole long evening of Love [sic]," where "a kiss is good for an act with playwright Dodie Smith." The play is not worthy of the talent, he argued. "It is very British, very chin-up, and everybody is off'ly decent when it comes to falling in love with the wrong party." He suggested that the story should be told in twenty-nine installments in a ladies' magazine (B330).

*New York World-Telegram* (11/30/43)--Alton Cook liked the play and thought the supporting cast was "flawless." Massey's presence was "masterful," which made a "completely harmonious entity" with Miss Cornell's "mettlesome femininity." Moreover, he thought their performances were matched by the other players. "Ingredients such as these in the sagacious directorial control of Guthrie McClintic in a pair of stunning settings designed by Motley--what do you want for your money?" he asked (B337).

## Commentary
Considering the critics' negative comments, the play's success was surprising. Herrick Brown of the *New York Sun* panned it for failing to approach "the stature of its two chief players" (B322). Lewis Nichols of *The New York Times* agreed that, without that cast, the play "would be an insufferable bore" (B442). Other critics found it to be "trite" and overly long. Louis Kronenberger of the *New York Newspaper PM*, who saw little to like about it, quipped that McClintic's careful direction could not keep the play "from seeming to go on forever" (B398).

Although Robert Garland, *New York Journal American*, did not understand why Miss Cornell had chosen Miss Smith's "would be high-comedy," he and most other critics were not displeased with her or her cast (B371). Herrick Brown thought that Miss Cornell made the role of Stella "attractive, intelligent and gracious" (B322). Despite their gibes at the play, both critics and the public were happy to see Miss Cornell back on stage even in a trivial, polite, drawing room comedy.

******

## S55    THE BARRETTS OF WIMPOLE STREET
Overseas Tour of the European War Zone: August 11, 1944-January 31. 1945. (Opened: Santa Maria, near Naples, Italy; 143 performances in Italy, France and Holland)

## Credits
| | |
|---|---|
| Playwright | Rudolf Besier |
| Director | Guthrie McClintic |
| Stage Manager | Elaine Perry |
| Stage Technician | William Noon |
| Production Assistant | Nancy Hamilton |

General Manager                                                Gertrude Macy

Presented by                                        SOS-NATOUSA Special Service
                                               in cooperation with USO CampShows
                                                    and The American Theatre Wing

## Cast

| | |
|---|---|
| Doctor Chambers | Guthrie McClintic |
| Elizabeth Barrett Moulton-Barrett | Katharine Cornell |
| Wilson | Brenda Forbes |
| Henrietta Moulton-Barrett | Emily Lawrence |
| Arabel Moulton-Barrett | Margalo Gillmore |
| Octavius Moulton-Barrett | Erik Martin |
| Alfred Moulton-Barrett | Chester Stratton |
| Charles Moulton-Barrett | Robert Ross |
| Henry Moulton-Barrett | Roger Stearnes |
| George Moulton-Barrett | Keinert Wolff |
| Edward Moulton-Barrett | McKay Morris |
| Bella Hedley | Betty Brewer |
| Henry Bevan | Roger Stearnes |
| Robert Browning | Brian Aherne |
| Doctor Ford-Waterlow | Robert Ross |
| Captain Surtees Cook | Chester Stratton |
| Flush | Himself |

## The Play's History

With her original production, in 1931, Miss Cornell had established *The Barretts* as her most successful theatrical venture. Even during the deepest part of the Depression it had played to packed houses in New York and on its countrywide tours. Critics had hailed her revivals as being richer than the previous ones, especially her portrayal of Elizabeth. Despite the flaws in the structure of the play itself, which became more evident with time, it remained popular with audiences because of the quality of acting.

Antoinette Perry of the American Theatre Wing was looking for a stage production which would represent the best of American theatre to send to the armed services in Europe. She asked the opinion of her friend Margalo Gillmore who immediately suggested Katharine Cornell. Miss Cornell agreed providing Brian Aherne was available and she could take *The Barretts*.

Even though the American Theatre Wing was financing the undertaking, the Special Service Division (SDS) objected to the Victorian costume drama. They did not think it would appeal to GIs. Miss Cornell remained adamant and the SSD insisted that the play be screened at Mitchell Field in Long Island. The reception of the 2500 servicemen in the audience was overwhelmingly favorable so the SSD condescended--with one condition. A ribald farce, if possible, should be prepared in the event that *The Barretts* failed, as they were sure it would.

Under orders to the North African Theater of the United States Army (NATOUSA) the troupe sailed on the S.S. *General Meigs*, on August 11, 1944, and disembarked in Naples, Italy.

<u>Synopsis</u>
See *The Barretts of Wimpole Street*, 1931 (S35).

<u>Commentary</u>
Needless to say, the actors had some misgivings after the gloomy predictions about soldiers' reactions to a romantic love story. At the start there were tense moments when Dr. Chambers recommended that Elizabeth go to Italy for her health, when Flush entered and when the Barrett brothers kissed their sister. By holding the action for the hooting, yelling and boisterous laughter, the actors kept control and the hecklers were soon quiet.

As Margalo Gillmore wrote in her account of the tour, "Kit had a shining light in her. With that sixth sense of the actor...she had been aware of the gradual change out front from a dubious indifference to the complete absorption of interest...line by line she had felt them...give themselves up to the play...." Describing the response of the audience, Gillmore said, "At the curtain call, 'we stood before what seemed to be a solid wall of applause...and something like a great wave of affection came surging over us, and we sent back our hearts in return'" (B075, p. 49).

After the first four performances, the top brass conceded that the play was a success and the company (unit 391) was invited to stay 6 months rather than the two weeks they had planned. Servicemen lined up hours early for each performance and flocked backstage after the performance where they were greeted warmly by the cast. Between performances the actors visited and entertained the sick and wounded in the hospital wards.

For months Miss Cornell received an outpouring of gratitude from the men and their families, teachers and friends to whom they had written. They thanked her for bringing to them "yearned-for femininity" and for "the most nerve-soothing remedy for a weary G.I. [sic]" (B163, p. 467). News of *The B.O.W.S.*, as they came to be known, even spread to the South Pacific.

When the war was over, men who had seen her in *The Barretts* went to her plays and then backstage to thank her again for what she had done for them. She told S. J. Woolf of *The New York Times* that, "whatever sacrifices women make will be small compared with those that are being made today on the battlefields and behind the lines" (B242, p. 40). Taking *The B.O.W.S.* to the war zone had been the most inspiring and thrilling experience in her career--and the most successful.

\*\*\*\*\*\*

**S56**    **THE BARRETTS OF WIMPOLE STREET**
(Opened: March 26, 1945, at the Ethel Barrymore Theatre, New York; 11 weeks of performances)

<u>Credits and Cast</u>
See *The Barretts of Wimpole Street*, Overseas Tour of the European War Zone, 1944, (S55).

## The Play's History
While still playing to full houses in 1931, Miss Cornell's original production in New York was closed in order to go on tour. In 1933-34 it was taken on a long transcontinental repertory tour which also included *Candida* and *Romeo and Juliet*. After a revival in 1935, nearly ten years later it had just returned from being taken overseas where it helped to entertain the fighting forces for six months in 1944. Lewis Nichols noted that the history of Miss Cornell's productions of *The Barretts* has been "one of unbroken success" (B440).

## Synopsis
See *The Barretts of Wimpole Street*, 1931, (S35).

## Reviews
*The New York Times* (4/1/45)--Lewis Nichols declared that Miss Cornell "could spend the rest of her life as Elizabeth Barrett, and the world would like it very much." On the opening night the audience had offered her "an applause that comes only once or twice a year...." The flaws in the dramatic construction of the play were becoming more apparent with time, Nichols observed, and the burden of its success or failure is cast upon the actors. "Miss Cornell's performance is such that there can be no question of the latter; she is realistic and sure her Elizabeth is fully alive" (B440).

*Variety* (5/16/45)--In its 7th week in New York, *The Barretts* was still "very good" and making $18,000 a week, reported the trade paper. It would run 3 more weeks; the finale had been announced for June 9. V-E Day celebrations and a rainy season accounted for the decline in Broadway receipts. A flock of closings were expected (B293).

## Commentary
After the troupe returned from the European war zone, Miss Cornell decided to present *The Barretts* in Boston and New York in order for the actors to earn some money. It ran in Boston for one week where it grossed almost $47,000 and broke the record for legitimate drama at the Boston Opera House.

After opening in New York, it ran for 11 weeks and closed June 9, 1945. It grossed over $19,000 per week for 10 of those weeks.

Two years later *The Barretts* was taken on tour of the west coast. In Des Moines, Iowa, a radio version of the play was broadcast on April 14, 1947. While on that tour Miss Cornell played Elizabeth for the 1,000th time in San Francisco on June 7, 1947. By the end of the tour she had played Elizabeth in 1,019 performances (B512, pp. 81-82).


******


S57     ANTIGONE
(Opened: February 18, 1946, at the Cort Theatre, New York; 4 weeks of performances)

## Credits

| | |
|---|---|
| Playwright | Jean Anouilh |
| Adapted by | Lewis Galantiere |
| Director | Guthrie McClintic |
| Settings | Raymond Sovey |
| Costumes | Valentina |
| Producers | Katharine Cornell |
| | with Gilbert Miller |

## Cast

| | |
|---|---|
| Chorus | Horace Braham |
| Antigone | Katharine Cornell |
| Nurse | Bertha Belmore |
| Ismene | Ruth Matteson |
| Haemon | Wesley Addy |
| Creon | Cedric Hardwicke |
| First Guard | George Mathews |
| Second Guard | David J. Stewart |
| Third Guard | Michael Higgins |
| Messenger | Oliver Cliff |
| Page | Albert Biondo |
| Eurydice | Merle Maddern |

## The Play's History

When playing in *The Barretts of Wimpole Street* for the troops in Europe, Miss Cornell saw *Antigone and the Tyrant*, Jean Anouilh's modern version of the Sophocles classic, at the Antoine Theatre in Paris, and decided she wanted to do it. Gilbert Miller joined her in presenting it. Anouilh's version, first produced in Paris in 1943, was still running there at the time of Miss Cornell's opening of an adaptation by Lewis Galantiere.

The tryout run was not encouraging. The original title, *Antigone and the Tyrant*, which had been retained, was shortened before the New York opening. A loss of $2500 made the play's receipts the poorest of any previous tryout.

In New York, receipts dropped after the first week and *Candida* was revived to play in repertory with *Antigone*. Beginning April 3, 1946, *Antigone* played only on Fridays and Saturdays with *Candida* playing the other four days. The two plays ran through May 4, 1946, and were then taken on tour to Chicago and the east coast for 5 weeks.

## Synopsis

Introduced by Chorus, an interlocutor, the characters foretell their travails. When Oedipus, father of Antigone and Ismene died, he left his two sons Eteocles and Polynices to reign in alternate years over Thebes. After the first year Eteocles refused to give over the reign to Polynices, civil war broke out and the brothers killed each other in combat, leaving the throne to their Uncle Creon.

To crush the uprising and establish his authority King Creon gave Eteocles, with whom he sided, a hero's burial and ordained the body of Polynices to be left uncovered. The stench was to remind the "rabble" of King Creon's power.

For defying Creon and burying her brother's body, Antigone expected to be put to death. She is arrested and Creon decrees that she marry his son Haemon, with whom she is in love, and produce a son. However, Antigone chooses death rather than Creon's terms for happiness: "fear, lying and compromise."

She is taken to a cave where she is walled in to die. As the last rock is put into place Haemon's cry is heard from the cave where he has joined Antigone, only to find her already dead. Ordering the cave entrance to be opened, Creon begs his son to leave with him. Haemon stabs himself and dies beside his beloved Antigone. Queen Eurydice, hearing the news, also takes her life.

The cause for which Antigone has died and for all those who are to follow her, Chorus explains, "is always the same--a passionate belief that moral law exists, and a passionate regard for the sanctity of human personality."

### Reviews

*New York Journal American* (2/19/46)--Robert Garland found little merit in the play. He thought Katharine Cornell was "doing her biggish bit for the art of the theatre," but that "all art and no play can make theatre-going [sic] a duty rather than a pleasure." He did credit her with giving more to the Greek than the Greek had given back to her, and said, "She is also strangely beautiful!" (B367).

*New York World-Telegram* (2/19/46)--One of the most favorable reviews of *Antigone* came from Burton Rascoe who confessed that he sat "in rapt attention, with a lump once in my throat, and with unqualified admiration for the perception and skill with which Guthrie McClintic has directed it and the dignity and finesse with which Katherine [sic] Cornell and her company enact it" (B459).

### Commentary

Critics respected Miss Cornell for her excellent acting and for having the courage to experiment with a modernization of the Greek classic which most of them found interesting, but not satisfying. Written to symbolize the French resistance to the tyrannical Nazi occupation, the play's symbolism did not evoke the emotional excitement in Broadway audiences that it had in France, said Louis Kronenberger of *PM Exclusive*. The play, somewhat "a dead weight," in his opinion, strengthened Creon's role and weakened Antigone's (B402).

Lewis Nichols of *The New York Times* found the characters poorly defined and lacking "logical motivation" and the play "empty" (B439). In the *New York Daily News*, John Chapman's stated that it was "less than effective" (B326). Although Ward Morehouse reported in *The Sun* that Miss Cornell's portrayal was both beautiful and poignant, he thought that the text made her "inordinately stubborn and the loser...with Creon" (B431). He suggested she turn to *Macbeth* or *Antony and Cleopatra*.

Although *Antigone* could be considered an artistic success, it could not have survived as long as it did without the drawing power of *Candida*. Whether or not she was heeding the advice of Kronenberger or simply fulfilling a long-held dream, it was not long before she did *Antony and Cleopatra* which was to be one of her "crowning achievements" (B512, p. 96).

\*\*\*\*\*\*

**S58     CANDIDA (Fifth Version)**
(Opened: April 3, 1946, at the Cort Theatre, New York; 4 weeks of performances)

**Credits**

| | |
|---|---|
| Playwright | G. Bernard Shaw |
| Director | Guthrie McClintic |
| Producers | Katharine Cornell with |
| | Gilbert Miller |

**Cast**

| | |
|---|---|
| Miss Proserpine Garnett | Mildred Natwick |
| James Mavor Morell | Wesley Addy |
| Alexander Mill | Oliver Cliff |
| Mr. Burgess | Cedric Hardwicke |
| Candida | Katharine Cornell |
| Eugene Marchbanks | Marlon Brando |

**The Play's History**

The first version of *Candida* was in 1925. The second was done in repertory with *The Barretts of Wimpole Street* and *Romeo and Juliet* in the long tour of 1934-35; the third was alternated with *The Wingless Victory* in 1937. Her definitive all-star revival in 1942 was her fourth version. This one, the fifth, was alternated with *Antigone* in New York, then taken on tour.

**Synopsis**

See *Candida*, 1925 (S30).

**Reviews**

*Journal American* (4/4/46)--Although Robert Garland said he preferred other Shavian plays, there was no doubt that *Candida* is the "playgoing public's favorite." He still marveled at the "wit and wisdom, its comedy and tragedy" even though others did not. With this production, he wrote, "the theatre came back to life, all bright and beautiful and shining with what is surely the most all round satisfactory performance of 'Candida' Broadway has so far known" (B368).

*New York World-Telegram* (4/4/46)--Making it clear that he didn't like the play which seemed to him "the most sentimental sort of shenanigans," Burton Rascoe was glad that Shaw hadn't seen it. "Candida is not supposed to deliver her lines like a sermon by Morrell. But that is what Miss Cornell did" (B461).

**Commentary**

In the view of biographer Mosel, the new Marchbanks, Marlon Brando, and the ultimate *Candida* gave historical significance to this production. A student of the Stanislavski method of acting (a method for which McClintic had little tolerance) Brando represented the new psychological realism, or "naturalism," practiced earlier by Mrs. Fiske, while Miss Cornell was still the epitomy of romanticism. As Mosel said, it was a "meeting ground" of the theatre that was "passing" and that which was "yet to come" (B163, p. 472).

The critics' reactions to the play were mixed. Burton Rascoe of the *New York World-Telegram* observed that the audience had a "grand time" but he could see nothing good about the play except for Cedric Hardwicke (B461). On the other hand, Robert Garland of the *Journal American* judged Brando to be a superb Marchbanks. In fact he thought this was the "most satisfactory performance of *Candida* that Broadway has so far known" (B368). Louis Kronenberger of *PM Exclusive* liked this production of the play but thought it "showed up the faults as much as its virtues" (B400). Ward Morehouse of *The Sun* judged that the quality of Miss Cornell's playing was that of her earlier presentations but wished for Burgess Meredith and Raymond Massey to be playing with her (B430). Although he found that Miss Cornell retained the freshness of her role, *New York Times* critic Lewis Nichols thought the production fell short of the "brilliance" of the 1942 revival (B441).

In Mosel's opinion, Miss Cornell was too inflexible to bridge the decades or adapt to postwar tastes. Her characters were, he believed, frozen at a certain age, and the time when she could not find suitable roles was just ahead. At any rate, this was to be her final *Candida*.

******

## S59    ANTONY AND CLEOPATRA
(Opened: November 26, 1947, at the Martin Beck Theatre, New York; 16 weeks of performances)

### Credits

| | |
|---|---|
| Playwright | William Shakespeare |
| Director | Guthrie McClintic |
| Settings | Leo Kerz |
| Costumes (Women's) | Valentina |
| Costumes (Men's) | John Boyt |
| Music | Paul Nordoff |
| Producer | Katharine Cornell |

### Cast

| | |
|---|---|
| Philo | Alan Shayne |
| Demetrius | Theodore Marcuse |
| Antony | Godfrey Tearle |
| Cleopatra | Katharine Cornell |
| A Messenger | David J. Stewart |
| Dolabella | Robert Duke |
| Proculeius | Charlton Heston |
| Iras | Maureen Stapleton |
| Charmian | Lenore Ulric |
| Alexas | Oliver Cliff |
| Diomedes | Eli Wallach |
| Enobarbus | Kent Smith |
| Mardian | Joseph Wiseman |
| Octavius Caesar | Ralph Clanton |

| | |
|---|---|
| Lepidus | Ivan Simpson |
| Agrippa | David Orrick |
| Pompey | Joseph Holland |
| Menas | Martin Kingsley |
| Varrius | Barnet Biro |
| Ventidius | Bruce Gordon |
| Octavia | Betty Low |
| Canidius | Dayton Lummis |
| Eros | Douglas Watson |
| Silius | Charles Nolte |
| Thyreus | Robert Carricart |
| Taurus | Gilbert Reade |
| Gallus | Rudulph Watson |
| An Old Soldier | Bruce Gordon |
| Scarus | Anthony Randall |
| Euphronius | Ernest Rowan |
| Dercetas | Martin Kingsley |
| A Clown | Oliver Cliff |
| Slaves, Guards, Servants, Soldiers: | John Russo, Peter Barno, |
| | Drummond Erskine, Milfred Hull, |
| | Orrin Redfield, Charles Holt, |
| | James Grudier, Lawrence Perron |

## The Play's History

Shakespeare's source for *Antony and Cleopatra*, printed around 1608, was Plutarch's *Life of Marcus Antonius*, which was translated by Sir Thomas North from Amyot's French version (B170, p. 1244). Shakespeare compressed the action which actually covered a ten-year period from Fulvia's death in 40 B.C. to the deaths of Antony and Cleopatra in 30 B.C. The time between the battle of Actium and the deaths of Antony and Cleopatra was diminished from months to days; their deaths also occurred several days apart. He omitted events which did not bear on the theme (the struggle of Rome against Egypt and the part that Antony's love affair with Cleopatra played in the outcome). Important persons such as Octavius Caesar and Octavia were background figures and the time that Antony remained in Rome after his marriage to Octavia was reduced to a brief interval.

As Mosel noted, this is the most difficult of Shakespeare's plays to perform and "one of the most consistent failures" (B163, p. 480). It had been produced on Broadway only three times, the first with E. H. Sothern and Julia Marlowe in 1909, which reportedly was a disaster. Jane Cowl and Tallulah Bankhead had done the most recent productions when each was much younger than Miss Cornell.

The memory of John Mason Brown's scathing review of the latter "hung over" the Cornell cast. He had written: "Tallulah Bankhead barged down the Nile last night as Cleopatra--and sank." In addition to that reminder, McClintic encountered Jane Cowl at Sardis only a couple of hours before the opening on November 26, 1947. Instead of wishing him well, she must have shaken his confidence with her parting remark, "Remember, I have done this play. And I have never felt sorrier for two people in my life than I do for you and Kit tonight" (B163, p. 481).

Miss Cornell took a 7-week tryout tour during which the play lost $14,580.

After the New York run, the company went on a 9-week tour of 4 major cities.  With a total of 251 performances, *Antony and Cleopatra* enjoyed the longest run in its history.

## Synopsis

Egypt's Queen Cleopatra and Rome's Antony, joint ruler with Octavius Caesar, fell in love when they met at Tarsus and he had followed her to Alexandria.  There, when news comes to him that his wife Fulvia and his brother are making war against Caesar and that Fulvia has died suddenly, he returns to Rome.  In disfavor with Caesar, Antony reconciles their differences by marrying Octavia, Caesar's widowed sister.  The two triumvirs divide the Roman empire, Antony taking the eastern provinces.

To make amends with Cleopatra, Antony relinquishes large portions of the eastern empire to her.  His power threatened, Caesar persuades the Roman senate to divest Antony of his authority and engage him in battle at Actium.

After Antony loses the sea-fight and his honor, Cleopatra persuades him that they can regain their power if he goes to battle against Rome once more.  As he prepares to leave, he learns that his ships are damaged and cannot sail.  Believing that Cleopatra has betrayed him, he rages against her.  To win his sympathy again, she sends word by her attendant that she has taken her life for him.  Bereft, Antony asks his friend Eros to kill him.  Unable to carry out his friend's command, Eros kills himself instead.  Antony then falls on his own sword and Cleopatra, who has had misgivings about his reaction to her ploy, returns to find him near death.  He dies in her arms.

Cleopatra learns that Caesar, who had promised to treat her with compassion, intends to lead her in chains through  the streets of Rome.  Dressed in her royal robes, she takes her own life with the poisonous asp brought to her in a basket of figs.  Caesar orders that she be buried by her Antony for, as he said,
"No grave upon the earth shall clip in it
A pair so famous."

## Reviews

*New York Times* (11/27/47)--Brooks Atkinson found it unpleasant to report that the production was formal and somewhat pedantic and thought Miss Cornell had too much good taste to portray a "royal slut."  He praised her for playing the tragic scenes, particularly her last one, with nobility and radiance.  Her last scene, he wrote, was her grandest, and added that the qualities her audiences admired in her are not those of Cleopatra (B287).

*Journal American* (11/28/47)--In the opinion of Robert Garland, the McClintics had "reached down into William Shakespeare's grab-bag of a drama and pulled out a masterpiece."  He praised the production for moving swiftly through the "kaleidoscopic scenes" and for its "bite, clarity and dispatch" as well as "humor" (B369).

## Commentary

Despite the dubious well-wishers, Cornell's fans did not let her down nor did she fail them.  Even when transportation was shut down in December by a blizzard, she tramped through the snow to reach the theatre and a New Jersey couple walked through the Lincoln Tunnel to see her show.

Not only is the play difficult but it was also the most expensive of Miss Cornell's productions and the first for which she had needed outside financial backing.  The McClintics spared nothing in casting and staging the chronicle.  The result was, as

Ward Morehouse reported in *The Sun*, "something really magnificent" (B433).

Critics praised Miss Cornell's courage for presenting a play which, in the opinion of many, was not well written. There are too many themes, personages and conflicts and the multiple scenes jump around the eastern Mediterranean. Indeed, it is not an easy play to understand.

William Hawkins, in the *New York World-Telegram*, praised her production, saying that although she had done everything possible to make it great, the Bard had "let her down." He found the play to be "a monumental bore" (B380). Although most critics acknowledged weaknesses in the play itself, they expressed appreciation for the splendid production. Robert Coleman of the *New York Daily Mirror* called it "a superlative production" (B333). Robert Garland of the *Journal American* found it to be "the most exciting theatrical event of this or practically any other recent season" (B369).

The McClintics had, as usual, selected a company of outstanding actors. There was some disagreement about the performances of some members of the cast, but highest credits went to the fine acting of Godfrey Tearle and Kent Smith.

As for Miss Cornell's Cleopatra, critics had much praise and some criticism. She was lovely, her acting was impressive, she had distinguished herself and, for Ward Morehouse, she had conveyed all the facets of Cleopatra's character (B433). On the other hand, Louis Kronenberger and Brooks Atkinson found her lacking in passion and wickedness (B399; B287).

As pointed out by Harley Granville-Barker and Louis Kronenberger, one of the difficulties for the actress playing Cleopatra is the fact that the part was written to be played by a boy. Shakespeare avoided direct sex-appeal. Therefore, there is little physical touch and Shakespeare's Cleopatra masters Antony with "wit, malice, or subtle mischief" rather than voluptuousness (B083, p.327; B399). Whether her fidelity to the script, or simply her innate sense of good taste guided her, is not known. At any rate, perhaps her portrayal was what she believed and thought her fans would want--a woman who died for love.

******

## S60    THAT LADY
(Opened: November 22, 1949, at the Martin Beck Theatre; 10 weeks of performance)

**Credits**

| | |
|---|---|
| Playwright | Kate O'Brien |
| Director | Guthrie McClintic |
| Settings and Costumes | Rolf Gerard |
| Producer | Katharine Cornell |

**Cast**

| | |
|---|---|
| Rodrigo | Douglas Watson |
| Anichu | Jada Rowland |
| Bernardina Cavero | Esther Minciotto |
| Pablo, a Footman | Peter Barno |
| Juan De Escovedo | Joseph Wiseman |

| | |
|---|---|
| Another Footman | Anthony Radecki |
| Philip II, King of Spain | Henry Daniell |
| Ana de Mendoza y de Gomez | Katharine Cornell |
| Antonio Perez | Torin Thatcher |
| Cardinal Gaspar de Quiroga | Henry Stephenson |
| Estaban, a Servant | Richard Sterling |
| Paca, A Maidservant | Lita Dal Porto |
| Don Mateo Vesquez | Will Kuluva |
| King's Footman | Wallace Chadwell |
| Manuel Ortega | David J. Stewart |
| Anichu, at 18 | Marian Seldes |
| A Doctor | Oliver Cliff |

### The Play's History

That Lady was dramatized by Kate O'Brien from her novel *For One Sweet Grape* at the request of the McClintics. She admitted that it had been a challenge which caused her "a lot of trouble--and much fun and happiness too" (B174, p. viii). She added that the McClintics and she would soon know if her work would justify Miss Cornell's belief that the love story would make a good play.

After a 4-week tryout period in four cities *That Lady* was opened in New York on November 22, 1949, and closed January 28, 1950, a 10-week run. It made a small profit because of the low operating costs and the reduction of the director's and playwright's royalty fees. After closing in New York, the play was taken on tour through Texas and the south. The average weekly grosses were the lowest made by any of the C. & M. C. plays that had ever been taken on an extended tour (B512, p. 125).

### Synopsis

Throughout sixteenth century Europe during the reign of Philip II in Spain, the Inquisition is at its height with power struggles, intrigue, violence and bloodshed, an era replete with melodrama. Since the death of Ruy Gomez, Philip's Secretary of State, his widow Ana De Mendoza has lived on her country estate. The beautiful daughter of one of Spain's noblest families, Ana wears a black patch over the eye she had lost as a young girl in a dueling accident.

Because her husband and the King had grown up together, a close friendship had developed with the family. When Philip recalls her to Madrid to manage her family affairs, his action gives rise to rumors of a romance between them, which he would have liked, but Ana remains loyal to the memory of her husband.

When she is thirty-seven, however, she becomes the mistress of her husband's successor, Antonio Perez. The vengeful, jealous King Philip plans that Antonio Perez will be blamed for the murder of Escovedo, who has informed Philip of the love affair and is also plotting against the King. Philip orders Antonio and Ana to be imprisoned where Antonio is tortured and Ana's deprivation brings her near death.

Philip offers to pardon Ana with the condition that she will never again communicate with Antonio, but her demand for Antonio's freedom angers him further and seals her fate. The King orders her to live out the remainder of her life in the darkness of her walled palace room.

## Reviews

*Daily Mirror* (11/23/49)--Robert Coleman commented on Miss Cornell's flair for melodrama to which, he says, she almost gives "the illusion of drama." She has invested this "essentially tawdry and empty role" with "a semblance of meaning and merit. She makes dross glitter suspiciously like gold" (B332).

*New York Post* (11/23/49)--Richard Watts Jr. wrote that Miss Cornell is "as always a vital and dramatic figure" but he could not help "thinking it is the fault of the play that the love of which she is the central figure never seems properly moving or tragic" (B497).

## Commentary

Despite the effort and expense (over $60,000) of producing Kate O'Brien's romantic drama, it "drew a tepid set of adjectives" and the Spanish heroine "languished and expired within the confines of the legitimate theatre" (B169). In an article reprinted from the *New York Times* as a preface to the published play, O'Brien described her struggle in writing the play to make the characters' "spiritual progressions and failures" clearly highlighted by the outer plot (B174, p. ix). Unfortunately, Richard Watts of the *New York Post* thought her efforts resulted in characters who lacked "credibility and dramatic drive" (B497).

The critics were not only unenthusiastic but they were also harsh and sometimes caustic in their comments. Robert Coleman of the *Daily Mirror* judged the play to be "shoddily melodramatic" (B332). Howard Barnes of the *Herald Tribune* called it "highly uninteresting" as well as "episodic and loquacious" (B298).

Except for Howard Barnes and John Chapman of the *Daily News*, who had nothing positive to say, critics were kinder in their comments about the acting, settings and direction. Robert Coleman found Rolf Gerard's costumes and settings to be "stunning" and "pictorially magnificent." William Hawkins reported in the *World-Telegram* that the production was "one of the most beautiful things to look at of many a day, glamorously lighted..." (B382). He also applauded the direction, the lighting and the cast. As for the acting, Brooks Atkinson praised Miss Cornell for a fine performance although he thought the drama itself did not come alive. Comparing it to *The Barretts of Wimpole Street*, also a romantic drama and her most successful production, Atkinson found the fault to be in the writing (B286).

******

## S61     CAPTAIN CARVALLO

(Opened: December 6, 1950, Buffalo, New York; 3 weeks of performances)

## Credits

| | |
|---|---|
| Playwright | Dennis Cannon |
| Director | Guthrie McClintic |
| Settings | Rolf Gerard |
| Costumes | Motley of London |
| Producers | Katharine Cornell with |
| | Laurence Olivier |

## Cast

| | |
|---|---|
| Anni | Hope Cameron |
| Smilja Darde | Katharine Cornell |
| The Baron | Nigel Bruce |
| Professor Winke | Cedric Hardwicke |
| Private Gross | Walter Starky |
| Captain Carvallo | John Buckmaster |
| Casper Darde | Robert Emhardt |

## The Play's History

The tryout of *Captain Carvallo* opened in Buffalo in December, 1950, while it was playing successfully in London with Diana Wynyard in the female lead. It had been presented at the Bristol Old Vic Theatre, London in March, 1950, with Allan Davis as the director. Laurence Olivier directed the show at the St. James's Theatre which opened in August, 1950. Miss Cornell's production was not taken to Broadway.

## Synopsis

In early summer the action takes place in the farmhouse kitchen of Smilja and Caspar Darde located on "disputed territory" in a country vaguely described as "midway between East and West." It is the last summer of a long war between the Partisans and the enemy. While Darde, a Partisan, is away on an undetermined mission Professor Winke appears, dressed in Darde's clothes, claiming to have exchanged identity with him. When Captain Carvallo and his attendant come to the door demanding food, bath, and billet, Winke pretends to be Smilja's husband.

Both Carvello and Winke make romantic overtures to Smilja. Winke catches Carvello consoling Smilja who is overwrought by the whole situation, and her real husband, Caspar, arrives unexpectedly to find Winke clasping her in his arms.

Carvallo holds a court of inquiry to determine who is the real husband and puts Winke under fake arrest since each has found the other making advances toward Darde's wife. All is forgiven and the three men drink together in celebration.

Winke and Darde receive instructions from Baron, the commanding officer, to kill at least one enemy in honor of the anniversary of the Foundation of the Republic. They fake the killing of Carvallo and his attendant by blowing up the stable when the two men are not in it.

To get Carvallo away from the stable Smilja makes an "assignation" with him. Darde, who is elected to set off the explosives, suffers injuries. When Baron returns to investigate the explosion he is told that both Carvallo and his attendant died in the explosion. Smilja is left alone with the Baron who suggests that, with her husband incapacitated, they could get together.

## Reviews

*Buffalo Courier-Express* (12/7/50)--Rollin Palmer described the play as "sometimes embarrassingly inept" and thought it arouses "new wonders over that marvelous thing--the British cousin's sense of humor." The play was "sadly lacking in theme or situation," he stated, and "it appears nothing can be done to save it." He said there was one short speech in which "the Cornell magic glows" but Captain Carvallo was "not her dish" (B450).

Buffalo Courier-Express (12/8/50)--The reviewer stated that it was generally agreed that Captain Carvallo was "unworthy of the talents of the first lady of the theater. She has little more to do than appear as a glorified servant" (B324).

## Commentary
It is difficult to understand what attracted the McClintics to this play. Mosel suggests that McClintic wanted to do it because Laurence Olivier had produced it in London, and that Miss Cornell wanted to wear her beautiful Bavarian dirndl (B163, p. 501). Whatever the reasons for producing this unlikely choice, something went amiss at the Buffalo opening, McClintic's volatility surfaced and the show was not taken to Broadway. The critics were justifiably disappointed in the play and generally agreed it was not worthy of Miss Cornell's talents. Headlines in the *Detroit Times* summarized the general reaction: "Katharine Cornell's New Play Is Poor." The critic, Harvey Taylor, compared the play to "the first effort of a gifted but immature college boy" (B480). Ruth Elgutter of the *Toledo Times* asked why they didn't know this play was not right for Miss Cornell. The title of her review gave the answer: "Katharine Cornell Play Proves Even Theater Folks Are Fallible" (B358).

\*\*\*\*\*\*

## S62    THE CONSTANT WIFE
(Opened: December 8, 1951, at the National Theatre, New York; 17 weeks of performances)

### Credits
| | |
|---|---|
| Playwright | Somerset Maugham |
| Director | Guthrie McClintic |
| Settings | Donald Oenslager |
| Producer | Katharine Cornell |

### Cast
| | |
|---|---|
| Mrs. Culver | Grace George |
| Bentley | Liam Sullivan |
| Martha Culver | Gertrude Musgrove |
| Barbara Fawcett | Eva Leonard-Boyne |
| Constance Middleton | Katharine Cornell |
| Marie-Louise Durham | Nan Martin |
| John Middleton, F.R.C.S. | Brian Aherne |
| Bernard Kersal | John Emery |
| Mortimer Durham | Claude Horton |

### The Play's History
The Central City Opera House in Colorado invited Miss Cornell to bring a production to their annual festival in August, 1951. She selected *The Constant Wife*, in which Ethel Barrymore had been successful, and engaged Brian Aherne to play the leading man and Grace George for the role of Mrs. Culver. The total gross of the receipts for the performances, which ran for 4 weeks from August 4 to September 1,

1951, was $93,000. Because of the success in Central City, the McClintics decided to take the production to New York after a 3-week tryout in Columbus where it grossed over $65,000.

The show opened in New York at the National Theatre on December 8, 1951, with $7.50 as the top ticket price. After 17 weeks with receipts averaging just over $21,000 per week the play closed on April 5, 1952. From there the company went on tour of three eastern cities for 6 weeks. The next season *The Constant Wife* toured 35 cities in 31 weeks, the first long tour since *No Time for Comedy*. For the two seasons *The Constant Wife* realized the largest profit, almost $146,000, of any show since *The Barretts of Wimpole Street* (B512, p. 116). It was, in fact, Miss Cornell's only postwar financial success.

## Synopsis

Everyone knows except Constance--so they think--that her handsome, successful husband is having an affair with her "greatest" friend, Mary-Louise Durham. When John carelessly leaves his cigarette case in the Durham bedroom, Mortimer Durham finds it and confronts the Middletons. Constance claims that she had borrowed the cigarette case and unknowingly dropped it. Mortimer appears to be the fool, face is saved for John and Mary-Louise, the Durham marriage is salvaged, at least for the time being, and Constance decides to take a job as an interior decorator.

A year later the Durhams have returned after a year's absence. The infatuation between John and Mary-Louise is ended. Actually, he's "fed up" with her and she's "absolutely mad" about a young man from India.

Constance, who is ready to leave for a holiday trip to Italy without John, tells him that she is paying her own way on the trip and she has also deposited money in his account for her past year's board and lodging. As long as she was a parasite giving so little to their marriage she could not protest his little affair. She has forgotten to mention to him that she will not be alone on the trip but with Bernard, an old flame who has been madly in love with her for years.

Outraged, John cannot understand her violation of the double-standard in marriage, but Constance assures him that she "is doing no more injury to him" than he had done to her a year ago. Their marriage has simply grown stale. Furthermore, she expects him to be as charming to Bernard as she has been to Mary-Louise, for as she says, "I may be unfaithful, but I am constant." Does John want her to come back? His answer is an emphatic "yes."

## Reviews

*Daily News* (12/10/51)--Except for Oenslager's stylish set and Grace George, John Chapman could find little about the play to like. He supposed that Miss Cornell's "worshippers" will be furious with him "for regarding both the comedy and the actress as pallid" (B328).

*New York World-Telegram* (12/10/51)--William Hawkins viewed Miss Cornell's production of *The Constant Wife* as "a rarity in the season." He thought she avoided "all the pitfalls inherent here, of being too elaborately gracious, too obvious or arch, or even of seeming to have too good a time." Such an attitude would have made the play "dated nonsense." Because of the "incredibly good cast" and Miss Cornell's honesty, she and the comedy were believable (B384).

## Commentary

Although there were critics who thought Miss Cornell's production lacked the brightness of Ethel Barrymore's hit, they were outnumbered by the favorable responses. Robert Coleman of the *Daily Mirror*, who had not liked the civilized comedy when he saw Barrymore in it, now viewed it as "a veritable gem" in a season sadly lacking in "sparkle" and "wit" (B334). Although he thought she was more at home in drama, Coleman reported that Miss Cornell delighted her audiences. On the other hand, John Chapman of the *Daily News* thought the play a "warmed-over 'Candida'" (B328).

Brooks Atkinson has compliments for all members of the stellar cast, Grace George being singled out for "her impish humor" in this "artificial comedy" (B266). Walter Kerr commended Brian Aherne for preserving "the comic style" without losing a laugh. He found the play to have "surprising durability" and Miss Cornell's style to be suited to the times. Its success was proof of its appeal to audiences (B392).

******

## S63    THE PRESCOTT PROPOSALS
(Opened: December 16, 1953, at the Broadhurst Theatre, New York; 20 and one-half weeks of performances)

### Credits

| | |
|---|---|
| Playwrights | Howard Lindsay and Russel Crouse |
| Director | Howard Lindsay |
| Settings | Donald Oenslager |
| Costumes | Main Bocher |
| Producer | Leland Hayward |

### Cast

| | |
|---|---|
| Mary Prescott | Katharine Cornell |
| Kathleen Murray | Emily Lawrence |
| Emma | Helen Ray |
| Elliott Clark | Lorne Greene |
| Jan Capek | Bartlett Robinson |
| Sir Audley Marriott | Felix Aylmer |
| Paul-Emile D'Arceau | Roger Dawn |
| Dr. Ali Masoud | Minoo Daver |
| Alexis Petrovsky | Ben Astar |
| Miguel Fernandez | Edward Groag |
| Alan Draper | Robert M. Culp |
| Miroslav Babicka | Boris Tumarin |
| Russian Aide | Jan de Ruth |
| British Aide | J. P. Wilson |
| Precis-Writer | John Drew Devereaux |

Experts and Aides to the
United Nations Delegates:

Bijou Fernandez, Joe Masteroff,
John Leslie, Sheppard Kerman,
Richard Bengali, Ward Costello,
Bernard Reines, Hubert Beck

## The Play's History

The play was written for Miss Cornell and it was the first time in 25 years that her husband, McClintic, had not been involved in a show in which she starred. A 5-week tryout began in New Haven on November 11, 1953. After the first 6 weeks, during which the receipts topped $20,000, they began to drop steadily. Because expenses were so much higher than for previous shows, the authors and director waived part of their royalties to break even. The production had run for 16 weeks when it closed with a total loss of over $104,000 (B512, p. 121).

## Synopsis

In her New York apartment Mary Prescott, a delegate to the U.N. who is sponsoring the Prescott Proposals for solving world problems, is expecting three of her committee members to stop for cocktails. Before their arrival Jan Capek, a Communist Czechoslovakian who had once been Mary's lover, puts both her and himself in jeopardy when he appears to renew their "friendship." He collapses and dies of a heart attack in her dressing room.

When her guests arrive, Mary solicits their help. Before they can remove the body, the uninvited Russian committee member Petrovsky, who has followed Capek, appears and is shown the body. Learning of her past relationship with Capek, Petrovsky generously offers to help avoid a scandal. Swearing themselves to secrecy, the delegates move the body to the Czechoslovakian headquarters and issue a false report of the death.

The matter seems settled until the City of New York demands an autopsy, and a newspaper publishes rumors about the circumstances of Capek's death. It is apparent that someone in the group has broken their mutual vow of secrecy.

Elliott Clark, a television news commentator who is in love with Mary and has long kept the secret of her affair with Capek, warns her against trusting Petrovsky. Clark knows that Petrovsky sent Nina Simonova, the woman he loved, to death for putting her love for him above the state.

One of the delegates discovers that Petrovsky feigned his support of Mary and the Prescott Proposals for Russia's gain and also broke the stories to the press. Promising to reveal Mary's connection with Capek in his address to the General Assembly, Petrovsky makes a slip, calling Mary "Nina." Unnerved by his slip, he loses his resolve to discredit Mary. This convinces her that he is human and that Communism will be defeated by the "human spirit."

She proved her point with Elliott Clark who asks her to dine. Her acceptance implies the promise of a new romance.

## Reviews

*New York Daily News* (12/17/53)--Except for the Oenslager sets, John Chapman could not "make a cheerful report" on Lindsay and Crouse's venture. In his opinion, they had made "the United Nations a great bore and Miss Cornell a defeated actress." He was never able to figure out what the Prescott Proposals were and thought the director kept "Miss Cornell loping around the stage like an ostrich" (B329).

*New York Herald Tribune* (12/17/53)--Of the play Walter Kerr said, "The aura of all those flashy old romances does cling to it, and the very schmaltz which robs it of pertinence gives it a kind of footlight gayety [sic]." He attributed this to Miss Cornell's "personal splendor" and the excellent actors who gave her support. However, he thought it was "markedly lightweight" as a serious drama (B395).

## Commentary

The reviews of *The Prescott Proposals* were mixed. Walter Kerr said it "plays all of this fond and foolish romancing with a perfectly straight face" (B395). In *The New York Times* Brooks Atkinson commented that the staging was brilliant and the play "exciting" with "a lot of suspense." However, he expressed disappointment that the political aspect was superficial and intellectually unstimulating. On the other hand, he thought Miss Cornell was superb (B276).

Some critics were kinder than Atkinson; others decidedly unfavorable. They did grant that the costumes, cast and settings were admirable. However, they generally agreed that the play, although sometimes fun, was disappointing. Some fans who wrote Miss Cornell found her "warm" and "gracious" as well as "moving," but thought the play was neither well-written nor well-directed.

Because her later plays had not been financially profitable, Miss Cornell had sought the outside backing of Leland Hayward for this show. It, too, lost money and when Hayward refused to continue as producer after the New York run, Miss Cornell could not afford to take it on the road.

******

**S64**    **THE DARK IS LIGHT ENOUGH**
(Opened: February 23, 1955, at the ANTA Theatre, New York; 8 and one-half weeks of performances)

## Credits

| | |
|---|---|
| Playwright | Christopher Fry |
| Director | Guthrie McClintic |
| Settings and Costumes | Oliver Messel |
| Producers | Katharine Cornell |
| | and Roger L. Stevens |
| | by arrangement with |
| | H. M. Tennent, Ltd. |

## Cast

| | |
|---|---|
| Kassel | William Podmore |
| Jakob | Donald Harron |
| Belmann | John Williams |
| Stefan | Paul Roebling |
| Bella | Eva Condon |
| Willi | Charles Macaulay |
| Gelda | Marian Winters |
| Richard Gettner | Tyrone Power, Jr. |

| | |
|---|---|
| Countess Rosmarin Ostenburg | Katharine Cornell |
| Colonel Janik | Arnold Moss |
| Count Peter Zichy | Christopher Plummer |
| Beppy | Ted Gunther |
| Rusti | Sydney Pollack |
| Third Soldier | Jerome Gardino |
| Fourth Soldier | Dario Barri |

### The Play's History

The play, written in verse form for Edith Evans, was published in 1954. Miss Cornell chose this play, as well as Fry's *The Firstborn*, because she was then in her late fifties and the roles were suitable to her age.

The tryout tour, opening in Buffalo, November 24, 1954, was 11 weeks with a lay-off period of two and one half weeks between the end of the tour in Washington, D.C. and the New York opening. Although the play made a profit on the tour, attendance in New York dropped significantly after the fifth week so the show was closed on April 23, 1955. It was then taken on to Boston for another two weeks, making its total run twenty-one and one half weeks. The play's loss was just under $53,500 (B512, p. 123).

### Synopsis

The play is set in the country house of Countess Rosmarin in the winter of 1848-49, during the Hungarian uprising against Austrian rule. The Countess, an independent and compassionate lady, drives alone in a snowstorm toward the Hungarian army to rescue Capt. Gettner, a deserter and former husband of her daughter Gelda.

Stefan, son of the Countess, is furious with Gettner, who is generally regarded as a scoundrel, for prevailing upon his mother to save him from the firing squad. His presence in their house puts them at great risk from the advancing army. When soldiers are heard at the door, Gettner hides and the Countess refuses to allow Col. Janik to search her home. Janik holds Gelda's husband Peter as prisoner and offers to exchange him for Gettner, but neither the Countess nor her daughter will disclose Gettner's hideaway.

Col. Janik, agreeing not to search for Gettner if he keeps out of the way, takes possession of the house for his men and moves the Countess to the stable. He also allows Peter, under guard, to be with them. Gettner makes things difficult for everyone and wounds Peter in a duel.

In the final act the Countess, now ill, and Stefan are re-established in their house. They learn that the government is hanging every Hungarian who fought; this time the Countess hides fugitive Col. Janik. Gettner had left, but learning of her illness, returns to propose marriage to the Countess; she refuses because she has never loved him. With soldiers hammering at the door, she dies.

### Reviews

*New York Post* (2/24/55)--Critic Richard Watts, Jr., an admirer of Fry, found himself "unable to like his new play." He thought the author was "so bemused by the impressive sound of his own words" that he had become "pretentious, ponderous, even a bit pompous." This had "drained away" the "dramatic forcefulness" of the play. He wished that the author had been "more dramatic" in the lines he had written for Miss Cornell who, Watts thought, "offers one of her loveliest and most gracious performances" (B492).

*New World-Telegram* and *The Sun* (2/24/55)--William Hawkins was even more critical of Fry's script than Watts. He said it "rides on the brink of obscurity most of the time," and went on to indict Fry for abhorring "a simple statement of fact." He found the characters to be "flippant on the surface", and the actors unable "to give the Fry lines the glitter they need" (B381).

## Commentary

Louis Kronenberger, editor of *The Best Plays*, was critical of the play and thought Tyrone Power to be "woefully miscast" (B123, p. 9). The play, he commented, was neither "very dramatic" nor "very deep philosophically." Atkinson also found Fry's writing to be lacking and much of the play to be obscure. He concluded that Fry had written without much "passion or enthusiasm." From Brooks Atkinson's point of view, Miss Cornell "is the essence of theatre in the grand manner." As for Power, his performance is "vigorous" and "forthright" (B268).

The difficulty that Miss Cornell was having in getting well-written plays was apparent in *The Dark is Light Enough*. The casting also illustrates that her only gesture to commercialism, when she asked Tyrone Power to come back from Hollywood to appear as Gettner, was a mistake (B163, p. 491).

******

## S65  THE FIRSTBORN

(Opened: April 10, 1958, at the Coronet Theatre, New York; 6 weeks of performances; July 3-10, 1958, in Tel Aviv; July 12 in Jerusalem)

### Credits

| | |
|---|---|
| Playwright | Christopher Fry |
| Director | Anthony Quayle |
| Settings | Boris Aronson |
| Costumes | Robert Fletcher |
| Lighting | Tharon Musser |
| Music | Leonard Bernstein |
| Production Associate for Mr. Stevens | George Hamlin |
| Production Stage Manager | Keene Curtis |
| Producers | Katharine Cornell and |
| | Roger L. Stevens |

Under the auspices of the America-Israel Cultural Foundation

### Cast

| | |
|---|---|
| Anath Bithiah | Katharine Cornell |
| Teusret | Kathleen Widdoes |
| A Guard | Jack Betts |
| Kef | Chris Gampel |
| Seti II | Torin Thatcher |
| Rameses | Robert Drivas |
| Moses | Anthony Quayle |
| Aaron | Michael Strong |

| Miriam | Mildred Natwick |
| Shendi | Michael Wager |
| Overseers | Jack Betts |
| | Philip Robinson |

## The Play's History

A biblical drama, *The Firstborn,* was written in verse by Christopher Fry and first produced at the Edinburgh Festival in 1948. After a 4-week tryout in Cleveland, it opened in New York, April 30, 1958, at the Coronet Theatre. Following that, *The Firstborn* was taken to Israel to celebrate its tenth anniversary, sponsored by the American-Israeli Committee. The production was given at the Habima Theatre in Tel Aviv, running from July 3 through July 10, 1958. On July 12 it played in Jerusalem, making the total run of the show 10 weeks.

*The Firstborn* was another of Miss Cornell's financial failures. The play's New York engagement was cut short because of high running expenses and low boxoffice receipts. Even with royalties being waived by the designers and playwright during the third week in New York, the play lost money. The cost of production was over $85,500 and, at the end of the tour to Israel, the total losses were just under $97,000 (B512, p. 124). For the tour Miss Cornell and Anthony Quayle received only $150 each and the cast members $75 in addition to their round trip fares.

## Synopsis

In the summer of 1200 B.C. Moses, once a military hero, returns to the palace of the Pharaoh, Seti the Second, in Egypt, after ten years in exile. The Pharaoh has been seeking him to lead armies against invasion by the Libyans.

Moses, however, has returned to lead the Hebrews into the wilderness where they may worship their own god and escape the Pharaoh's inhuman treatment. Among those subject to the Pharaoh's severe discipline and deprivation are Moses' sister Miriam and her son Shendi.

Anath, sister of the Pharaoh who had found Moses among the bulrushes, is torn by the danger she sees in her brother's power and her son's mission. Strongly influenced by his uncle Moses, the Pharaoh's young son Rameses and successor to the throne, treats the citizens as equals much to the displeasure of his father. He intercedes with his father to give Shendi a position in the palace.

Life for Miriam and Shendi improves and they become angry with Moses for risking what they have gained. Moses promises them that their slavery will be over at midnight when God will "descend and obliterate the firstborn of Egypt" and spare those of Israel. When God's descent occurs, Moses stops Shendi from returning to the palace but is too late to warn Rameses whose father has just named him the new Pharaoh and granted Moses permission to lead the Hebrews away. Moses has accomplished his mission but cannot stop the death of Rameses, one of the firstborn.

## Reviews

*New York Herald Tribune* (5/1/58)--Walter Kerr perceived that the "essential theatrical failing" of the play was lack of dramatic confrontation. He said that "the personal moment, the moment that may shed very human light on the political battle that is going on, never comes" (B393).

*Variety* (5/7/58)--The *Variety* reviewer noted that, although films have been successful in "turning the Bible into gold...religious dramas have generally been poor pickings for the stage." This is particularly true when there is no "apparent viewpoint" and the play is "static." Moreover, the trade paper sees little general interest in the play for Broadway. The script suffers from lack of theme, the playwright's wordiness and lack of drama. The performance is impressive but the play itself is "slow and heavy, and has an exasperating way of side-stepping what should be the big scenes--the crucial conflict." *Variety* compliments Quayle for a "potent performance" and Miss Cornell for her regality although her characterization, which is insufficiently explained, offers her only one big scene. The reviewer concludes that "it's a lot of production, but not much entertainment" (B472).

## Commentary

As usual, Miss Cornell had selected a superb cast. Anthony Quayle did an excellent job of portraying Moses and, as director, he imbued the performance with vigor and movement. In fact, Brooks Atkinson credited him for having breathed "life into a rather colorless script and made something bold and beautiful out of a well-loved Bible story" (B288). Richard Watts also praised Quayle for playing Moses "with eloquence and dignity" (B493).

As Anath, not a central role, Miss Cornell again exemplified her ability to support fellow actors in roles more dominant than hers, which she did with Anthony Quayle and others. Her performance was reserved, regal and moving. In the *Journal American,* John McClain reported that she didn't "look a day older than the lad [Moses] who she reared" (B424).

Having commended the actors for their portrayals, the critics disagreed on the power of the script itself. McClain found it "deeply moving;" Robert Coleman described it in the *Daily Mirror* as "stirring" (B424; B336). Others, such as Richard Watts of the *New York Post,* found it "strangely lacking in dramatic power and emotional warmth" (B493).

\*\*\*\*\*\*

**S66    DEAR LIAR**
(Opened: March 17, 1960, at the Billy Rose Theatre, New York; 6 and one-half weeks of performances)

## Credits

| | |
|---|---|
| Letters by | G. Bernard Shaw |
| | Mrs. Patrick Campbell |
| Adaptation by | Jerome Kilty |
| Director | Jerome Kilty |
| Settings | Donald Oenslager |
| Costumes | Cecil Beaton |
| Lighting | Jean Rosenthal |
| Music | Sol Kaplan |
| Producers | Guthrie McClintic with |
| | Sol Hurok |

## Cast

G. Bernard Shaw                                                        Brian Aherne
Mrs. Patrick Campbell                                          Katharine Cornell

### The Play's History

  *Dear Liar*, a comedy of letters, was adapted by Jerome Kilty from *Bernard Shaw and Mrs. Patrick Campbell: Their Correspondence*, edited by Alan Dent and published in 1952. Not really a play, it is more a series of readings interspersed with the dialogue of the two characters who speak for Mr. Shaw and Mrs. Campbell.

  The presentation has only two acts; the first takes place in the period between 1899 and 1914, and the second between 1914 and 1939. The dialogue takes place in a very simple setting consisting of an entrance, a French window, a desk and chair for each of the actors, and a stool. On a small table between Shaw and Mrs. Campbell is a hatbox containing the letters.

  Before the production was taken to New York, it toured for 7 weeks in the spring of 1959, to cities in Arizona and the southern states. Miss Cornell was still enthusiastic about touring, a pace that few actors could tolerate. Brian Aherne hated the road, but was so supportive of Miss Cornell that he agreed to be her co-star. As he said, "She's wedded to the road, and I'm wedded to her" (B208 p. 53).

  At the Sombrero Theatre in Phoenix, *Dear Liar* played 9 performances to capacity crowds, even turning away about a thousand patrons for whom there were no seats. Additional seats were installed to accommodate 225 more customers. The show was taken to 9 cities in Arizona and the southern states and performed 43 times.

  After a summer break, the tour was resumed through the east, midwest and west coast in the fall of 1959. While waiting for a suitable theatre in New York, the tour continued until March 17, 1960, with the best boxoffices in Washington, D.C. and Chicago. The New York opening at the Billy Rose Theatre was on March 17, 1960, where the presentation did poorly at the boxoffice. In fact, it ran for only six and one-half weeks with the average gross being the lowest of Miss Cornell's productions in New York since 1935. After closing on April 30, 1960, Miss Cornell took the show to Boston where receipts increased and she was able to recover a small portion of her New York losses. The total gross for *Dear Liar* was $650,000 (B512, p. 112).

  When the show closed, the curtain had fallen for the last time on Miss Cornell as actress-manager. It marked the end of an era in the theatre.

### Synopsis

  The actors introduce themselves and together open the hatbox of letters. Their story begins when she is at the peak of her acting career and he is just starting to write plays after ending his career as a music and drama critic. His first letter to her, in 1899, is an invitation to talk about the new play he is writing, *Caesar and Cleopatra*. Unable to meet him, she does not hear from him again until 1911, when he calls to discuss *Pygmalion* and falls "head over heels in love" with her. The reading of the letters that pass between them over the next forty years chronicle an apparently unconsummated love affair through stages of giddiness, intensity, quarrelsomeness, anger, hurt and waning interest.

  Critical points in their relationship occur in the successful production of *Pygmalion,* in which Stella plays Eliza, and her marriage to George Corwallis-West. Shaw is deeply hurt by her marriage even though he himself has no intention of divorcing his long-suffering wife for Stella Campbell.

The war closes the theatres in London where *Pygmalion* is having great success. Mrs. Campbell brings it to America where it is not well received. Returning to England in 1916, she finds Shaw morose and disagreeable. Her own life is filled with the grief of losing her son and George's divorce from her.

The relationship with Shaw takes "a tragi-comic turn" as they argue over what to do with the letters that both have kept. Their correspondence grows nasty when he refuses to let her publish his letters. She publishes some of them and attempts to reconcile their differences, to little avail.

Seven years pass. They age, become more cantankerous, suffer ill health and grow farther apart. Her effort to succeed in Hollywood has failed; his film *Pygmalion* has been a great success as the flame flickers out for what Mrs. Campbell called "the lustless lions at play."

## Reviews

*New York Herald Tribune* (3/18/60)--Walter Kerr likened the evening to a social occasion. "It's tea-time, perhaps with a few shredded vegetables as canapes, rather than a late and lively hour of the night," he commented. Shaw was probably inconsiderate, Kerr remarked, to have written "such splendidly tart plays," and spoiled his audiences for *Dear Liar* in which the letters were less carefully shaped. The evening was pleasant, but lacked the "sense of combat" expected of the lovers (B394).

*New York World-Telegram and The Sun* (3/18/60)--Frank Aston, a more enthusiastic critic, viewed the play as "pure gold, freshly and stimulatingly novel." He suggested that anyone familiar with Shaw "should have a blissful time" seeing *Dear Liar*. He thought that the passages worked "like magic" because of the "sound artistry" and "acute training" of Cornell and Aherne (B262).

## Commentary

In the *New York Mirror*, Robert Coleman reported that the dramatized correspondence failed to create an exciting evening and Aherne seemed more successful than Cornell in breathing a spark into Shaw (B335). Richard Watts noted in the *New York Post* that Shaw's letters were more entertaining than Campbell's which gives Aherne a "livelier role" (B495). Moreover, as Brooks Atkinson pointed out, Miss Cornell lacked the "aggressiveness" of Stella Campbell and thus reduced the "dramatic tension" that existed between the couple (B269).

Critics generally liked the presentation, but found the letters wordy and somewhat tedious. Most agreed that Aherne and Cornell could have conveyed the nastiness of the characters.

The ending of *Dear Liar* in some ways symbolizes the flickering out of Miss Cornell's career. She had set an enviable record in the quality, variety and success of her productions but after the war, audiences were not interested in her kind of grandeur. Beginning with *Antony and Cleopatra* and with one exception, *The Constant Wife*, her shows failed financially. She had survived because of the "expert" financial supervision of Griffis, Goodyear, and Macy, outside financial backing and her loyal fans on the road. However, even though on her last tour *Dear Liar* was breaking records, her audiences were thinning out. In addition, suitable, well-written plays were difficult to find and critics were less forgiving of her shortcomings. Moreover, the years were beginning to take their toll. When the final curtain fell on *Dear Liar*, it marked the ending of an auspicious career.

# Radio, Film, Television, Recordings

## RADIO

**R01**    *The Barretts of Wimpole Street* (April 14, 1947)

This radio broadcast on KRNT was made in Des Moines, Iowa, when the company was on tour. It was given as a benefit performance.

**R02**    *The Barretts of Wimpole Street* (January 10, 1951)

The Council of the Living Theatre sponsored this presentation of *The Barretts* for the bicentennial of the American professional theatre.

**R03**    *Candida* (May 6, 1951)
("Theatre Guild on the Air," *U.S. Steel Hour*; WNBC Radio Premiere; running time: 60 minutes)

**Credits**
Playwright                                                                    G. Bernard Shaw

**Cast**
Rev. James Mavor Morell                                                          Wesley Addy
Eugene Marchbanks                                                                Alfred Ryder
Candida                                                                     Katharine Cornell

**The Play's History**
        Miss Cornell first played Candida in the Actors' Theatre production, directed by Dudley Digges, in 1924. Guthrie McClintic directed the play when it was revived for the repertory tour in 1933-34. Three years later *Candida* (1937) was revived to go into repertory with *The Wingless Victory* to boost the declining boxoffice receipts. *Candida* did so well that it was continued alone for 2 weeks before the plays were taken on a repertory tour.
        When *Rose Burke*, which was scheduled to open in New York in the spring of 1942, was closed on its tryout tour, Miss Cornell revived *Candida* (1942) with an all-

star cast for a series of 5 performances.  Sponsored by the American Theatre Wing as a benefit for the Army and Navy Relief Fund, it was so successful that 1,000 mail orders were rejected each day.  The play was extended to 27 performances.

On the fifth occasion of its revival *Candida* (1946) was run in repertory with *Antigone* which did not have the drawing power to meet its expenses.  *Candida* was able to offset the losses of *Antigone*.  Although Miss Cornell had retained the freshness of the role, critics thought the play had lost some of the "brilliance" of the 1942 all-star production.  Except for this radio version, it was not revived again.

## Synopsis

(See *Candida*, 1924, S30).

## Reviews

*Newsweek* (5/14/51)--Miss Cornell, who had heretofore shunned radio because she didn't believe she could serve two masters at the same time, had readily consented to play *Candida*, the reviewer stated.  It had been possible to produce a "trimly cut version" of Shaw's play only because his will had not put a specific ban on cutting or radio productions.  The playwright had never allowed adaptations of his full-length works.

By broadcast time, Miss Cornell's apprehension about "radio's constant fading in and out and the lack of theatrical tricks...had departed." *Newsweek* reported that it was "a delightful program" and Miss Cornell was considering the idea of a movie on Florence Nightingale (B056).

## Commentary

No comments were found in *New York Times*, *Time* magazine or other sources.


# FILM


F01     *Stage Door Canteen* (United Artists)
        (Released: June, 1943; black and white; running time: 120 minutes)

## Credits

| | |
|---|---|
| Original screen play | Delmer Daves |
| Director | Frank Borzage |
| Producer | Sol Lesser |
| Presented by | Sol Lesser |
| | in association with American Theatre Wing |
| Songs | Al Dubin, Jimmy Monaco, Richard Rodgers, |
| | Lorenz Hart, Johnny Green and Gertrude Lawrence |

## Cast

| | |
|---|---|
| Eileen | Cheryl Walker |
| "Dakota" Ed Smith | William W. Terry |
| Jean | Marjorie Riordan |
| "California" | Lon McCallister |
| Ella Sue | Margaret Early |
| "Texas" | Michael Harrison |

| | |
|---|---|
| Mamie | Dorothea Kent |
| "Jersey" | Fred Brady |
| Lillian | Marion Shockley |
| The Australian | Patrick O'Moore |
| The Captain | Louis Jean Heydt |

and

| | |
|---|---|
| Judith Anderson | Otto Kruger |
| Henry Armetta | June Lang |
| Benny Baker | Betty Lawford |
| Kenny Baker | Gypsy Rose Lee |
| Tallulah Bankhead | Alfred Lunt |
| Ralph Bellamy | Bert Lytell |
| Edgar Bergen and | Harpo Marx |
| Charlie McCarthy | Aline MacMahon |
| Ray Bolger | Elsa Maxwell |
| Helen Broderick | Helen Menden |
| Ina Claire | Yehudi Menuhin |
| Katharine Cornell | Ethel Merman |
| Lloyd Corrigan | Ralph Morgan |
| Jane Darwell | Alan Mowbray |
| William Demarest | Paul Muni |
| Virginia Field | Elliott Nugent |
| Dorothy Fields | Merle Oberon |
| Gracie Fields | Franklin Pangborn |
| Lynn Fontanne | Brock Pemberton |
| Arlene Francis | George Raft |
| Vinton Freedley | Lanny Ross |
| Lucile Gleason | Selena Royle |
| Virginia Grey | Martha Scott |
| Helen Hayes | Cornelia Otis Skinner |
| Katharine Hepburn | Ned Sparks |
| Hugh Herbert | Bill Stern |
| Jean Hersholt | Ethel Waters |
| Sam Jaffe | Johnny Weissmuller |
| Allan Jenkins | Arleen Whelan |
| George Jessel | Dame May Whitty |
| Roscoe Karns | Ed Wynn |
| Tom Kennedy | |

and the bands of    Count Basie, Xavier Cugat, Benny Goodman, Kay Kyser, Guy Lombardo, Freddy Martin.

### The Film's History

The screen play, which was original, was produced in New York and the west coast to support the Stage Door Canteen, a recreation center set up by theatre people to entertain servicemen. It opened in the basement of the Forty-Fourth Street Theatre, just west of Broadway in New York, on March 1, 1942.

## Synopsis

The scenes, for the most part, take place inside the Stage Door Canteen where lonesome, homesick young men and women in uniform come for a few hours of good cheer. They are entertained by actors, actresses, musicians and other volunteers who serve food, act, sing, talk and try to give the men a spell of happiness. Young women volunteers dance with them to the big bands of Benny Goodman, Kay Kyser and others.

A romance between a soldier and hostess (Cheryl Walker and William Terry) heightens the interest and demonstrates the bravery of young people in wartime. It also tugs at the heartstrings.

## Reviews

*New York Times* (6\25\43) -- Bosley Crowther described Stage Door Canteen as a servicemen's place for "a taste of fun and entertainment" which the public can share through this "bulging and generally heart-warming film." As Crowther said, "virtually every actor and entertainer in the business did a stunt." You will see Katharine Cornell giving an orange to Ron McCallister and reciting from *Romeo and Juliet* and Alfred Lunt washing dishes. Almost all of the profits from the movie go to the support and advancement of the American Theatre Wing. It's good entertainment for a good cause, stated Crowther. It may not appeal to the sophisticates, "but it will fetch honest thrills, tears and laughter from millions throughout the land" (B354).

## Commentary

The Stage Door Canteen in New York did much to help wartime morale. The film gave families and friends in other parts of America a glimpse of the environment where their sons, husbands and sweethearts sought friendship, comraderie, laughter and fun as they tried to forget for a few hours what might lay ahead for them. To be sure, they did not see such a concentration of celebrities but they did see show people who were giving their time and talents toward the war effort. The scene with Katharine Cornell and Lon McCallister is touching; one wishes it could have been longer. (A photograph of this scene appears in Blum's *Pictorial History of the American Theatre*). The film captures the feelings of loneliness, bravado, laughter and sadness that characterized the atmosphere in the Stage Door Canteen. The movie, which sometimes appears on TV, is nostalgic for those of us who were there or had someone in the services.

The American Theatre Wing sent entertainers to men in the services, wherever they were. Miss Cornell's overseas tour with *The Barretts of Wimpole Street* was made possible through this organization after this movie was made. The warm reception *The Barretts* company received from the GIs encouraged the Wing to send other entertainers to war zones.


## TELEVISION

T01    ***The Barretts of Wimpole Street***
       (NBC-TV), *Producer's Showcase*; aired: April 2, 1956; running time: 90 minutes; color).

## Credits
Director                                                    Vincent J. Donehue

| | |
|---|---|
| Production Supervisor | Guthrie McClintic |
| Settings | Otis Riggs |
| Costumes | Jerome Boxhorn |
| Musical Director | George Bassman |
| Producer | Guthrie McClintic |

## Cast

| | |
|---|---|
| Elizabeth Moulton-Barrett | Katharine Cornell |
| Robert Browning | Anthony Quayle |
| Edward Moulton-Barrett | Henry Daniell |
| Henrietta | Nancy Coleman |
| Arabel | Margalo Gillmore |
| Wilson | Brenda Forbes |

and

Donald Harron, Geoffrey Lumb, Edward Hunt, Lisa Daniels, William Podmore, Charles McCauley, Charles Forsythe, Roderick Walker, Kendall Clark and others.

## The Play's History

  *The Barretts* was first played in England at the Malvern Festival on August 19, 1930. After at least 27 producers had rejected the play on the basis that the public would have little interest in the Victorian love story, it seemed a propitious time for the McClintics to form their own company in order to produce plays of her choice. *The Barretts* was Miss Cornell's greatest success, launching her on a stage career in which she was to become a "genuine giant" (B179).

  After several revivals, long tours and her 6-month overseas tour of the European was zone, it broke house records for legitimate drama at the Boston Opera House (1945). On May 22, 1947, in San Francisco, Miss Cornell played Elizabeth for the 1000th time. By the end of that tour (June 7, 1947), she had played the role 1, 019 times. Because it was the play she knew best and because *The Barretts* had reached its 25th anniversary, she selected it for her TV debut.

## Synopsis

  (See *The Barretts of Wimpole Street*, 1931, S35)

## Reviews

  *New York Times* (4/3/56)--Jack Gould thought television had accentuated the play's weaknesses. The close-ups and intimacy of the camera put emphasis on the psychological narrative rather than the larger mood of *The Barretts*. Miss Cornell was both "ethereal and quietly indomitable" and the love scenes were played with tenderness and inspiration, Gould reported. "The episodic camera treatment, however, did not give her full opportunity to sustain...the glowing magic of a woman in love."

  Anthony Quayle was "more courtly than impassioned," and the drama was "never deeply gripping," in Gould's view. He directed his disappointment toward the medium, saying, "More could have been done with the cameras to implement her artistry." His hope was that, even if this was a little disappointing, Miss Cornell would appear on TV again (B081).

*Variety* (4/4/56)--The trade journal called the show "an incandescent gem." The reviewer proclaimed it to be "one of the top, magnificent performances in the whole catalog of 90-minute "Producer's Showcase color spectaculars....No finer vehicle could have been chosen for Miss Cornell's TV debut." Describing Miss Cornell's "warm, expressive genius," her vocal control, "the frugality of movement" and lack of "any affectation," the reviewer stated that "it was well nigh inconceivable that this was her first television performance." Quayle as Browning, and Daniell as the sadistic father as well as Gillmore, Coleman and Forbes received commendation for superb performances (B300).

*Newsweek* (4/9/56)--The reviewer said that Miss Cornell blazed a new trail in presenting the 8th version of her role as Elizabeth on television. More people saw this portrayal than all those who had seen it in her many stage performances. She had taken 3 years to decide to try TV but the idea of a huge audience and the celebration of the 25th anniversary of the play's Broadway opening had overcome her resistence. She toned down her gestures and facial expression by at least 50%, she said. She admitted she would like to do *Candida* and *The Doctor's Dilemma* if *The Barretts* proved to be popular on TV (B082).

## Commentary

The critics' comments identify the pitfalls of television: the difficulty of building and sustaining emotions and the overall mood of a drama. The weaknesses in the scenario and camera techniques can be attributed to the early stage in the development of television. This TV special and the only other television appearance she made (T02) remain in kinescope form (B179).

******

T02    *There Shall Be No Night*
       (NBC-TV, *Hallmark Hall of Fame*; aired: March 17, 1957; color & black & white; running time: 90 minutes).

## Credits

| | |
|---|---|
| Playwright | Robert E. Sherwood |
| Screen Adaptation | Morton Wishengrad |
| Director | George Schaefer |
| Producer | George Schaefer |

## Cast

| | |
|---|---|
| Dr. Kurloy Valkay | Charles Boyer |
| Miranda Valkay | Katharine Cornell |
| Dave Corween | Ray Walston |
| Eric Valkay | Bradford Dillman |
| Katalin Tor | Phyllis Love |
| Uncle Vlayhoc | Theodore Bikel |
| Major Rutowski | Karel Stepanek |
| Frank Olmstead | Gerald Hilken |
| Gus Shuman | Val Avery |

## The Play's History

Sherwood made Finland the original setting of the play during the 1930 Soviet invasion of that country. In 1940, Alfred Lunt and Lynn Fontanne starred in it on Broadway. In his adaptation for television, Wishengrad changed the scene to Hungary just before the uprising in the spring of 1956, and included events of the previous 17 years. Characters remain the same.

## Synopsis

A distinguished man of science and winner of the Nobel Prize for his study of the mind fights against the belief in war. A man with enormous Christian faith and optimism, he is forced to take up a gun after he loses his son in the fighting. He also dies courageously. In the end his wife is waiting with a rifle to defend her home.

## Reviews

*New York Times* (3/18/57)--In the process of altering the events in the play, "much of Sherwood's specific eloquence and indignation was vitiated," wrote Jack Gould. The fast moving events left little opportunity "to explore the soul-searching anguish of the scientist." Mr. Boyer's part did not allow for the "fuller and more intellectual perspective that exists in the original." Gould was disappointed in Miss Cornell's role as well. The climactic scene in which she reads her husband's last letter was touching, but her part, in general, lacked "dimension." Furthermore, Gould noted that Mr. Sherwood had been "articulate about the Communist premordial beast" but this revival had merely "wrung its hands" (B080).

## Commentary

It was not customary for the camera crew to break into spontaneous applause when a show went off the air, but that is what the crew did. Miss Cornell did not realize the honor they had paid her. For both this play and *The Barretts* she had reached audiences of 28 million people, more than she had reached with her stage performances.

This was Charles Boyer's debut in a dramatic part on live television although he had appeared in shows filmed for television and was a partner in a Hollywood company that produced many of them. After two weeks of rehearsal, he thought appearing on a live show was less trying than movie work.

Why did Miss Cornell not continue with TV? No explanation was made, but one can imagine that there may have been several reasons. Perhaps television cameras intensified the stagefright that she had always experienced before a performance. Perhaps, too, she feared that the intimate scrutiny of the camera would confirm what she had been told as a child--that she was not attractive. Or, maybe it was just too late to begin the mastery of a new medium. Whatever the reason, Miss Cornell did not make another appearance on TV, so she is only a memory for the fortunate ones who saw her on stage or in one of these television appearances.

## RECORDINGS

In 1974, Paul Kresh, a contributing editor to "Stereo Review" in *The New York Times*, did a check of archives for recordings of the "charismatic voices" of theatre's "Great Ladies." He found disks and cylinders of Sarah Bernhardt and speculated that records of Eleanora Duse or Nazimova could be located. He found, also, that British actresses Judith Anderson, Edith Evans, Sybil Thorndike and Margaret Webster have left legacies of albums, records and cassettes.

Of American great ladies, at that time, no recordings of Helen Hayes seemed to be available, although her voice is preserved on film.  Moreover, when Katharine Cornell died in June of 1974, she left only one record on the market, a Caedmon disk (D10 and D11 listed below).  On one side it features Miss Cornell in  the three love scenes from *The Barretts of Wimpole Street* with Anthony Quayle; the other side records her readings of Elizabeth Barrett Browning's *Sonnets from the Portuguese*.  The neglect of these great ladies "is undeserved," Kresh laments (B122).

A search of current catalogs indicates that the situation has changed very little.  In "Spoken Arts" section, the popular *Schwann Spectrum* (Winter 1992/93) lists Elizabeth Barrett Browning: *Sonnets from the Portuguese*, but the reader is not Katharine Cornell.  A computer search indicates that, in addition to the Caedmon disk, several other recordings exist and may be found in some libraries.  Information is incomplete.

**D01**      **"Actors Talk About Acting"   7923-A**

Katharine Cornell.  Dramatic Publishers (Phonodisc).

**D02**      **Adventures in Reading**

Katharine Cornell.  Harcourt, Brace.  1963.

**D03**      **An Interview with Katharine Cornell**

Dramatic Publishers.  1960.

**D04**      **Tribute to Ethel Barrymore**

At Miss Barrymore's seventieth birthday celebration the voice of Miss Cornell is recorded along with the voices of many other notables.  The recording of her two-sentence tribute is held in the Michigan State University Voice Library at East Lansing, Michigan.


******


Following is a chronological list of the recordings which are held in the *Rodgers & Hammerstein Archives of Recorded Sound* at The New York Public Library for the Performing Arts at 40 Lincoln Center Plaza, New York City.  Information includes recording dates, the label name and issue number (for commercial releases) and the Library's classmark number.  Recordings are available for on-site listening.  The library may be able to provide professional quality phonocopies of the commercial recordings if copies cannot be found at out-of-print dealers.  Copies of private tapes cannot be made without explicit written permission from the proprietary rights owners.  The label name and number follow the entry number (i.e. D02).

**D05**      *The Barretts of Wimpole Street*. **Selections.  2299**

Katharine Cornell and Brian Aherne in selections from the play. Rehearsal recorded October 28, 1940, from acetates. (1 tape reel; 7.5 ips; mono.; 10 inch).

**D06**      *The Barretts of Wimpole Street. Selections.* **2299**

With the Army Hour, Katharine Cornell and Brian Aherne. Rehearsal, recorded November 4, 1940, from acetate. (1 tape reel; 7.5 ips.; mono.; 10 inch).

**D07**      **Army Hour**    **2299**

USO program, featuring Katharine Cornell, Dinah Shore, Bob Hope, Jack Benny, Jane Froman, and others. Broadcast October 14, 1945, over KFI, Los Angeles (NBC network). From acetate. (1 tape reel; 7.5 ips.; mono; 10 inch).

**D08**      **Victory Clothing Collection**    **2300**

From World Broadcasting System transcription (master no.:BB 44565/6), produced by Ken Thomas. Broadcast January 1946 (?). Contents include *"Homecoming"* starring Katharine Cornell. (1 tape reel; 7.5 ips.; mono.; 10 inch).

**D09**      *The Barretts of Wimpole Street.* **2296-2297**

Katharine Cornell and Anthony Quayle, in *Producers' Showcase* television production, 1954. From acetates. (2 tape reels; 7.5 ips.; mono.; 10 inch).

**D10**      *The Barretts of Wimpole Street: The Three Love Scenes.* **LRXS 112**

Read by Katharine Cornell and Anthony Quayle. Caedmon TC1071 (Phonodisc). 1957. (1s.; 33.3rpm; 12 inch).

**D11**      **Elizabeth (Barrett) Browning,** *Sonnets from the Portuguese.* **LRXS 112**

Read by Katharine Cornell are sonnets 1, 2, 5, 6, 7, 8, 10, 14, 16, 18, 20, 21, 22, 23, 26, 28, 33, 38, 43, 44. Caedmon TC 1071 (Phonodisc). 1957. (1s; 33.3rpm; 12 inch).

**D12**      *Dear Liar*    **151-153**

Adaptation of letters by Jerome Kilty with Katharine Cornell. (3 reels; 15 ips.; 7 inch).

\*\*\*\*\*\*

Following is a list of some of the recordings from the Nancy Hamilton sound recording collection in which the participation of "K.C." is identified. This collection has not been catalogued and information is sketchy.

**D13**    **Katharine Cornell Reads Kirsten Flagstad Translations**

Apparently these are translations of songs or arias from the soprano's repertory. 1962 and 1963. (12 tapes, 3 being marked "Master tapes").

**D14**    **Cornell and Hardwicke Interview about *Antigone***

May 7, 1946. (1 tape reel; 5 inch).

**D15**    **K. C. Message to Will Gibson**

No date. (1 tape reel, 5 inch). (Will Gibson unidentified).

**D16**    **K. C. Broadcast: *Florence Nightingale***

1951. (1 tape reel, 5 inch; 1 tape reel, 7 inch). (No information located about this broadcast).

**D17**    **K. C. First Practice Recording: Narration for Helen Keller Film**

March 8, 1953. (1 tape reel, 7 inch).

**D18**    **Rosalind Russell Birthday Message to K. C.**

September 13, 1974. (1 tape reel, 7 inch).

# Bibliography

This bibliography represents an extensive listing of the print references to Katharine Cornell. It contains a listing of books, magazine, journal and newspaper articles that give insight into her life, her career and the plays she produced. Because she was a very private person who led a quiet life, she was not an exciting personality for the press. However, Ray Henderson realized the public's desire to admire a woman of good breeding and by focusing on these qualities, he kept her public interested and eager to see her next show. He discussed her thoughts, her plans, the honors she received, her activities and her audiences.

Critics' reviews, many of which have not been included, make up about half of more than 500 items in this bibliography. Miss Cornell's name also appears in a number of theatre books which have not been listed. Titles of newspapers are reported as they appeared in the source in which they were found.

## Books, Journals, Periodicals and Newspaper Articles

B001    "Actress of the Month." *Theatre Magazine* 42 (August 8, 1925):8.

The caption under her photograph claims that Cornell has won the position of one of America's most significant actresses and imparts to a role a "spiritual fire."

B002    "Actresses Honored at Elmira Exercises." *New York Times* (June 15, 1937):11:2.

Katharine Cornell and Helen Hayes received honorary degrees of Doctor of Letters at Elmira College, in New York. Dr. Peter Cornell represented his daughter, who was unable to receive the honor in person.

B003    Adams, Mildred. "Mrs. Browning on Broadway." *Woman's Journal* (March, 1931):12.

Calls Cornell's production of The Barretts "romance incarnate." Her portrayal of Elizabeth is "moving, vivid, and lovable."

**B004**     Aherne, Brian. *A Proper Job*. Boston: Houghton Mifflin, 1969.

Aherne reveals himself as a vital, yet genteel and hardworking man in his account of a varied life of acting which he undertook to make a living. He expresses gratitude to all who helped him, particularly the McClintics, and pays tribute to a great friend, Miss Cornell. He relates experiences with Orson Welles, Tyrone Power and other actors he met while working with Miss Cornell. He feels Welles had some animosity toward him when McClintic gave Aherne the part of Mercutio which Welles expected to play.

**B005**     "American Academy Arts & Letters Award to K. Cornell." *New York Times* (May 21, 1959):28:2.

Miss Cornell receives the Medal for Good Speech, an award intended to bring attention to correct and natural diction.

**B006**     "...And Juliet is the Sun." *Literary Digest* 119 (January 5, 1935):19.

Describing Miss Cornell's *Romeo and Juliet* as "a living, breathing drama," the critic compliments her for her grace, voice and understanding of Juliet which she played with "burning ardor."

**B007**     "Antony and Cleopatra." *Life* 23 (December 1, 1947):76-78.

Discusses the cost of the most expensive of the 16 plays Cornell had produced. Describes her Spartan discipline and routine on tour.

**B008**     Arce, Hector. *The Secret Life of Tyrone Power*. New York: Morrow, 1979.

As expected from the title, the biography focuses on the private life, particularly the personal turmoil and unhappiness Power experienced. It does mention Miss Cornell and Power's gratitude for her help with his career.

**B009**     Atkinson, Brooks. "Katharine Cornell in the Barretts." In *American Theatre as Seen by Its Critics, 1752-1934*. Edited by Montrose Moses and J. M. Brown. New York: Norton, 1934, pp. 295-297.

These samples of reviewers' criticisms span almost a century of plays. The first-hand reactions help "to capture a sense of what our theater of the past has been like." Among them is Atkinson's February 22, 1932 review of *The Barretts* in which he points out her gifts as an actress and challenges her to leave her mark on drama by selecting roles responsibly. He proclaims her Elizabeth to be a "masterpiece;" it leaves the audience with a "feeling of exultation."

**B010**     Atkinson, Brooks. "Lady of the Theater." *New York Times* (June 10, 1974):34:1.

In this tribute to Katharine Cornell upon the event of her death, Atkinson said, "she made something beautiful and exhilarating out of the theater....Her productions were on the highest possible artistic level." Although she lacked self-confidence, when she stepped on stage "that quiet splendor filled the stage."

**B011**    Atkinson, Brooks and Albert Hirschfeld.   "S. N. Behrman, No Time for Comedy." In *The Lively Years 1920-1973*. New York: Association Press, 1973, pp. 144-147.

In this outline of plays, the authors discuss Behrman's intent in *No Time for Comedy*, which they consider to be his best play.

**B012**    Bailey, Ralph S. "The Curtain Rises." *Independent* (November 12, 1927):482.

Expresses disappointment in Maugham's play, *The Letter*, but judges Cornell's acting to be "superb."

**B013**    Banham, Martin, ed. *The Cambridge Guide to World Theatre*. Cambridge: Cambridge University Press, 1988.

A comprehensive view of the history and present worldwide theatre. In a short summary on Cornell the editor states that she could create the illusion that "a memorable play was being witnessed when in fact the vehicle was weak."

**B014**    "Barretts of Wimpole Street." *Life* 18 (April 16, 1945):105-108.

Reviews the production and reports Cornell to be "the most absorbing personality" among U.S. actresses.

**B015**    Barrow, Kenneth. *Helen Hayes: First Lady of the American Theatre*. Garden City, New York: Doubleday & Co., 1985.

Barrow states that Helen Hayes "always shunned the title of 'First Lady'" which she claimed should go to Katharine Cornell. A number of complimentary references to Miss Cornell are made.

**B016**    Barrymore, Ethel. *Memories: An Autobiography*. New York: Harper & Bros., 1955.

Chronicles Barrymore's experiences, her marriage to Russell Colt, birth of her children and stage appearances. Among her successes was *The Constant Wife*, which she played for three years. Reveals a talented woman before her demise. Refers to Cornell as "that lovely, glowing creature."

**B017**    Barton, Ralph. "Theatre." *Life* 95 (February 28, 1930):18.

Expresses disappointment in *Dishonored Lady* and criticizes Cornell for being too artistic.

**B018**     "Baylor U. in Tribute to Robert Browning." *New York Times* (December 3, 1951):7:8.

Special tribute was paid Robert Browning at the dedication of Baylor University's Armstrong-Browning library at which Mr. Aherne and Miss Cornell received honorary degrees.

**B019**     "Baylor U. Dedicates Its Browning Library." *New York Times* (December 4, 1951):42:5.

At the dedication ceremony of Baylor University's new Armstrong-Browning library, Katharine Cornell and Brian Aherne were a chief attraction.  They did a scene from *The Barretts*, received honorary Doctor of Law Degrees, and were honored at a luncheon following the exercises.

**B020**     Beyer, William.  "The State of the Theater: Mid-season High Lights." *School & Society* 67 (January 31, 1948): 85-86.

Points out the weaknesses in *Antony & Cleopatra* and praises Cornell's acting.

**B021**     Block, Maxine, ed.  *Current Biography.*  New York: Wilson, 1941.

Contains a comprehensive biographical sketch of Cornell's life and career.  States that her "psychic sensitiveness" is her principal artistic asset.

**B022**     Blum, Daniel and John Willis.  *A Pictorial History of the American Theatre, 1960-1980.*  5th ed.  New York: Crown Publishers, 1981.

The history of each year begins with an opening text and photographs.  Includes a full-page photograph of Cornell as Elizabeth.

**B023**     Bordman, Gerald.  *Oxford Companion to American Theatre.*  New York: Oxford University Press, 1984, pp. 166-167.

A listing with brief explanations of Cornell's plays.  Her performance as Candida, in 1924, "consolidated her reputation and was followed by two of her most sensational roles," Iris March and Leslie Crosbie.  Bordman reports that, as one of the greatest actresses of her era, she was more willing than other actresses to extend her range and attempt classics.

**B024**     Boyd, Ernest.  "Broadway Reveries." *Theatre Guild Magazine* 6 (May, 1929):15-16.

Review of good things in the theatre, one being *The Age of Innocence*.

**B025**     Brady, Frank.  *Citizen Kane: A Biography.*  New York: Chas. Scribner's Sons, 1989.

Brady maintains that, being a Shakespearean scholar, Welles's "presence gave assurance to the McClintics in their first Shakespearean venture." Miss Cornell scolded him for his bizarre behavior in public as well as other infractions. He did not receive the acclaim he expected for his portrayal of Tybalt, except from director John Houseman.

**B026**    Bronner, Edwin. *The Encyclopedia of the American Theatre 1900-1975.* New York: A.S. Barnes, 1980.

Contains information about plays produced on and off Broadway; 22 entries about plays in which Cornell appeared. Also lists awards and honors.

**B027**    Brown, John Mason. *Dramatis Personnae.* New York: Viking Press, 1963.

Includes reviews of Cornell as Joan d'Arc, Juliet and Cleopatra. As the Maid, Brown says her performance  flamed with an "inner radiance," her Juliet was "youth incarnate," and as Cleopatra "she has never given a more enchanting performance."

**B028**    Brown, John Mason. "Katharine Cornell Presents Bernard Shaw's 'Saint Joan.'" *Theatre Arts* 20 (June, 1936):463- 464.

Brown compliments McClintic for the direction, the extraordinary casting and Cornell "who glows with all the radiant qualities of the text" for "one of the finest things she has done."

**B029**    Brown, John Mason. "Seeing Things: Overseas Edition of the Brownings." *Saturday Review* 28 (April 7, 1945):20-22.

Brown reviews Cornell's revival of *The Barretts* seen by the GIs in the European war zone. States that it "continues to be the finest of her many fine performances." Her "spirit" overcomes whatever may be wrong with the play and the times. Asking why this play was an inspired selection for "men facing death," Brown can only guess at the reasons.

**B030**    Brustein, Robert. "Chekhov's Dramaturgy in 'The Three Sisters.'" In *Anton Chekov's Plays*, trans. and edited by K. Bristow. New York: Norton, 1977.

Brustein explains how Chekhov subordinates plot to characters, highlights inertia and irresponsibility and uses rhythmic sound effects to evoke poetic illusion. He functions as a realist and a moralist.

**B031**    Bryant, Mary. "Teenagers Interview Katharine Cornell." *St. Louis Times Star* (March 8, 1949).

Miss Cornell warned the teenagers who were aspiring to careers in the theatre that it is a hard life.

**B032**    "Canteen in London Opens Doors Tonight." *New York Times*, August 7, 1944, 7:9.

Announces the opening of the American Theatre Wing in London and reports a cable from Cornell with the message that the first overseas performance of *The Barretts*, at Naples Opera House, was "very thrilling."

**B033**     Carb, David. "The Letter." *Vogue* (November 15, 1927):166.

Suggests that Cornell's radiance may save the play, if it can be saved.

**B034**     Carmody, Deidre. "Katharine Cornell Stars in the Role of Raconteur." *New York Times* (January 11, 1974):18:1.

Because of Miss Cornell's failing health, the presentation of the American National Theater and Academy (ANTA) award took place in her New York town house in the presence of a few close friends. Given as "an expression of gratitude from a nation for continued artistic excellence," the medal had been given only once before--to Alfred Lunt and Lynn Fontanne in 1972. Like "a raconteur who knows how to tell a good story," Miss Cornell reminisced about herself and clowned when having her picture taken.

**B035**     Carrier, Jeffrey L. *Tallulah Bankhead.* New York: Greenwood Press, 1991.

In a bio-bibliograpy of Bankhead, Carrier gives an overview of the life and career of the actress who played with Katharine Cornell in *Nice People.* He mentions the huge success that Cornell was having in *The Green Hat* at the same time that Miss Bankhead's version in London was not being so fortunate.

**B036**     Cheney, Sheldon. *The Art Theater.* 2d ed. rev. and enlarged. New York: Knopf, 1917, 1925.

Discusses the conditions of major aspects of the Art theater as differentiated from commercial theater. Representative talented young actresses, including Cornell, were eager to break away to have "the permanency and wider artistic opportunity of repertory."

**B037**     Chinoy, Helen Krich and Linda Walsh Jenkins, eds. *Women in American Theatre.* Revised and expanded edition. New York: Theatre Communications Group, 1981, 1987.

The editors cite Miss Cornell as one of the actresses who had sought more personal control over her performances by forming her own company as Mrs. Fiske and Eva Le Gallienne had done. In this way they were able to perform "personally & culturally meaningful plays."

**B038**     Churchill, Allen. "Behind the Curtain." *Saturday Review* 38 (October 22, 1955):21.

Description from McClintic's biography *Me and Kit* of the difficulties both he and Miss Cornell had overcome to reach success.

**B039**     Cocroft, Thoda. "It's in the Stars." *Theatre Magazine* 52 (January, 1931):37-38.

Despite critics' dismissal of *Dishonored Lady* as "cheap melodrama," Cocroft predicts it will draw audiences because of Cornell's exoticism and "emotional magic."

**B040**    Coe, Richard L.  "Cornell: It Had To Be The Best." *Courier-Journal & Times*, June 23, 1974.

Coe pays tribute to Miss Cornell following her death. He decribed her as "quality." She did nothing that was "chintzy," but selected the best casts, designs, and the unknowns she chose were "winners." He described her voice as being "of brown velvet," and said her Juliet "sparkled with youthful wonder."

**B041**    Cole, Toby and Helen K. Chinoy. *Actors on Acting*. New York:Crown, 1954.

Cornell is selected as one of the great actresses of the time to explain her acting theory and techniques.

**B042**    "College to Honor Stage Figures." *New York Times* (May 30, 1956):13:2.

Kenyon College in Gambier, Ohio, awarded honorary Doctor of Literature degrees to Katharine Cornell and Guthrie McClintic.

**B043**    Collins, Charles. "Katharine Cornell's Plans for World Tour Brings Tragedy." *Chicago Tribune* (October 10, 1937).

Announces the death of Ray Henderson whose plane crashed while he was arranging for Miss Cornell's world tour.

**B044**    Corey, Melinda & George Ochoa. *A Cast of Thousands: A Compendium of Who Played What in Film*. New York: Stonesong Press, 1992.

Lists movies, dates, producers, directors and casts.

**B045**    "Cornell, Hardwicke Bring Yule Surprise to Critic." *New York Times* (December 24, 1950):36:2.

After Miss Cornell closed *Captain Carvallo* because she felt it was not good enough for Broadway, she and five members of the company gave a performance at the home of ailing critic William F. McDermott. It came as a delightful Christmas surprise to the critic, who could be "discerning and caustic." This time he said, "Magnificent, wonderful," probably expressing his pleasure at the thoughtful gesture rather than the play itself.

**B046**    Cornell, Katharine and Alice Griffin. "A Good Play Will Always Find a Good Audience." *Theatre Arts* 38 (May, 1954):27-29.

Believing that many people throughout America want and appreciate good plays, Cornell praises the receptiveness and astuteness of audiences she meets on tours.

**B047**     Cornell, Katharine and Ruth Woodbury Sedgwick. *I Wanted to Be An Actress*. New York: Random House, 1938, 1939.

An "as told to" autobiography. Cornell reminisces to Sedgwick about her life and career, highlighting her sketchy story with experiences and feelings. The book is somewhat vague about details and dates; the second half consists of credits, casts and reviews of her plays, the last being *The Wingless Victory*. Sedgwick pays Cornell the highest tribute for her ability to give a role a "fresher, deeper, truer interpretation" with each performance. Believes she alone fuses her "genius, physical and vocal endowment, technique, discipline and responsibility to the public."

**B048**     Cornell, Katharine. "Actress-Manager." *Scholastic* 36 (April 8, 1940):17-19.

Taking from her autobiography, Cornell discusses the formation of her company, *The Barretts,* and her health problems.

**B049**     Cornell, Katharine. "Audiences I Have Known." *New York Sun*, November 19, 1924.

She discusses the actors concerns about audiences and their effect on the actors. Comparing opening night playgoers to those who attend a closing performance, she explains some of the factors, such as current events and holidays that affect audience responses.

**B050**     Cornyn, Stan. *A Selective Index to Theatre Magazine*. New York: Scarecrow Press, 1964.

A useful index of articles. Contains approximately 45,000 references to authors, subjects, dramatic works. Articles selected for scholarly interest.

**B051**     Crothers, Rachel. "Nice People." In *Best Plays of 1920-21*, edited by Burns Mantle. Boston: Small, Maynard, 1921: 224-268.

Excerpts from the play with comments of the critics who considered the play to be one of the best plays of the season, at least in the first two acts.

**B052**     "Curtain Going Up." *Time* 62 (August 31, 1953):59.

Discusses the forthcoming *Prescott Proposals* with a brief synopsis of the play.

**B053**     Dane, Clemence. *Will Shakespeare: An Invention*. New York: 1924.

Dane's play about Shakespeare depicts him as an insignificant but gifted writer who is merely a pawn in the hands of his wife, Mary Fitton and the Queen.

**B054**     De Casseres, Benjamin. "Does Stage Realism Really Reflect Life?" *Theatre Magazine* 50(July, 1929):14-15.

The author observes that plays which are closer to realism are more apt to become hits and have long runs. *The Age of Innocence* is realistic romance in which "the beautiful and bewitching Cornell, with her gowns and her hats" lured crowds to the Empire Theatre.

**B055**    De Casseres, Benjamin. "Broadway to Date." *Arts & Decoration* 34 (March-April, 1931):46.

Discusses Elizabeth Barrett, Cornell's finest role yet.

**B056**    "Debut of Veterans." *Newsweek* 37 (May 14, 1951):69-70.

Comments on Miss Cornell's radio presentation of *Candida* on "Theatre Guild on the Air." Calling it "a delightful program," *Time* reports that Miss Cornell is considering the idea of her first full-length movie from biography of Florence Nightingale.

**B057**    Dimmit, Richard Bertrand. *Title Guide to the Talkies.* New York: Scarecrow Press, 1965.

A good reference for locating early movies.

**B058**    "Dog That Never Missed Cue on Broadway Dies." *Baltimore Sun* (July 4, 1937).

Flush, Elizabeth Barrett's dog, became the favorite dog of the decade, and played 709 performances. News of his death was broadcast worldwide.

**B059**    Douglas, Kirk. *The Ragman's Son: An Autobiography.* New York: Simon & Schuster, 1988.

Douglas candidly relates his early life as the son of an immigrant Russian-Jewish ragman and his later life in becoming an actor. The discrimination he suffered as a poverty-stricken Jew motivated him to succeed. In *The Three Sisters* he overplayed his bit part. Coveting another role, he felt duly chastised by Miss Cornell, but was grateful for the opportunity to work with great artists.

**B060**    "Drama, Music & Sleuthing on the Radio." *New York Times* (May 6, 1957):X9.

A radio performance of *Candida* with Katharine Cornell, Wesley Addy and Alfred Ryder, to take place that evening, is announced.

**B061**    Duerr, Edwin. *The Length and Depth of Acting.* New York: Holt, Rinehart & Winston, 1963.

In his history of acting, Duerr gives attention to the theories of acting and the two opposing schools of thought, one stressing the protean quality of an actor and the other the actor-rhetorician. Gives insight into technical and psychological problems in acting.

**B062**     "Dykstra Depicts Tyranny by Vote." *New York Times* (May 24, 1938):17:1.

At the 113th commencement of Hobart College where her grandfather and great-grandfather had been trustees, Miss Cornell was awarded an honorary Doctor of Letters degree. Dr. Clarence Dykstra, president of the University of Wisconsin and commencement speaker, also received an honorary degree. The award to Miss Cornell was in recognition of her "paving the way for a revival of a great cultural institution."

**B063**     Eaton, Walter Pritchard. "Reviewing the American Theatre." *Theatre Guild Magazine* (October, 1928):15.

In 1928, Eaton writes that taking a company on the road is an exception because movies are more attractive and the successful Broadway plays have lost appeal for large parts of the country. Eaton suggests that intelligent plays with good companies producing them should be brought to the patrons.

**B064**     Eustis, Morton. "An Actor Attacks His Part--V, Katharine Cornell." *Theatre Arts* 21 (January, 1937):37-51.

Cornell explains her approach to acting. To her it is the creation of "an illusion of reality" which is destroyed by personal exhibitionism. She believes an actor must accurately select "significant things." McClintic's coaching is a great help to her.

**B065**     Eustis, Morton. "The Director Takes Command." *Theatre Arts* 20 (February, 1936):114-120.

Eustis interviews McClintic who explains his philosophy of directing and his belief in the "higher value" of a play. He visualizes scenes in color, gives greatest care to casting and maps out action as actors read their parts.

**B066**     Eustis, Morton. "New Hope for the Road." *Theatre Arts* 18 (February, 1934):943-951.

Discusses Broadway wiseacres' pessimism about Cornell's plan for her 1933-34 tour. When she grossed $700,000 in the first 6 months, she "paved the way for a rebirth of the once prosperous road." At least 6 other companies followed her example with extensive tours. Eustis concludes that if good, well-acted plays are taken on tour, audiences will see them.

**B067**     Fergusson, Francis. "A Month of the Theatre." *Bookman* 73 (April, 1931):182-83.

Not a fan of Cornell or *The Barretts*, Fergusson says that, with her "taste for trailing skirts, sofas and suffering," she should have been born earlier.

**B068**     "Film Highlights of the Week." *New York Times* (March 28, 1937):XI:29:4.

Reports the rumor that Miss Cornell might consider doing a movie, possibly *Wingless Victory,* if the script pleases her.

**B069**  Forbes, Bryan. *Dame Edith Evans, Ned's Girl.* Boston: Little, Brown & Co., 1977.

Her father's favorite, Evans was called Ned's girl. One of the Great English actresses of this century, Evans was playing the Nurse in Cornell's *Romeo and Juliet* when her husband died. Cornell found Evans to be "an absolute dream to work with." In reflecting on her early life, Evans learned much about herself and, hopefully, realized that she was leaving a rich legacy for her readers.

**B070**  "Friends, Neighbors Gather in Miss Cornell's Memory." *Vineyard Gazette.* Martha's Vineyard, Mass. (June 28, 1974).

A description of the service held in memory of Miss Cornell in Association Hall which she had renovated. Recordings of her voice were interspersed with music as grieving friends reminisced about their associations with her.

**B071**  Funke, Lewis and John E. Booth. *Actors Talk About Acting.* New York: Random House, 1961.

The authors interview 14 stars for this book. Cornell discloses family influences that helped her develop self-discipline, describes her routine and process in developing a role. It requires hard work, struggle, and imagination.

**B072**  Gage, Freda, ed. *Who's Who in the Theatre.* 14th ed. London: Pitman, 1967, 1972.

Information about Katharine Cornell is similar to that in other encyclopedias.

**B073**  Gassner, John, ed. *A Treasury of the Theatre.* 3rd ed. New York: Simon & Schuster, distrib. by Holt, Rinehart & Winston, 1935, 1965.

Discusses Shaw and his plays. He stated that Shaw revealed "a spirit highly responsive to the nobility and loneliness of exceptional people." His mastery of characterization in *Candida* and *Saint Joan* is "beyond dispute."

**B074**  Gelman, Morris. "A Theatre Portrait: Katharine Cornell." *The Theatre* (January, 1960):17.

Gelman calls Cornell "a living legend," who seeks perfection and is "imbued with a magnetic and inspirational something." In approaching a role, Cornell becomes absorbed in the part she is doing at the moment. She has no past favorites.

**B075**  Gillmore, Margalo and Patricia Collinge. *The B.O.W.S.* New York: Harcourt, Brace, 1945.

Gillmore, who was in the overseas company, kept an account of the actors' experiences as they toured with *The Barretts of Wimpole Street* to the front lines in the European war zone.  Collaborating with Collinge, she relates the experiences and portrays Miss Cornell as a real trouper.

**B076**    Golden, Sylvia B.  "America's First Civic Theatre." *Theatre Magazine* 48 (October, 1928):20-21.

The history of Jessie Bonstelle's civic theatre, which became a vital part of the city's culture, reveals Bonstelle's desire to revive the love for spoken drama.  It was in this theatre that Cornell got invaluable training.

**B077**    Goodrich, Marc.  "Who is the Best American Actress? *Theatre Magazine* 42 (December, 1925):9.

Enumerating the plays in which Cornell has appeared,  Goodrich considers them mediocre except for *Candida*.  He believes her personality accounts for her popularity.

**B078**    Gordon, Ruth.  *An Open Book.*  New York: Doubleday, 1980.

In a "freewheeling" style Gordon recalls the lessons of a lifetime that she learned from "her life's many stages."  She reminisces about an outline she wrote for a comedy about 23 Beekman Street, based on what one would see if the front wall were removed from the McClintic's brownstone house.  She wrote what maybe went on and sent it to the McClintics.  Makes references to *The Three Sisters*.  She was a hit in it and married Garson Kanin during the play's run.

**B079**    Gordon, Ruth.  *My Side: The Autobiography of Ruth Gordon.*  New York: Harper & Row, 1976.

Written at age 80, Gordon's story of her barnstorming days, her movie roles and stage successes includes her role as Natasha in *The Three Sisters*.  Interwoven are the stories of theatre people including Katharine Cornell and Guthrie McClintic to whom Gordon felt she owed "half of her career."

**B080**    Gould, Jack.  "TV: Play by Sherwood." *New York Times* (March 18, 1957):56:6.

Gould reviews the modernized version of Robert Sherwood's *There Shall Be No Night*, adapted by Morton Wishengrad for TV.  The severe trimming of the parts allowed little opportunity for giving dimension to characters.  Moreover, the outrage at Communist aggression which Sherwood articulated was merely "hand wringing" in the adaptation.

**B081**    Gould, Jack.  "TV: Katharine Cornell Makes Debut." New York Times, April 3, 1956, 71:1.

Gould reports on Cornell's TV adaptation of *The Barretts*. The camera tended to emphasize the psychological narrative, thus losing the enveloping mood of the play. The cameras could have done more to "implement her artistry." He would have liked to see more of her facial reactions as she responded to Browning.

**B082**    "Grand Entrance." *Newsweek* 47 (April 9, 1956):104.

Reports Cornell's television appearance on the 25th anniversary of *The Barretts*. If successful, the McClintics indicated they would be eager to do other shows on television.

**B083**    Granville-Barker, Harley. "Shakespeare's Dramatic Art." In *A Comparison to Shakespeare Studies*, edited by Harley Granville-Barker and G. B. Harrison. Cambridge: Cambridge University Press, 1966.

This volume was intended as an extension of Shakespearean study. The scholarly essays, representing diversified opinions, focus on the poet-dramatist: his life, his art, the theatre and social background of the times and other information which provides understanding of the man and his work.

**B084**    Granville-Barker, Harley. "Romeo and Juliet--The Conduct of Action." In *Twentieth Century Interpretations of Romeo and Juliet*, edited by Douglas Cole. Englewood Cliffs: Prentice-Hall, N. J., 1970.

Included in a volume of articles on "Romeo and Juliet," Granville-Barker's essay explains how Shakespeare made dramatic use of time and action to give passionate life to this tragedy of circumstance. He judges Shakespeare's artistry to be "immature."

**B085**    "Great Katharine." *Time* 33 (April 3, 1939):23.

Discusses the release of Cornell's autobiography and judges it acceptable but, by failing to communicate her personality, Cornell's words lack sparkle.

**B086**    Guinness, Alec. *Blessings in Disguise*. New York: Alfred A. Knopf, 1986.

When in the Navy during World War I, Guinness saw *The Barretts* which he had thought to be "quite dreadful." With the exception of Kit Cornell, the actors "played down to the troops." He could not "be as effusive as was expected."

**B087**    Hall, Gladys. "Why Broadway's Greatest Star--Katharine Cornell--Won't Act for the Movies." *Motion Picture Magazine* 44 (October, 1932):34-35,92. Illus.

Cornell explains that she prefers the immediate audience contact unique to theatre rather than the movie camera.

**B088**    Hartnoll, Phyllis, ed. *The Oxford Companion to the Theatre*. 4th ed. London: Oxford University Press, 1983.

The brief biography includes only some of Cornell's plays. Less comprehensive summary of her career than in earlier editions.

**B089**    Harvey, Jackson. "To the Ladies." *Theatre Magazine* 51 (April, 1930):24.

For her "ceaseless energy" in her performances, Cornell is rated as one of the foremost dramatic actresses.

**B090**    Hayes, Helen with Katharine Hatch. *My Life in Three Acts.* New York: Harcourt Brace Jovanovich, 1990.

Hayes visualizes her life in "theatrical terms" as a kind of mosaic, combining many varicolored pieces which reflect "different worlds, events, people, places." She discusses the rivalry that McClintic assumed to exist between her and Kit, which neither woman felt. She is highly complimentary of Miss Cornell.

**B091**    Hayes, Richard. "The Limits of Lyricism." *Commonweal* 68 (May 23, 1958):205-206.

Hayes finds *The Firstborn* to be too lyrical, and lacking in lucidity and urgency. He wishes Cornell could admit "more moral ambiguity, soil and grit."

**B092**    Herendeen, Anne. "The Lady of Two Legends." *Theatre Guild* 3 (April, 1931):18-21.

Expressing discontent with Cornell's roles before *The Barretts*, Herendeen commends her for her sense of audience, compassion and sincerity. She finds compassion to be one of her striking traits. Compares her development of a part to that of a deepsea diver descending into the depths of the water.

**B093**    Herndon, Richard. "The American Theatre is at is Zenith." *Theatre Magazine* 49 (April 1929):13.

Herndon thinks the theatre is at its zenith, showing rich promise with better playwrights, actors, directors, scene designers and mechanical experts. He has, however, witnessed a decline in decency and thinks producers are poor business men.

**B094**    Holden, Anthony. *Lawrence Olivier: A Biography.* New York: Athenaeum, 1988.

Holden discusses Olivier's relationship with the McClintics and their hospitality on several occasions. He explains the incident when they released Olivier from rehearsals so that he could to fly to Hollywood to see the distraught Vivien Leigh. They stayed with the McClintics after Leigh's filming was completed and until Olivier's play closed.

**B095**    Holland, Norman. *The Shakespearean Imagination.* New York: Macmillan, 1964.

Contains chapters on Shakespeare's theatre and *Romeo and Juliet.* For background and insight into his plays.

**B096**     Hollis, Alpert. *The Last of the Barrymores.* New York: Dial Press, 1964.

In this enlightening account of the Barrymores, Hollis relates the event of Ethel's 70th birthday party at which many notables, including Cornell, recorded their greetings in one of the biggest tributes ever given an actress.

**B097**     Hornblow, Arthur. "Mr. Hornblow Goes to the Play." *Theatre Magazine* 39 (April, 1924):15. (Review of "The Way Things Happen").

In this play Miss Cornell proves to Hornblow that she has great potential and "emotional power" that will enable her to attempt any role. She may be a future Eleanora Duse.

**B098**     Hornblow, Arthur. "Mr. Hornblow Goes to the Play." *Theatre Magazine* 42 (November, 1925):15. (Review of "Tiger Cats").

Hornblow compares Miss Cornell's acting in *The Green Hat,* which he thought she acted well, to *Tiger Cats,* a role which he found unsuitable for her.

**B099**     Hornblow, Arthur. "Mr. Hornblow goes to The Play." *Theatre Magazine* 39 (May 24, 1924):15.

In reviewing *The Outsider,* Hornblow finds the controversy between the medical profession and quackery to be timely and effectively presented. The acting is good; Miss Cornell's Lalage is sincere, appealing and touching.

**B100**     Hosmer, Howard S. "Hobart to Honor Noted Star." *Rochester Times Union* (May 20, 1937).

Notice of the honorary degree that Hobart College was presenting to Katharine Cornell.

**B101**     Houghton, Norris. *Entrances and Exits. A Life In & Out of the Theatre.* New York: Limelight Editions, 1991.

Having had a long and eventful life associated with the theatre which he helped to change by co-founding the Phoenix Theatre, a spearhead of the Off-Broadway movement, Houghton knew many renowned theatre people, including the McClintics. He explains that Miss Cornell may have been drawn to *The Age of Innocence* by her friendship with Edward Sheldon. He also comments on what made the McClintic team work so well.

**B102**     Hughes, Glenn. *History of the American Theatre 1700-1950.* New York: Samuel French, 1951.

Hughes compresses 250 years of theatre activity into 562 pages. He gives an overview of the times, brief sketches of the stars and dramatists, managers, forms of theatre and the fight for survival after W.W.II. Concluding with the "Perils of Prophecy," he states that "If the human spirit is worth ennobling, then the theatre is worth preserving. For in no other way has man expressed himself more profoundly or more inspiringly than in the drama." Refers to Cornell's *Antony & Cleopatra* as a "sumptuous revival."

**B103**    "Husband-and-Wife Teams." *New York Times* (January 12, 1947):VI,7:9.

Of these teams, Cornell was the only actress-manager and McClintic had staged 73 plays. Gives insight into how the couples work together.

**B104**    Hutchens, John. "Nominating Katharine Cornell." *New York Times* (February 15, 1931):VIII:1:8.

Upon the event of Miss Cornell's new venture into management with *The Barretts of Wimpole Street*, Hutchens reviews her career accomplishments, her attitude toward touring, her idea about management and plays she would like to try. He puts her on "that select plane reserved for First Ladies."

**B105**    Hutchens, John. "In School, In Love, In Prison." *Theatre Arts* 14 (April, 1930):283-284.

In a review of *Dishonored Lady* Hutchens praises Cornell for her voice, intelligence, magnetism and body control, but thinks her plays exploit her personality and name.

**B106**    Hynes, Betty.  "Katharine Cornell Offered $300,000 for One Picture." *Washington Herald* (July 15, 1938).

Hollywood was doing its best to lure Miss Cornell to the movies. She was unimpressed by the handsome sum offered her.

**B107**    Isaacs, Edith J. R.  "Coat of Many Colors: Broadway in Review." *Theatre Arts* 21 (February, 1937):89-95.

Pointing out the difficulties of playing Oparre, Isaacs praises Cornell's voice and memorable acting in the second and third acts.

**B108**    Isaacs, Edith J. R.  "Merry Feast of Play-going: Broadway in Review." *Theatre Arts* 19 (April, 1935):258.

Views the role of Elizabeth as the beginning of Cornell's ascent in powerful, beautiful performances.

**B109**    Isaacs, Edith J. R.  "Ring Out the Old: Broadway in Review." *Theatre Arts* 19 (February, 1935):92-94;101-102.

Cornell's performance as Juliet is richer than the previous year. She erases the memory of those before her, Isaacs says. "Of the whole performance there is no more to say than that it is the East and Juliet is the sun!"

**B110**  Isaacs, Edith J. R. "Saints and Lawmakers: Broadway in Review." *Theatre Arts* 20 (May, 1936):333-38.

Synopsis of *Saint Joan* with a critique of the play and praise for Cornell's masterful portrayal of the Maid.

**B111**  Isaacs, Harold. "Queen of the Theatre." *Newsweek* 31 (January 19, 1948):82-83.

Sketches Cornell's career and commends her for her crowning accomplishment, *Antony and Cleopatra*.

**B112**  "Katharine Cornell to Get Degree." *New York Times* (June 4, 1941):19:8.

Clark University, Worcester, Massachusetts, announces that Miss Cornell will receive an honorary Doctor of Fine Arts degree. Radio news commentator Lowell Thomas also received an honorary degree.

**B113**  "Katharine Cornell's Estate Valued at over $500,000." *New York Times* (July 9, 1974):30:1.

Reports value and recipients of Miss Cornell's estate.

**B114**  "Katharine Cornell Returns to Last Spring at Tashmoo." *Vineyard Gazette*, June 14, 1974.

In his tribute to Miss Cornell, the writer mentions the film on Helen Keller's life, *The Unconquered*, which Miss Cornell narrated, and the play *Lucrece*, which she produced because "she believed in its moral grandeur."

**B115**  "Katharine Cornell at the War Front." *Stage* 2 (Spring, 1945):4.

Comments on the ironic acceptance of a romantic love story by 225,000 GIs in Italy and France.

**B116**  "Katharine Cornell Is Cited as 'Woman of the Year.'" *New York Times* (December 30, 1959):14:2.

The Woman's Division of the American Friends of the Hebrew University cited Miss Cornell as "Woman of the Year" for "her outstanding contribution to the American cultural scene." Miss Cornell, who was playing in *Dear Liar* in Washington returned to New York for the event.

**B117**    Kaufman, Wolfe. "Where Do Critics Come From?" *Variety* (January 1, 1936):208.

Kaufman introduces the outstanding critics of the day, what makes them critics, where they come from and how they got the way they are. Includes Atkinson, Brown, Gabriel, Garland, Hammond, Lockridge and Mantle.

**B118**    Kennedy, John B. "The Lady Learns to Shoot." *Collier's* (March 24, 1928):22.

Discusses Cornell's background and her role in *The Letter* in which she shoots her lover.

**B119**    Keyishian, Harry. *Michael Arlen*. Boston: Twayne, 1975.

Background of the author and novel from which *The Green Hat* was adapted.

**B120**    Klink, William R. *S. N. Behrman: The Major Plays*. Amsterdam: Rodapi N. V., 1978.

In analyzing Behrmann's plays, Klink judges his dialogue to be suave but monotonous and unilluminating in *No Time for Comedy*. He sees his characterization as the major flaw. The male lead lacks credibility as a good playwright. Klink says Behrman attempts "to generate humor from a play in a chaotic time; and he nearly succeeds."

**B121**    Kraft, Irma. *Plays Players Playhouses*. New York: Dobsevage, 1928.

Identifies actresses with qualities of Duse, and places Cornell as the greatest of American actresses. Kraft thinks what is so potent about the acting of these women is what they do not say.

**B122**    Kresh, Paul. "Those Legendary Ladies Speak Again." *New York Times* (Sunday, December 22, 1974):31.

Kresh laments the fact that the "Great Dames" of the English theater (Judith Anderson, Edith Evans and Sybil Thorndike) have made a number of albums whereas two of America's Great Ladies (Helen Hayes and Katharine Cornell) have not. He located only one record of Miss Cornell (*The Barretts* and "Sonnets from the Portuguese"), an undeserved neglect of a musical, expressive voice.

**B123**    Kronenberger, Louis, ed. *Best Plays 1952-53 through 1960-61*. New York: Dodd, Mead, 1952-61.

Kronenberger succeeds Burns Mantle as editor of this series. The book includes summaries of Broadway, Chicago and London seasons as well as 10 best plays. Later Paris, California and an index of producers, directors, designers and stage managers were added. In his summary of the 1954-55 Broadway season Kronenberger thought *The Dark is Light Enough* to be worthy of the best ten plays, despite its shortcomings. It was neither "very dramatic" nor philosophically deep, and Tyrone Power was "woefully miscast."

**B124**    Krutch, Joseph Wood. "The Crisis in the Theater." *Nation* (September 7, 1932):211-212.

Describing the demise of theatre in New York, Krutch believes that a few theatres where excellent plays are produced are needed. As theatres are dismantled, he recommends reorganization and less lavish spending. Thinks the depression may be good for the theatre, if it survives.

**B125**    Krutch, Joseph Wood. "Drama From A to B." *Nation* (April 24, 1935): 490-491.

Krutch is very critical of van Druten's writing in *The Flowers of the Forest* and his narrow range of emotional expression in serious drama. Says van Druten's style is best suited to the drawing room.

**B126**    Krutch, Joseph Wood. "Off Broadway--Then & Now." *Theatre Arts* 43 (January 1959):12-14, 72.

Discusses why Washington Square Players, Provincetown Players and Neighborhood Playhouse were important to New York theatre. Katharine Cornell probably was the most famous of the actors who emerged from the Washington Square Players.

**B127**    Krutch, Joseph Wood. "Shaw's Classic." Nation 142 (March 25, 1936): 392.

Krutch considers *Saint Joan* one of Shaw's finest works and one of Miss Cornell's the finest performance of her career. Her interpretation "is simple, flexible, and amazingly varied. Somehow the girl and the saint are both there."

**B128**    Kunitz, Stanley J. and Vineta Colby, eds. *European Authors 1000-1900*. New York: H. W. Wilson, 1977.

In their brief sketch of Friedrich Hebbel whose play *Herodes and Mariamne* (written in 1849) was adapted by Clemence Dane, the editors explain Hebbel's conception of society. Reflecting the influence of Hegel's "categorical imperative," (a force that determines a person's destiny) he viewed "dramatic conflicts as historical or historically determined processes." His tragedies marked a change from the idealism to realism, determinism and psychological drama.

**B129**    Lady with the Lorgnette. "Mirrors of Stageland." *Theatre Magazine* 39 (May, 1924):22.

Discusses Cornell's unique qualities, her marriage and the fact that she always has a job.

**B130**     Le Gallienne, Eva. *With a Quiet Heart: An Autobiography*. New York: The Viking Press, 1953.

This follows Le Gallienne's first book, *At 33*, after the explosion which left her hands in shreds and nearly took her life. Praises Cornell for her kindness when she was recuperating. Le Gallienne courageously resumes her career as she witnesses the theatre's loss of old values and its power "to spread beauty out into life."

**B131**     Leaming, Barbara. *Orson Welles: A Biography*. New York: Viking, 1985.

When he was playing in Miss Cornell's company, the sophomoric behavior of Orson Welles often created problems. He was late for rehearsals, even missed a train to the next booking, and embarrassed the company with public antics. His flamboyance was appropriate for the character of Mercutio, but his general behavior was not professional.

**B132**     Leiter, Samuel L., ed.-in-chief. *Encyclopedia of the New York Stage*, 1920-1930. Westport, Ct.: Greenwood Press, 1985.

Contains information about New York plays: types, authors, directors, producers, theatres and opening dates, with short comments from reviews and a brief synopsis of each. Excellent resource. See for short summary of "Jealousy."

**B133**     Leonard, William Torbert. *Theatre: Stage to Screen to Television*. Metuchen, New Jersey: Scarecrow Press, 1981.

Contains credits, casts, and reviews of American plays that have been produced in the three mediums. Extremely helpful as far as it goes.

**B134**     Lewisohn, Ludwig. "Myth & High Romance." *Nation* 116 (January 24, 1923):102.

Lewisohn says that, in *Will Shakespeare*, Cornell does not avoid "cheap theatricality," nor does she disguise "the touch of genius that is hers." As Mary Fitton she has "a wild, natural, never unrestrained eloquence of speech, rhythm, gesture...."

**B135**     "Lippman Urges Search for Truth." *New York Times* (June 21, 1937).

Walter Lippman was speaker for the commencement exercises of Smith College in Northampton, Massachusetts, when Miss Cornell was presented an honorary degree.

**B136**     "Little 'Women' to Cleopatra." *New York Times Magazine* (February 15, 1948):20-21.

Reviews Cornell's career on her 50th birthday. Cites her favorite lines from *Will Shakespeare*. Illustrated with photographs of her in various roles.

**B137**     Lovett, Robert M. "Criticism After the Play." *New Republic* 29 (December 28, 1921):130.

In *A Bill of Divorcement*, Lovett finds that the double motives have created ambiguity and weakened the play's "dramatic value as a universal appeal." For the most part, Cornell played the most difficult role admirably.

**B138**     "Lucrece's Tragedy Miss Cornell's Triumph" *Stage* 10 (February, 1933):16-17.

Although shortlived, author says *Lucrece* was an important event in that it established Cornell's position among the outstanding tragic actresses of our time. "In pose and gesture, in voice, and above all in her amazingly mobile face, she lived...through Lucrece's experience." Eight photographs by Maurice Goldberg capture her emotions in the rape scene.

**B139**     Malvern, Gladys. *Curtain Going Up*. New York: Julian Messner, 1943.

For this biography Malvern has gotten first-hand information from Miss Cornell and her autobiography *I Wanted to be An Actress*. Malvern develops accounts of Cornell's life and career in greater detail and depth than Cornell had done. Malvern also covers a longer time period which ends with Cornell's consideration of *Antony and Cleopatra* as her next production. The book does not contain credits, casts and reviews of plays as did her autobiography. It emphasizes the dedication of both Guthrie McClintic and Miss Cornell to the theatre, the added sense of responsibility that becoming a star entails, and her love of dogs. The "Foreword" to the book, written by Miss Cornell, appears in Appendix C.

**B140**     Maney, Richard. "Exile by Choice." *Christian Science Monitor Magazine* (April 20, 1938):3.

Cornell's year of recess from the stage was prompted by Henderson's death, the subsequent cancellation of a world tour and her need for "rest, relaxation and reflection."

**B141**     Mantle, Burns, ed. *Best Plays of 1920-21*. Boston:    Small, Maynard, 1921.

Mantle comments on the success of *Nice People* with the public, but not with critics, and includes a summary with excerpts from the play.

**B142**     Mantle, Burns, ed. *Best Plays of 1921-22*. Boston: Small,  Maynard, 1922.

In a commentary on *The Bill of Divorcement* Mantle explains Pollack's fascination with the play and his success in persuading the owners he could play the role of Hilary. Includes a summary and excerpts of the play.

**B143**     Mantle, Burns, ed. *Best Plays of 1932-33*. New York: Dodd, Mead, 1933.

Ranks Cornell's Elsa Brandt in *Alien Corn* between her Elizabeth and Lucrece. Includes a summary and excerpts.

**B144**    Maxwell, Perriton.  "Don't Worry About the Theatre's Future."  *Theatre Magazine* 50 (August, 1929)30.

In discussing the impact of film on theatre, Maxwell believes smaller and more numerous intimate playhouses are a solution to dwindling audiences.  He sees no need to cry over theatre's death so long as people want to escape the humdrum of life.

**B145**    McClintic, Guthrie.  "Directing Chekhov."  *Theatre Arts* 27 (April, 1943):212-215.

McClintic explains how he came "to tackle" *The Three Sisters*, a play he considers to be a "director's dream."  He had been waiting since 1936 to find a cast that could do it justice.  He found a talented cast who worked "entirely for the play and not for personal aggrandizement."  McClintic also worked closely with Alexander Koiransky, a Russian drama critic, on a new translation.  When soldiers from Ft. Meade came to see the play and cheered at the end of the performance, they "evoked from Miss Cornell her one and only curtain speech."

**B146**    McClintic, Guthrie.  "Fry's Finest: The Dark is Light Enough."  *Theatre Arts* 39 (March, 1955):26-27.

Written before the New York opening, McClintic praises the play, which was not to be a great success.

**B147**    McClintic, Guthrie.  "Kit and I."  *American Magazine* (November, 1935):23,164-167.

McClintic gives insight into Kit's private life which is really private, her shyness, her fears, her childhood, and love of dogs.  He explains her insecurity about being unattractive, her ability to be beautiful through feeling, her need to maintain her composure before a performance and his own penchant for raving and storming.

**B148**    McClintic, Guthrie.  "A Letter from Guthrie McClintic."  *Theatre Arts* (April, 1943):212-15.

Discusses *The Three Sisters* and the impressive number of young people who were attending performances.

**B149**    McClintic, Guthrie.  *Me and Kit.*  Boston: Little, Brown, 1955.

As he relates his life and career, McClintic reveals his great admiration for his wife as a person and his conviction that she belongs in the theatre.

**B150**    McDermott, William F.  "Cornell's Juliet."  *Stage* 12, (January, 1935):32-33.

Praises the production of *Romeo and Juliet* for the force of its presentation, delineation of characters and welding of  diverse elements into "a rich panorama of Renaissance life."

**B151**     Meredith, Burgess. "A Marchbanks Fondly Recalls His Candida." *New York Times*, (June 16, 1974):3.

Meredith reminisces about the first time he met Miss Cornell "sitting there looking quite beautiful; a gentle-mannered lady, very quiet." He thought McClintic had "a kind of stagedoor crush on her."

**B152**     "Middlebury Honors 8." *New York Times* (June 14, 1955):15:5.

At the 155th commencement exercises Dr. Samuel S. Stratton, president of Middlebury in Vermont, conferred an honorary Doctor of Humanities on Miss Cornell. Seven distinguished men also received honorary degrees.

**B153**     Miles, Carlton. "Shakespeare a Stage Hero." *Theatre Magazine* (March, 1922):238-161, 196.

Discusses the London production of *Will Shakespeare*, the event of the season. After a great "outlay" was expended on the production, critics attacked it with savagery.

**B154**     "Miss Cornell Triumphs Over the Play." *Literary Digest* 115 (January 7, 1933):15.

Complimentary of Cornell's acting in *Lucrece*.

**B155**     "Miss Cornell Gets Drama League Medal." *New York Times* (May 18, 1935):20:2.

Actor-manager Daniel Frohman presented the Delia Austrian Medal to Miss Cornell for her acclaimed performance in *Romeo and Juliet*. Members of the Drama League had voted the play the most distinguished performance of the year. Two hundred attended the ceremony at the Central Park casino.

**B156**     "Miss Cornell Will Produce an Ibsen Drama Next Season." *Buffalo News* (June 22, 1937).

Reports Miss Cornell's intention to produce *Rosmersholm*.

**B157**     "'Mister Roberts' Wins Perry Award: Judith Anderson, Katharine Cornell & Jessica Tandy Reward for Roles." *New York Times* (March 29, 1948):23:6.

Twenty-five Antionette Perry awards were presented at the Waldorf-Astoria. Miss Cornell received an award for her distinguished performance in *Antony and Cleopatra*.

**B158**     Moore, Ruth C. "What a voice!" *Collier's* (June 29, 1935):28.

Praises the quality and flexibility of Cornell's voice.

**B159**     Morehouse, Ward. "Queen Katharine." *Theatre Arts* 42 (June, 1958):9-11.

Discusses the "special kind of excitement" Cornell brings to plays and her longing, at age 60, to play many more roles.

**B160**     Morrdan, Ethan. *The American Theatre.* New York: Oxford University Press, 1918.

Morrdan's aim is to recount events that shaped American drama. Contains a number of references to Cornell.

**B161**     Morrison, Hobe. "Tribute to Miss Cornell." Passaic, New Jersey: *Herald News* (June 22, 1974).

The reporter wrote that Miss Cornell's death was the end of an era. "Even before her long, lingering illness, her sort of theater had ceased to exist."

**B162**     Morrow, Anne. "Katharine Cornell, a Sketch and a Prophecy." *Woman Citizen* (October, 1925):17.

Predicting that Cornell will be a great actress, Morrow reflects on her magnetism, sense of theatre and devotion to it.

**B163**     Mosel, Tad and Gertrude Macy. *Leading Lady: The World and Theatre of Katharine Cornell.* Boston: Little, Brown, 1978.

This biography of Cornell encompasses her entire life and career. The elusiveness of the dates and details of some events is understandable inasmuch as the McClintics were vague and often in disagreement about them. The elimination of five years from Cornell's age added to the difficulty in achieving chronological accuracy. Anecdotal material supplied by Macy, who knew her as well as anyone, and Mosel's interpretations of Cornell's motives and abilities add interest even though one may not agree with them.

**B164**     Motherwell, Hiram. "Those Broadway Blues." *Theatre Guild Magazine* 6 (February, 1929):11-13.

Describes the state of the theatre as bankrupt. Among the poor theatre fare is Cornell's "The Age of Innocence." He attributes the collapse of theatre to competition, cost, high prices of tickets, poor acting and poor plays.

**B165**     Mullett, Mary B. "Unhappiness Has Its Own Magic." *American Magazine* (June, 1926):34.

Mullett suggests that Cornell's efforts to compensate for an unhappy childhood taught her compassion and is the secret of her "genius."

**B166**     Nathan, George Jean   "The Autumn Drama." *Arts & Decoration* 24 (November, 1925):51.

Review of *The Green Hat* in which Nathan claims that Cornell understands "the art of acting."

**B167**    Nathan, George Jean. "Besier's Barretts." *Vanity Fair* (March, 1931):5.

Nathan describes *The Barretts* as an ably, often glowingly written play in which drama is motivated within the character. Despite faults, the "body of the play sings and hammers out the story with a genuine power...as provocative a play as has come out of England for several years."

**B168**    Nathan, George Jean "Critical Sagacity." *American Mercury* 16 (February, 1929):249-50.

Nathan calls *The Age of Innocence* a bad play which fails to capture the spirit of the novel. He does not consider Cornell a boxoffice star and does not understand why audiences patronize her plays.

**B169**    Nathan, Paul S. "Books into Films." *Publishers' Weekly* 159 (May 5, 1951):1882.

Comments on the failure of *That Lady* and Cornell's interest in the Florence Nightingale story. He also announces her radio dramatic debut as Candida on Theatre Guild of the Air.

**B170**    Neilson, William A. and Charles J. Hill, eds. *The Complete Plays and Poems of William Shakespeare.* New York: Houghton-Mifflin, 1942.

In addition to the plays, this volume contains a summary of Shakespeare's life, a chronology of his works, his opportunity and accomplishments. An introduction, which precedes each play, contains factual information and critical comments.

**B171**    *New York Theatre Critics' Reviews*, vols 2-19. New York:  New York Theatre Critics Reviews, 1941-1960.

Beginning in 1940, these volumes contain theatre critics' reviews from the New York newspapers. A primary and invaluable resource for critics' reactions to plays and actors.

**B172**    *New York Times Theater Reviews*, vols 1-7. New York: New York Times and Arno Press, 1971.

These volumes contain theater reviews that appear in *The New York Times*. Volumes 1-7 contain reviews of Cornell's plays. A primary resource for this book.

**B173**    "No Time for Comedy." *Stage* 16 (April 15, 1939):22.

Complimentary of both Cornell and McClintic. The play got perfect direction from McClintic whose particular forte is "pace, rhythm, taste, unself-conscious ease, the attention to exquisite and relevant detail."

B174    O'Brien, Kate. *That Lady.* New York: Harper, 1946.

In her foreword to the play the author explains her concerns about dramatizing her book, *For One Sweet Grape.*

B175    "Obituary." *Time* 103 (June 24, 1974):62.

Describes Cornell as the "Empress of the American Theater," and her marriage to McClintic as the start of "one of the theater's most auspicious connubial collaborations." McClintic directed almost all of her roles during the 40 years of their marriage. She continued "her throaty-voiced performances" until his death in 1961, when she retired. "I couldn't do anything after that," she said. "He always gave me the security I needed."

B176    "Off Islanders--The Guthrie McClintics." *Harper's Bazaar* 76 (September, 1942):64-65. Illus.

Six photographs of the interior and exterior of East-West Chop, the McClintics island home which was "smote" by the 1938 hurricane. Gives a glimpse of Miss Cornell's retreat on Lake Tashmoo.

B177    Olivier, Laurence. *Confessions of An Actor: An Autobiography.* New York: Simon & Schuster, 1982.

Written at age 75, Olivier tells the story of his 60-year career as an actor, film maker, producer and director. It is also a personal account of his childhood and marriages, particularly the 20-year stormy marriage to Vivien Leigh. McClintics were very understanding and considerate of the Oliviers, who appreciated the friendship.

B178    Oppenheimer, George. "Obituary." *Newsday,* June 30, 1974.

Oppenheimer wrote of Miss Cornell that "...she possessed a kind of glamor....Hers was a combination of presence, an indefinable air of mystery, an elegance and refinement that set her apart and an appeal that lay not alone in her beauty but in her voice, in her gestures and in her intelligence."

B179    Osborne, Robert.  "Memories of Stage Giant Cornell on Centennial." *Hollywood Reporter* (February 16, 1993).

Ironically, 100 years after her birth and 19 years after her death, Katharine Cornell, who was virtually "a genuine giant as famous in her field as Disney and Garbo in theirs" is almost forgotten while the horse Trigger is becoming immortal. The reason? It was Miss Cornell's choice not to make movies, but it's sad that she should be forgotten so soon.

B180    Parish, James Robert & Vincent Terrace. *The Complete Actors' Television Credits, 1948-1988.* 2d ed. 3 vols. Metuchen, New Jersey: Scarecrow Press, 1989.

An important resource for finding performers and each episode of dramatic or comedy series in which he or she appeared. Also includes the network and televised date.

**B181**     Patterson, Ada. "Gaieties and Gravities." *Theatre Magazine* 50 (August, 1929):36.

Explains that Miss Cornell's nickname "Kit" was related to her love of the outdoors. Other sources credit her mother or grandmother with giving her the nickname because she looked like a boy after having scarlet fever.

**B182**     Patterson, Ada. "Two Innocents on Broadway." *Theatre Magazine* 41 (June, 1925):22.

Cornell credits McClintic with turning her "face toward the greater things of the theatre." He expressed his delight in watching her develop the womanly greatness he sensed in her on their first meeting.

**B183**     Pederson, Lucille. "Cornell, Katharine." In *Notable Women in the American Theatre*, edited by A. M. Robinson, V. M. Roberts, and M. S. Barranger. New York: Greenwood Press, 1989.

A brief biographical sketch of Miss Cornell's life and career appears in this comprehensive biographical dictionary of women who have been influential in the American theatre. Became the groundwork for this book.

**B184**     Pederson, Lucille. "The Exuberance of Young Love at Forty-five? Katharine Cornell as Juliet." *Ohio Speech Journal* 16 (1978):20-27.

Descriptive study of Cornell's preparation for the role of Juliet and her success in the part.

**B185**     Peters, Margot. *House of Barrymore.* New York: Alfred A. Knopf, 1990.

Peters reviews the triumphs and failures of each of the Barrymores as they pursue brilliant careers and succumb to the 'Barrymore Curse,' alcohol. Ethel had dreamed of being a concert pianist. Formal and standoffish in contrast to Cornell's generosity toward and consideration for her casts, Barrymore captured the public more than Cornell, Hayes or Fontanne.

**B186**     Phelps, William L. "As I Like It." *Scribner's Magazine* 89 (1931):569-70.

A student of Browning, Phelps urges Americans to see this powerful portrayal of the Barrett-Browning love story.

**B187**     Phelps, William L. "As I Like It." *Scribner's Magazine* 91 (1932):309.

After seeing *The Barretts* three times, Phelps evaluates it as "an emotional experience that will be remembered as long as life lasts." He advocates it to those going into a "gloomy and despairing" world.

**B188**     Pierre, Ray. "The First Lady of Chip Chop." *Christian Science Monitor Magazine* (October 9, 1943 ):10.

Describes the simple life at Cornell's island home on Martha's Vineyard where she escapes the rigors of her profession for peace and tranquility.

**B189**     "Playgoer's After Thoughts." *Stage* 10 (January, 1933):7.

With a full page photograph of Cornell as Lucrece. The critic praises Cornell's portrayal, especially in the ravishment and death scenes, but thinks the play suffers from have been "embalmed" too long.

**B190**     "Princeton Honors Bradley, 9 Others." *New York Times* (June 16, 1948):33:1.

Along with General Omar Bradley, Dr. Raymond B. Fosdick and others, Miss Cornell received the honorary degree of Doctor of Fine Arts for "her distinguished contribution to one of the great arts of all time and for the pleasure and deep satisfaction she has given us."

**B191**     "Producer's Showcase, Hallmark of Fame, Ford Star Jubilee." *New York Times* (April 12, 1956):63.

*Producer's Showcase* received an Emmy and a Peabody Award for dramatic entertainment. One of the "productions of interest" during the 1956 season was *The Barretts*.

**B192**     "Promised and Hoped For." *Stage* 14 (November, 1936):115-116.

Announces the McClintics' forthcoming production, *The Wingless Victory*, by Maxwell Anderson.

**B193**     Pulaski, Jack. "Road's Top Grossers in Past Ten Years, Helen Hayes Star; Lunts Top Money Team." *Variety* (January 7, 1943):187.

As to the most favored actress on the road, it's a "dead heat" between Helen Hayes and Katharine Cornell. Within ten years Miss Cornell had toured more often than any other star. Miss Hayes grossed the largest amount on tour, the Lunts were the most popular touring team.

**B194**     Pulaski, Jack. "The Road, Or What Road?" *Variety* (January 2, 1934):117.
Summarizes the exact state of the road during the early 1930s. Where there had been 1500 at one time on Klaw and Erlanger touring sheets, there was no road. Brokers said there were 200-300 playable theatres.

**B195**     Rand, Ellery. "A Study in Self-Mastery." *Personality* (July, 1928):20-24.

Rand discusses Cornell's instinctive good manners, punctuality, self-control and the "fire" one feels in speaking with her.

**B196**     Randall, Tony & Michael Mindlin. *Which Reminds Me.* New York: Delacorte Press, 1989.

Randall got his first acting job on Broadway after the war in *Antony & Cleopatra* with "the great Katharine Cornell." She suggested he not spend so much time preparing for his role some night. A student of Method acting under Sanford Meisner at the Neighborhood Playhouse, Randall took Cornell's suggestion and his performance was the same.

**B197**     Rathbone, Basil. *In and Out of Character.* Garden City, New York: Doubleday & Co., 1962.

Rathbone reveals a person of integrity and compassion who appreciates his friends. During the long tour with Cornell in 1933-34, he said the sign "Standing Room Only" was always outside the theater. At the end of the successful tour she gave every member of the company an extra week's salary. He thanks her for "as memorable an adventure in the theater as I have ever known or shall ever know."

**B198**     Rigdon, Walter, ed. *The Biographical Encyclopedia and Who's Who of the American Theatre.* New York: J. H. Heineman, 1966.

Contains detailed information on plays in Cornell's apprenticeship years with the Bonstelle company, awards  and honors as well as Cornell's life and career.

**B199**     Ross, L., ed. "Profiles: Interview." *New Yorker* 37 (October 28, 1961):82.

Explores Cornell's upbringing, her instinctual approach to acting, McClintic's influence and her struggle to get a part "right." She confesses that Mrs. Campbell in *Dear Liar* was one of the most difficult roles for her.

**B200**     Sedgwick, Ruth Woodbury. "Saint Joan." *Stage* 13 (April, 1936):30-33.

Sedgwick claims there are moments of emotional intensity in *Saint Joan* that "sear across the memory."

**B201**     Sedgwick, Ruth Woodbury. "Town Crier: Alexander Woollcott on the Air." *Stage* 12 (January, 1935):18-19.

Calls Woollcott "the emperor of radio's most high-toned kingdom." As a story-teller he is superlative with new tales as in the case of Cornell's Christmas story in Seattle (Dec. 25, 1933) which became almost as famous as Dicken's Christmas Carol. Woollcott is the "pet" of broadcasting.

**B202**     Seldes, Gilbert. "Producers and Playwrights of 1924-25." *Theatre Magazine* 42 (July, 1925):9.

Discusses Cornell in the role of Candida and predicts that her destiny will lead "to the highest place" in acting.

**B203**     Seldes, Gilbert. "The Theatre: 'The Letter.'" *The Dial* (February, 1928):166.

Seldes disliked *The Letter* and stated that it did not help Cornell's reputation.

**B204**     Seldes, Marian. *The Bright Lights: A Theatre Life.* Boston: Houghton Mifflin Co., 1978.

In this account of her career, Seldes discusses her experience when cast as Cornell's daughter Anichu in *That Lady.* Says critics did not like the play but audiences came to see Cornell. Cornell told her that "the only thing that lasted in the theatre was the memory held in the audience's consciousness." Seldes is impressed by the way Miss Cornell handled the situation when Guthrie lost his temper over a scene she was doing with Miss Cornell.

**B205**     Severo, Richard. "Cornell Room Dedicated Without Star." *New York Times* (April 25, 1974):46:1.

Miss Cornell was too ill with the flu to attend the dedication of a room in honor of her and her late husband. However, a gathering of several hundred friends and admirers attended the brief ceremony in which Brooks Atkinson said, "the theater becomes electric when she appears." A tape recording of the proceedings was made.

**B206**     Shanley, J.P. "Miss Cornell Discusses Her Premiere on TV." *New York Times* (April 1, 1956):13:8.

Before the premiere Miss Cornell admitted she had some misgivings about selecting *The Barretts* for television. Because Elizabeth Barrett sits on a couch through most of the play, she thought she might have chosen a play in which she had more movement. As a staff member said, "She's always been a worrier." She also relates the rewarding experience of taking *The Barretts* overseas to the GIs.

**B207**     Shaw, Bernard. *Seven Plays.* New York: Dodd, Mead, 1966.

Prefaces the text of the play, *Saint Joan*, with lengthy introductory information to help the playgoer understand it.

**B208**     "Shaw with Water." *Time* 73 (April 27, 1959):53.

In this brief article the reporter discusses *Dear Liar*, Cornell's love of touring and Aherne's loyalty to her.

**B209**     "Shaw's Saint." *Time* (March 23, 1936).

Comments on Cornell's "high-powered troupe of actors" in the cast of *Saint Joan.* States that "...Spectators found her full of the youthful fire that danced around her Juliet, approved the added touch of honest rusticity which brought a full flush of credibility to her Joan."

**B210**    Sherwood, Robert. "Footnote to a Preface." *Saturday Review* 32 (August 6, 1949):130-135.

Sherwood looks back to the 1920s when new ideas and talents were flourishing. Among the rising stars was Cornell, and McClintic was a trail-blazing director.

**B211**    Skinner, Richard D. "The Barretts of Wimpole Street." *Commonweal* 11 (February 25, 1931):469.

Congratulates Cornell for a play that "represents a pleasing and engaging contrast to most of her recent vehicles."

**B212**    Skinner, Richard D. "Dishonored Lady." *Commonweal* 11 (February 19, 1930):453.

Critical of the play, Skinner thinks Cornell's first-rate talent cannot withstand "theatrical rubbish" such as this play.

**B213**    Speicher, Eugene. "A Portrait of Katharine Cornell." *Life* 8 (April 29, 1940):47.

A brief summary of Cornell's career accompanies the half page photograph of her portrait as Candida, painted by Speicher.

**B214**    Straus, Henrietta. "Clemence Dane & Shakespeare." *New York Times Magazine* (January 27, 1934):6.

Discusses how Dane came to write her interpretation of Shakespeare's life in *Will Shakespeare*. Recurrent in his plays she found 3 types of women who influenced him. Anne stands for the blind, human love that is always faithful; Mary Fitton for the physical side; Queen Elizabeth for the intellectual side. Discusses Cornell whose technique she finds amazing.

**B215**    Talmay, Allene. "Katharine Cornell in 'The Wingless Victory.'" *Vogue* (February 1, 1937):56.

A striking full page colored photograph of Miss Cornell as Oparre in *The Wingless Victory*.

**B216**    Talmay, Allene. "Sufferin' Through." *Vogue* (March 15, 1936):89,127.

Miss Cornell leads a tranquil private life. Inside the theatre she is a sufferer: shoots, commits suicide, poisons, was raped in Lucrece and burned to ash in *Saint Joan*. "She suffers but does not whine."

**B217**    Taubman, Howard. "The Barretts Abroad: Katharine Cornell's Italian Campaign and Her Conquest of GI Joe." *New York Times* (September 17, 1944):II:1,2:3.

Written from "somewhere in Italy" when he was a private in the Army, Taubman relates the GIs' reactions to *The Barretts*. The play has been "enormously stirring to the parties of the first and second parts," he said. "The play grips its GI audiences....By the end of the play the audience is completely within its spell."

**B218**     Taubman, Howard. *The Making of the American Theatre*. New York: Coward McCann, 1965.

Taubman weaves "indelible memories" of great moments and disappointments into his history of theatre. One exalted moment was when Cornell as Elizabeth rose uncertainly from her sofa and walked again. A disappointment was her lack of passion as Cleopatra.

**B219**     Terrace, Vincent. *Encyclopedia of Television: Series, Specials, Pilots*. New York: Zoetrope, 1985-88.

This three-volume encyclopedia indexes performers and contains credits, cast, producer, date of production, and brief description of story. Excellent resource.

**B220**     "That Lady--Miss Cornell." *New York Times Magazine* (November 13, 1949):70-71.

This is a synopsis of the play, *That Lady*, in which Cornell was playing.

**B221**     "The Honors List." *Nation* (July 27, 1963):43.

Lists 1963 recipients of the Medal of Freedom, which was made official by President Kennedy, and the criteria for receiving it. It replaces the Medal of Freedom begun in 1945, which had been bestowed on those who acted meritoriously "in the interest of the security of the United States," when Miss Cornell received it.

**B222**     "Theatre Asides: Katharine Cornell." *Stage* 10 (December, 1932):25.

Comments that Katharine Cornell is busy with *Lucrece* in which she is "again a lovely, ruined lady, this time, noble, dignified, and compassionate." Portrait of Cornell by Martha Sawyers on the cover.

**B223**     "Three Star Classic." *Time* 40 (December 21, 1942): 45-46.

Reviews the diverse and miraculous roles Cornell has performed and announces *The Three Sisters* which will have the most "glittering cast the theatre has seen."

**B224**     "Two by Two Across the U.S." *Life* (December 21, 1959):61.

In the spring Cornell and Aherne toured 18,000 miles in a Land Cruiser, taking *Dear Liar* to 66 cities, many being difficult to reach by public transportation. It was a top boxoffice draw in Phoenix, Arizona, but poor in New York.

**B225**    "U of Pennsylvania to Honor Five." *New York Times* (May 29, 1938):II,5:2.

Miss Cornell was one of five persons who received honorary degrees at the University of Pennsylvania commencement exercise. She received the Doctor of Letters degree.

**B226**    "University Honor for Miss Cornell." *New York Times* (February 23, 1935):14:5.

In presenting the Chancellor's Medal to Miss Cornell for enriching "the life of her generation, Chancellor Capan said that in great acting the actor "fashions a thing of beauty or of power" out of "his own inner resources."

**B227**    Van Vechten, Carl. "An Ode to the Stage Door Canteen." *Theatre Arts* 27 (April 1943):229-231.

The Canteen had done much for servicemen and those who work there. Absolutely democratic in organization and social behavior, its a place where all races and cultures mingle, and stay perfectly sober (they serve no alcoholic drinks).

**B228**    Van Doren, Mark. "Early Victorian Father." *Nation* 132 (February 25, 1931):255.

Calls *The Barretts* "a meritorious play" in which the actors talk like human beings.

**B229**    Vernon, Grenville. "Romeo and Juliet." *Commonweal* 21 (January 4, 1935):291.

Claims that Cornell has "the wand of genius" and that no other Juliet of her generation has equaled hers.

**B230**    Vickers, Hugo. *Vivien Leigh, A Biography*. Boston: Little, Brown & Co., 1988.

A thoroughly researched study of the talented, complex Vivien Leigh. Vickers examines the relationships in her life, especially with Olivier, and her illnesses (tuberculosis and manic depression) which imposed cruel limits on the courageous woman. Mentions the kindness of Cornell in taking Leigh into her home during an illness. Discusses Miss Leigh's lovely Juliet which she played with "grace and eloquence," but which was a "resounding failure." The Oliviers spent $96,000, most of their savings from recent film successes.

**B231**    Warren, Wilson. "She Stood in Tears Amid the Alien Corn." *Stage* 10 (March 1933):12-13.

Reviews the story of *Alien Corn* and compliments Cornell for bringing back an American playwright who interprets native life with sympathy and understanding.

B232      *Washington Post* (June 23, 1951).

Reports that Cornell is still hedging on a movie debut of the life of Florence Nightingale.

B233      *Washington Times Herald* (May 2, 1951).

Cornell announces her intention to make a film of Florence Nightingale.

B234      "White House Fete for Miss Cornell." *New York Times* (March 30, 1937).

For outstanding achievement during the year, First Lady Mrs. Franklin D. Roosevelt presented the Chi Omega National Achievement Award to Miss Cornell, the first actress to receive it.  She was currently appearing in *Candida* and *The Wingless Victory*.

B235      Whitman, Alden.  "Katharine Cornell Is Dead at 81." *New York Times*, June
            10, 1974.

In his tribute Whitman said that Miss Cornell's acting was "quite as remarkable for the carefulness of its design as for the fire of her presence."  She had an astonishing hold on audiences.  Her final award was for having "elevated the theater throughout the world."

B236      *Who Was Who In The Theatre, 1912-1976*. Vol I.  Detroit, Michigan: Gale
            Research Company, 1978.

Contains detailed information about illustrious persons who qualify for the publication.  An impressive listing of Miss Cornell's accomplishments.

B237      "Who's Who Among Producers." *Theatre Arts* 26 (October, 1942):620.

Discusses Cornell's belief that audiences across the country want to see good theatre.

B238      Wilk, Max.  *The Golden Age of Television: Notes from the Survivors*.  New
            York: Delacorte Press, 1976.

Explores the history of television from its beginning in the 40s to the advent of videotape.  NBC was the first show able to lure the great Katharine Cornell into television when she did *The Barretts*, a *Producer's Showcase* Production.  This TV special remains in kinescope form (B179).

B239      Willis, Richard.  "In Search of an American Siddons." *Theatre Magazine* 38
            (December, 1923):12.

Views Cornell as a strong contender for the American Mrs. Siddons.

**B240**     Wilson, Garff. *Three Hundred Years of American Drama and Theatre*. 2nd ed. Englewood Cliffs, New Jersey: Prentice-Hall, 1982.

Wilson recalls the night he saw Cornell in *The Barretts* in Dijon, France, during the war. Elizabeth was an ideal role for her, but in other roles (Juliet and Cleopatra) Wilson found her deficient in passion.

**B241**     Wilson, Garff. *Three Hundred Years of American Drama and Theatre*. Englewood Cliffs, New Jersey: Prentice-Hall, 1973.

Wilson rates Cornell, along with Judith Anderson and Helen Hayes, as actresses of the classical school, for the integrity, devotion and quality they have given to their acting.

**B242**     Woolf, S. J. "When Wimpole Street Went to the Front." *New York Times Magazine* (February 25, 1945):14,40.

An interview with Cornell reveals her profound experience of taking *The Barretts* to the war theater. She expresses her great respect for the American GIs; they were inspiring, discriminating, and appreciative.

**B243**     Woolf, S. J. "Again That Cornell-McClintic Team." *New York Times Magazine* (February 21, 1943):17.

Woolf interviews the McClintic's about their philosophy of theatre and how they work together. They believe "the play's the thing" which lives through "the sparkle of fine acting."

**B244**     Woollcott, Alexander. "Miss Kitty Takes to the Road." *Saturday Evening Post* 207 (August 18, 1934):14-15; 70-72. (Also published in *The Passionate Playgoer* edited by George Oppenheimer. New York: Viking Press, 1958; *Christmas with Ed Sullivan* comp. by E. Sullivan and B. Precht. New York: McGraw-Hill, c1959).

This interesting article describes the experiences of touring and highlights the thrilling production of *The Barretts* in Seattle at Christmas.

**B245**     Young, Stark. "Casanova." *New Republic* 36 (October 10, 1923):180-181.

Young thinks the music haunting and the costumes magnificent but the play "does not really speak our language." The undertone is an irony that we do not understand.

**B246**     Young, Stark. "High Tor and Highty Tighty." *New Republic* 89 (February 3, 1937):411-412.

In a negative review of *The Wingless Victory*, Young calls the play "semi-tosh." He reserves his praise for Cornell.

**B247**     Young, Stark. *Immortal Shadows*. New York: Scribner's Sons, 1948.

A selection of Young's essays which includes *Candida, The Wingless Victory* and *Antigone*.

**B248**     Young, Stark. "Katharine Cornell's Juliet." *New Republic* 81 (January 9, 1935):252.

None could be better than Cornell's Juliet, Young claims. She is moved by real emotion and "makes you believe in love."

**B249**     Young, Stark. "It Is the Lark." *New Republic* 33 (February 14, 1923):321.

Young discusses Jane Cowl's performance of Juliet which he praised for simplicity, naturalness and beauty. He found the weakest spots to be in the scenes with the nurse. Cowl's portrayal was a challenge to Miss Cornell.

**B250**     Young, Stark. "The McClintics' Shaw." *New Republic* (March 25, 1936):198.

Miss Cornell really understands the role of Saint Joan, says Young. She has the ability to bring on stage a kind of trance in which she seems alone in the midst of the other players.

**B251**     Young, Stark. "Miss Katharine Cornell." *New Republic* 52 (October 12, 1927):207-08.

*The Letter*, poorly written, is neither credible nor good entertainment in Young's opinion. He advocates Cornell take the risk of selecting better plays that challenge her and have "richer dramatic substance."

**B252**     Young, Stark. "Two New Pieces." *New Republic* 57 (December 12, 1928):97.

Young did not think *The Age of Innocence* was commendable but could hardly say enough about Miss Cornell's acting. Her gift for achieving the "right emotional intensity" was indescribable. She was the only actress he would compare to the great Duse.

**B253**     Young, William C., ed. *Famous Actors and Actresses on the American Stage*. Vol. 1. New York: Bowker, 1975.

This 2-volume series documents American theatre history. The lengthy article on Miss Cornell includes biographical data and famous roles. It focuses on her two outstanding portrayals, Elizabeth and Juliet. Reviews from critics Brooks Atkinson and John Mason Brown testify to her great success in these portrayals. Her approach to a role, with excerpts from the article by Morton Eustis in *Theatre Arts Monthly* concludes the laudatory essay.

**B254**     Yurka, Blanche. *Bohemian Girl*. Athens, Ohio: Ohio University Press, 1970.

In an "Afterword," Brooks Atkinson discusses the value of Yurka's autobiography which reveals her total commitment to the theatre. Having played with Cornell in *Lucrece*, Yurka suggests what she thinks would have saved the play and commends Kit, whose "voice in the last act was of an unearthly beauty." Yurka replaced Edith Evans as Nurse in *Romeo and Juliet* and praises the production and players.

**B255**     Zolotow, Maurice. *Stagestruck: The Romance of Alfred Lunt and Lynn Fontanne*. New York: Harcourt, Brace & World, 1964 & 1965.

In the theatre between 1925 and 1950, the Lunts were the most spectacular boxoffice attraction. Passionately dedicated to acting, they were inseparable and, as Woollcott said, "better as a couple." Fontanne played in *Strange Interlude*, which Cornell had turned down. Both Fontanne and Lunt declined the invitation to appear in *Candida*, probably because McClintic asked her to play Miss Prism. The lead role of Candida was given to Miss Cornell.

### Newspaper and Trade Paper Reviews

**B256**     "Age of Innocence." *New York Times*, November 28, 1928.

**B257**     Anderson, John. "Lucrece." *New York Journal*, December, 1932. (Also in K. Cornell, *I Wanted to be An Actress*, 272-275).

**B258**     Anderson, John. "'The Three Sisters' Opens at Barrymore." *New York Journal American*, December 22, 1942.

**B259**     Anderson, John. "Katharine Cornell Stars in van Druten Play Attacking War." *New York Evening Journal*, April 9, 1935. (Review of "Flowers of the Forest").

**B260**     Anderson, John. "'Doctor's Dilemma' Revived by Cornell." *New York Journal and American*, March 12, 1941.

**B261**     Anderson, John. "Saint Joan." *New York Evening Journal*, March 10, 1936. (Also in K. Cornell, *I Wanted to be An Actress*, 317-319).

**B262**     Aston, Frank. "Cornell, Aherne Exchange Notes in Kilty's 'Dear Liar.'" *New York World-Telegram and Sun*, March 18, 1960.

**B263**     Atkinson, Brooks. "Candida." *New York Times*, March 21, 1937.

**B264**     Atkinson, Brooks. "Candida." *New York Times*, April 8, 1942.

**B265**     Atkinson, Brooks. "Candida." *New York Times*, May 3, 1942.

B266    Atkinson, Brooks. "The Constant Wife." *New York Times*, December 11, 1951.

B267    Atkinson, Brooks. "Cornell and Massey Appear in a Revival of Bernard Shaw's 'The Doctor's Dilemma.'" *New York Times*, March 12, 1941.

B268    Atkinson, Brooks. "The Dark Is Light Enough." *New York Times*, February 24, 1955.

B269    Atkinson, Brooks. "Dear Liar." *New York Times*, March 27, 1960.

B270    Atkinson, Brooks. "Dishonored Lady." *New York Times*, February 5, 1930.

B271    Atkinson, Brooks. "Elizabeth the Poet." *New York Times*, February 22, 1931. (Review of "The Barretts of Wimpole Street").

B272    Atkinson, Brooks. "Fleeing the Wimpole Street Ogre." *New York Times*, February 10, 1931. (Review of "The Barretts of Wimpole Street").

B273    Atkinson, Brooks. "Flowers of the Forest." *New York Times*, April 9, 1935.

B274    Atkinson, Brooks. "Flush & Co." *New York Times*, February 26, 1935. (Review of "The Barretts").

B275    Atkinson, Brooks. "Katharine Cornell, Massey and Meredith Appear in Revival of Shaw's 'Candida' for Army-Navy Relief." *New York Times*, April 28, 1942.

B276    Atkinson, Brooks. "Katharine Cornell is Starred in 'The Prescott Proposals' by Lindsay and Crouse." *New York Times*, December 17, 1953.

B277    Atkinson, Brooks. "Lucrece." *New York Times*, December 21, 1932. (Also in K. Cornell, *I Wanted to be An Actress*, 275-277).

B278    Atkinson, Brooks. "Maugham Plus Cornell." *New York Times*, December 27, 1927. (Review of "The Letter").

B279    Atkinson, Brooks. "Maxwell Anderson." *New York Times*, January 3, 1937. (Review of "Wingless Victory").

B280    Atkinson, Brooks. "No Time for Comedy." *New York Times*, April 18, 1939.

B281    Atkinson, Brooks. "The Play: 'Candida.'" *New York Times*, March 11, 1937.

B282    Atkinson, Brooks. "The Play: Misdirected Effort." *New York Times*, November 23, 1946. (Review of Eva Le Gallienne's "Rosmersholm").

B283    Atkinson, Brooks. "Presenting Katharine Cornell." *New York Times*, February 26, 1933. (Review of "Alien Corn").

**B284**   Atkinson, Brooks. "Romeo and Juliet." *New York Times*, December 21, 1934.

**B285**   Atkinson, Brooks. "Saint Joan." *New York Times*, March 15, 1936.

**B286**   Atkinson, Brooks. "That Lady." *New York Times*, November 23, 1949.

**B287**   Atkinson, Brooks. "At the Theatre: 'Antony and Cleopatra.'" *New York Times*, November 27, 1947.

**B288**   Atkinson, Brooks. "Theatre: 'The Firstborn.'" *New York Times*, May 1, 1958.

**B289**   Atkinson, Brooks. "Wingless Victory." *New York Times*, December 24, 1936.

**B290**   "B'way Grosses Slightly Lower, But 'Barretts' Exceeds Expectations." *Variety*, February 18, 1931, p. 63.

**B291**   "B'way Grosses Hit Low Marks After Holiday; 'Barretts' Weak at $11,000." *Variety*, March 6, 1935, p. 57.

**B292**   "B'way Sees Fair Influx Helping, but Probably Not Until June; 'Comedy' Near Lead with $21,000." *Variety*, April 26, 1939, p. 43. (Review of "No Time For Comedy").

**B293**   "B'way Sloughed by V-E, Rain But Biz Spurts Later; 'Carousel' Tops 'Ground' 6G, 'Carmen's Center Record." *Variety*, May 16, 1945, p. 45. (Review of "The Barretts").

**B294**   Baker, Colgate. "Katharine Cornell's Marvellous Acting in 'The Outsider.'" *New York Review*, March 22, 1924.

**B295**   Baker, Colgate. "Will Shakespeare Has His Say." *New York Review*, January 6, 1923.

**B296**   Baker, Gladys. "Cornell Aspires Shakespearean Role." *Birmingham News*, May 28, 1933. (Review of "Romeo & Juliet").

**B297**   Barnes, Howard. "Cornell and Chekov." *New York Herald Tribune*, December 22, 1942. (Review of "The Three Sisters").

**B298**   Barnes, Howard. "Period Romance, Period." *New York Herald Tribune*, November 23, 1949. (Review of "That Lady").

**B299**   Barnes, Howard. "Lovers and Friends." *New York Herald Tribune*, November 30, 1943.

**B300**   "Barretts of Wimpole Street." *Variety*, April 4, 1956, p. 29. (*Producers' Showcase* production).

**B301** "Barretts' in Buffalo Tops Cornell's 'Juliet.'" *Variety*, December 5, 1933, p. 55.

**B302** Beaufort, John. "Miss Cornell and Maugham." *Christian Science Monitor*, December 15, 1951. (Review of "The Constant Wife").

**B303** Beaufort, John. "Miss Cornell's 'Antony & Cleopatra.'" *Christian Science Monitor*, December 6, 1947.

**B304** Beaufort, John. "Actress in Costume Drama of Sixteenth Century Spain." *Christian Science Monitor*, December 3, 1949. (Review of "That Lady").

**B305** Beebe, Lucius. "Maurice Evans: Miss Katherine Cornell's New Romeo." *New York Herald Tribune*, 1935.

**B306** Bell, Nelson. "The Theater's First Lady is Favored by Role in New Drama." *Washington Post*, April 7, 1935. (Review of "Flowers of the Forest").

**B307** Bellamy, Francis R. "The Theatre." *Outlook and Independent*, December 26, 1928. (Review of "The Age of Innocence").

**B308** "Biz Looks Up Again: Cornell 'Joan' Clicks to Splendid $20,000, 1st Wk." *Variety*, March 18, 1936, p. 65. (Review of "Saint Joan").

**B309** Blade, Mark. "A One-Eyed Cornell Bores Critic in 'Tiresome' Play." *Toledo Blade*, November 27, 1949. (Review of "That Lady").

**B310** "Broadway Review: 'Nice People.'" *Variety*, March 11, 1921, pp. 16-17.

**B311** "Broadway Review: 'Will Shakespeare.'" *Variety*, January 5, 1923, p. 17.

**B312** Broun, Heywood. "It Seems to Me: 'Candida.'" *New York World*, December 13, 1942.

**B313** Broun, Heywood. "Review of 'Will Shakespeare.'" *New York World*, January 2, 1923. (Also in K. Cornell, *I Wanted to Be An Actress*, 189-193).

**B314** Broun, Heywood. "The New Play: 'Casanova.'" *New York Morning World*, September 27, 1923.

**B315** Brown, John Mason. "Cornell and Massey in 'The Doctor's Dilemma.'" *New York Post*, March 12, 1941.

**B316** Brown, John Mason. "Katharine Cornell Presents 'The Barretts of Wimpole Street' at the Empire." *New York Evening Post*, February 10, 1931.

**B317** Brown, John Mason. "Katharine Cornell Presents Mr. Shaw's 'Saint Joan.'" *New York Post*, March 10, 1936.

**B318** Brown, John Mason. "Katharine Cornell Starts Broadway Engagement in 'Flowers of the Forest.'" *New York Post*, April 9, 1935.

**B319** Brown, John Mason. "A Magnificent Revival of Mr. Shaw's 'Candida.'" *New York World-Telegram*, April 28, 1942.

**B320** Brown, John Mason. "The Play: 'Dishonored Lady.'" *New York Post*, February 5, 1930.

**B321** Brown, John Mason. "Review of 'Romeo and Juliet.'" *New York Post*, December 24, 1935. (Also in K. Cornell, *I Wanted to Be An Actress*, 310-315).

**B322** Brown, Herrick: "Katharine Cornell and Raymond Massey Return in 'Lovers and Friends." *New York Sun*, November 30, 1943.

**B323** Burr, Kate. "Nothing of the Dilettante about Katherine [sic] Cornell's Stage Work." *Buffalo Times*, March, 1922. (Review of "Bill of Divorcement").

**B324** "Captain Carvallo," *Buffalo Courier-Express*, December 8, 1959.

**B325** Carroll, Harrison. "Katharine Cornell Casts Spell over Biltmore." *Los Angeles Herald*, September 9, 1930. (Review of "Dishonored Lady").

**B326** Chapman, John. "Cornell's 'Antigone' Interesting Switch on Ancient Sophocles." *New York Daily News*, February 19, 1946.

**B327** Chapman, John. "Miss Cornell Shoots the Works, Cries with One Eye in 'That Lady.'" *New York Daily News*, November 23, 1949.

**B328** Chapman, John. "Katharine Cornell's New Vehicle is Maugham's Old 'Constant Wife.'" *New York Daily News*, December 10, 1951.

**B329** Chapman, John. "K. Cornell's 'Prescott Proposals' Looks & Sounds Important; Isn't." *New York Daily News*, December 17, 1953.

**B330** Chapman, John. "'Lovers and Friends' is Meager Vehicle for Katharine Cornell." *New York Daily News*, November 30, 1943.

**B331** Coe, Richard L. "Lindsay & Crouse Have a Grand Play." *Washington Post*, December 1, 1955. (Review of "Prescott Proposals").

**B332** Coleman, Robert. "Cast is Fine in 'That Lady,' But Play Isn't." *Daily Mirror*, November 23, 1949.

**B333** Coleman, Robert. "Cornell's Cleopatra Is a Triumph." *Daily Mirror*, November 27, 1947.

**B334** Coleman, Robert. "Cornell Makes a Gem of 'Constant Wife' Revival." *Daily Mirror*, December 10, 1951.

**B335** Coleman, Robert. "'Dear Liar' Shows Up Shaw." *Daily Mirror*, March 18, 1960.

**B336** Coleman, Robert. "'Firstborn' a Stirring Drama." *Daily Mirror*, May 1, 1958.

**B337** Cook, Alton. "'Lovers and Friends' a Cornell Hit." *New York World-Telegram*, November 30, 1943.

**B338** Corbin, John. "Invented Shakespeare." *New York Times*, January 2, 1923. (Review of "Will Shakespeare").

**B339** Corbin, John. "Pinero Phantasy." *New York Times*, April 2, 1923. (Review of "The Enchanted Cottage").

**B340** Corbin, John. "The Play: 'Neighbors.'" *New York Times*, December 27, 1923.

**B341** Corbin, John. "The Way Things Happen." *New York Times*, January 29, 1924.

**B342** "Cornell-'Burke' $18,500 in Frisco." *Variety*, January 28 1942, p. 51.

**B343** "Cornell in Balto First." *Variety*, March 13, 1935, p. 56. (Review of "Flowers of the Forest").

**B344** "Cornell Gets $23,500, Balto." *Variety*, April 14, 1939, p. 59. (Review of "No Time For Comedy").

**B345** "Cornell Sells Out Detroit, $28,000." *Variety*, December 23, 1936, p. 57. (Review of "Wingless Victory").

**B346** "Cornell 10G in Port." *Variety*, June 12, 1934, p. 1. (Review of "Rose Burke").

**B347** "Cornell's 'Herod' Big $22,000 in Detroit." *Variety*, November 9, 1938, p. 59. (Review of "Herod and Mariamne").

**B348** "Cornell's $650,000 Tour." *Variety*, June 12, 1934, p. 1.

**B349** "Critical Digest: 'Casanova.'" *Variety*, October 4, 1923, pp. 12,14.

**B350** Crowther, Bosley. "The Barretts of Wimpole Street." *New York Times Film Reviews*, January 18, 1957, 15:3.

**B351** Crowther, Bosley. "For Whom the Bell Tolls." *New York Times Film Reviews*, July 15, 1943, 25:2.

**B352**   Crowther, Bosley. "The Nun's Story." *New York Times Film Reviews*, June 19, 1959:30:1.

**B353**   Crowther, Bosley. "'Since You Went Away,' a Film of Wartime Domestic Life, with Claudette Colbert and Others, Opens at the Capitol." *New York Times Film Reviews*, July 21, 1944, 18:5.

**B354**   Crowther, Bosley. "Stage Door Canteen." *New York Times Film Reviews*, June 25, 1943.

**B355**   Dale, Alan. "Tiger Cats." *New York American*, October, 1924. (Also in K. Cornell, *I Wanted to Be An Actress*, 216-217).

**B356**   Dale, Alan. "'Will Shakespeare,' the Second Play by Clemence Dane Seen Here." *New York American*, January 21, 1923.

**B357**   Davies, Lawrence. "Rose Burke." *New York Times*, January 25, 1942.

**B358**   Elgutter, Ruth. "Katharine Cornell Play Proves Even Theater Folks Are Fallible." *Toledo Times*, December 21, 1950. (Review of "Captain Carvallo").

**B359**   Ervine, St. John. "The Age of Innocence." *New York World*, November, 1928. (Also in K. Cornell, *I Wanted to Be An Actress*, 245-249).

**B360**   "Firstborn." *Variety*, May 7, 1958, p. 10.

**B361**   Flexnor, Eleanor. "Get an Actor Talking about Actors." *New York Herald Tribune*, February 16, 1936. (Review of "Romeo and Juliet").

**B362**   Freedley, George. "Cornell's Production of 'Antony' Impressive but Not Very Exciting." *Morning Telegraph*, November 28, 1947.

**B363**   Furman, Gertrude. "Shaw's Classic Play Revived." *Argonaut*, March 1, 1935. (Review of "Candida").

**B364**   Gabriel, Gilbert W. "Candida." *New York Mail*, December, 1924.

**B365**   Gabriel, Gilbert W. "Catnip-and-Tuck: Robert Loraine and Katharine Cornell in an English Denunciation of French Félines." *Telegram Mail*, October 22, 1924. (Review of "Tiger Cats").

**B366**   Gabriel, Gilbert W. "The Wingless Victory." *New York American*, December 24, 1936. (Also in K. Cornell, *I Wanted to Be An Actress*, 329-333).

**B367**   Garland, Robert. "'Antigone' Offered at the Cort Theatre." *New York Journal American*, January 19, 1946.

**B368**   Garland, Robert. "'Candida' Presented at the Cort Theatre." *New York Journal American*, April 4, 1946.

**B369**   Garland, Robert. "Cornell Triumphs in Superb Offering." *New York Journal American*, November 28, 1947. (Review of "Antony and Cleopatra").

**B370**   Garland, Robert. "'Flowers of the Forest' at the Martin Beck by Katharine Cornell and Her Company." *New York World-Telegram*, April 9, 1935.

**B371**   Garland, Robert. "Katharine Cornell Opens in New Play." *New York Journal American*, November 30, 1943. (Review of "Lovers and Friends").

**B372**   Garland, Robert. "Romeo and Juliet." December, 1934. (Data incomplete).

**B373**   Garland, Robert. "Saint Joan." *New York World-Telegram*, March 10, 1936.

**B374**   Hall, Mordaunt. "Katharine Cornell Appears in George Bernard Shaw's Masterly Play, 'Candida'." *Boston Evening Transcript*, June 11, 1937.

**B375**   Hammond, Percy. "Alien Corn." *New York Herald-Tribune*, February, 1933. (Also in K. Cornell, *I Wanted to be An Actress*, 278-280).

**B376**   Hammond, Percy. "Casanova, the 'Arch Rogue' is Not So Very Wicked at the Empire." *New York Tribune*, September 28, 1923. (Also in K. Cornell, *I Wanted to Be An Actress*, 200-202).

**B377**   Hammond, Percy. "Mr. Atwill and Miss Cornell Act 'The Outsider,' a Play Much Better Than Most of Them." *New York Herald-Tribune*, March 4, 1924.

**B378**   Hammond, Percy. "Mr. Belasco Presents Robert Loraine & Miss Cornell in 'Tiger Cats,' A Despondent Sex Tragedy." *New York Herald Tribune*, October 23, 1924.

**B379**   Hammond, Percy. "Pinero's 'Enchanted Cottage' Informs Us How Magic Love May be When It is Blind." *New York Tribune*, April, 1923.

**B380**   Hawkins, William. "Cornell Spectacular in Role of Cleopatra." *New York World-Telegram*, November 28, 1947. (Review of "Antony and Cleopatra").

**B381**   Hawkins, William. "Fry's Wit Challenge to Cast." *New York World-Telegram & The Sun*, February 24, 1955. (Review of "The Dark Is Light Enough").

**B382**   Hawkins, William. "Patrician Cornell Portrays 'That Lady.'" *New York World-Telegram*, November 23, 1949.

**B383**   Hawkins, William. "'Proposals' Is Dignified Thriller." *New York World-Telegram*, December 17, 1953. (Review of "The Prescott Proposals").

**B384**   Hawkins, William. "Stage Is at Its Best With 'Constant Wife.'" *New York World-Telegram & The Sun*, December 10, 1951.

**B385**    Hutchens, John. "Nominating Katharine Cornell." *New York Times*, February 15, 1931. (First play as Actress-Manager).

**B386**    Hynes, Betty. "Katharine Cornell Offered $300,000 for One Picture." *Washington Herald*, July 15, 1938.

**B387**    "Jealousy." *New York Times Theater Reviews*, October 23, 1928, 32:2.

**B388**    "'Joan' Great Feat in Career of First Lady of Theater." *Buffalo Times*, February 13, 1936. (Review of "Saint Joan").

**B389**    "Kath Cornell $10,000, Pitts." *Variety*, December 18, 1934, p. 56. (Review of "Romeo & Juliet").

**B390**    "Katharine Cornell Opens in Cleveland." *New York Times*, November 30, 1932. (Review of "Lucrece").

**B391**    Kaufman, Wolfe. "Hinterland's Legit Best Since 1929." *Variety*, April 28, 1937, 1,66. (Review of "Candida").

**B392**    Kerr, Walter F. "The Constant Wife." *New York Herald-Tribune*, December 10, 1951.

**B393**    Kerr, Walter F. "The Firstborn." *New York Herald-Tribune*, May 1, 1958.

**B394**    Kerr, Walter F. "First Night Report: 'Dear Liar.'" *New York Herald-Tribune*, March 18, 1960.

**B395**    Kerr, Walter F. "The Prescott Proposals." *New York Herald-Tribune*, December 17, 1953.

**B396**    Kronenberger, Louis. "'Candida' Tops Season's Plays." *New York Newspaper "PM,"* April 4, 1942.

**B397**    Kronenberger, Louis. "Chekhov Gives Broadway a Lift." *New York Newspaper "PM,"* December 22, 1942. (Review of "The Three Sisters").

**B398**    Kronenberger, Louis. "Cornell Enlivens a Long Evening." *New York Newspaper "PM,"* November 30, 1943. (Review of "Lovers and Friends").

**B399**    Kronenberger, Louis. "A Great Masterpiece Is Effectively Revived." *PM Exclusive*, November 28, 1947. (Review of "Antony and Cleopatra").

**B400**    Kronenberger, Louis. "The Lady Who Had to Choose." *PM Exclusive*, April 4, 1946. (Review of "Candida").

**B401**    Kronenberger, Louis. "Shaw's Satire is Like His Beard--Neat but Long." *New York Newspaper "PM,"* March 12, 1941. (Review of "The Doctor's Dilemma").

B402    Kronenberger, Louis. "When Greek Meets Greeks." *PM Exclusive*, February 10, 1946. (Review of "Antigone").

B403    Lewis, Lloyd. "Katharine Cornell's 'Candida' is a Flawless Revival." *Chicago News*, May 21, 1937.

B404    Lockridge, Richard. "Candida." *New York Sun*, March, 1937. (Also in K. Cornell, *I Wanted to Be An Actress*, 338-340).

B405    Lockridge, Richard. "Chekhov's 'The Three Sisters' Is Revived at the Barrymore Theater." *New York Sun*, December 22, 1942.

B406    Lockridge, Richard. "Half a Browning." *New York Sun*, February 10, 1931.

B407    Lockridge, Richard. "Miss Cornell Revives 'The Doctor's Dilemma' at the Shubert Theatre." *New York Sun*, March 12, 1941.

B408    Lockridge, Richard. "Saint Joan." *New York Sun*, March 10, 1936.

B409    Lockridge, Richard. "The Stage in Review: Mr. van Druten Speaks Out." *New York Sun*, April 20, 1935. (Review of 'Flowers of the Forest").

B410    Macgowan, Kenneth. "A Bill of Divorcement." *New York Globe*, October 11, 1921.

B411    Macgowan, Kenneth. "The New Play: 'The Enchanted Cottage.'" *Globe & Commercial Advertiser*, April 2, 1923.

B412    Mantle, Burns. "'Candida' Revival Wins Cheers for Cornell and Her Co-Stars." *New York Daily News*, April 28, 1942.

B413    Mantle, Burns. "Cornell Inspired 'St. Joan.'" *New York News*, March 11, 1936. (Also in K. Cornell, *I Wanted to Be An Actress*, 321-323).

B414    Mantle, Burns. "'Enchanted Cottage' Pretty Fable." *New York News*, April, 1923.

B415    Mantle, Burns. "This New Candida Has a Mighty Tough Job." *New York Daily News*, March 26, 1925.

B416    Mantle, Burns. "'The Outsider' Tense and Well Acted Play." *Daily News*, March 4, 1924.

B417    Mantle, Burns. "Personality and Katharine Cornell." *New York News*, February 15, 1931.

B418    Mantle, Burns. "Review of 'Alien Corn'." *New York Daily News*, February, 1933. (Also in K. Cornell, *I Wanted to Be An Actress*, 280-283).

**B419**  Mantle, Burns. "'The Three Sisters' Revived by Cornell and a Starry Cast." *New York Daily News*, December 22, 1942.

**B420**  Mantle, Burns. "Ugly Duckling and the Drama." *New York Sunday News*, March 22, 1936. (Review of "Saint Joan").

**B421**  Mantle, Burns. "'Way Things Happen' & Katharine Cornell." *New York Daily News*, January 29, 1924. (Also in K. Cornell, *I Wanted to be An Actress*, 204-206).

**B422**  Mantle, Burns. "When Shakespeare was 'Will.'" *New York Daily News*, January 3, 1923.

**B423**  Marsh, Leo A. "Lowell Sherman is Star of 'Casanova.'" *New York Morning Telegraph*, September 27, 1923.

**B424**  McClain, John. "A Modern Classic on Moses Legend." *Journal American*, May 1, 1958. (Review of "Firstborn").

**B425**  McClain, John. "'The Prescott Proposals': Another Hit for Hayward." *New York Journal-American*, December 17, 1953.

**B426**  McDermott, W. F. "Katharine Cornell Brings Her New Play 'Herod & Mariamne' to the Hanna." *Cleveland Plain Dealer*, November, 1938. (Also in K. Cornell, *I Wanted to Be An Actress*, 357-359).

**B427**  Melvin, Edwin F. "Katharine Cornell Starring in New Lindsay-Crouse Play." *Christian Science Monitor*, November 17, 1953. (Review of "The Prescott Proposals").

**B428**  Metcalfe, James S. "Rare Acting." *Wall Street Journal*, December 16, 1924. (Review of "Candida").

**B429**  "Miss Cornell Plays Swift Moving Juliet." *New York Times*, November 30, 1933.

**B430**  Morehouse, Ward. "Katharine Cornell Again Plays Beautifully in 'Candida,' Revived at Cort." *The Sun*, April 4, 1946.

**B431**  Morehouse, Ward. "Miss Cornell's 'Antigone' Bold Experiment, but Not Very Stimulating Theater." *The Sun*, February 1, 1946.

**B432**  Morehouse, Ward. "Miss Kit Returns in Her 32nd Play." *New York World-Telegram*, December 16, 1953. (Review of "Prescott Proposals.")

**B433**  Morehouse, Ward. "Triumph for Miss Cornell." *The Sun*, November 28, 1947. (Review of "Antony and Cleopatra").

**B434**    "Mr. Arlen's 'Green Hat.'"  *New York Times*, September 16, 1925.

**B435**    Nathan, George Jean.  "Commercial Idealism."  *New York Journal-American*, January 3, 1954.  (Review of "The Prescott Proposals").

**B436**    Nathan, George Jean.  "The Green Hat."  *Morning Telegraph*, September, 1925.  (Also in K. Cornell, *I Wanted to Be An Actress*, 220-233).

**B437**    Nathan, George Jean.  "Star Spangled Drama."  *Judge*, November 15, 1924. (Review of "Tiger Cats").

**B438**    "New Play Produced Within Week on Broadway: 'Way Things Happen.'" *Variety*, January 31, 1924, pp. 16-17.

**B439**    Nichols, Lewis.  "Antigone."  *New York Times*, February 19, 1946.

**B440**    Nichols, Lewis.  "Barretts."  *New York Times*, April 1, 1945.

**B441**    Nichols, Lewis.  "Candida."  *New York Times*, April 4, 1946.

**B442**    Nichols, Lewis.  "Lovers and Friends."  *New York Times*, November 30, 1943.

**B443**    Nichols, Lewis.  "Romeo & Juliet."  *New York Times*, December 24, 1935.

**B444**    Nichols, Lewis.  "The Three Sisters."  *New York Times*, December 27, 1942.

**B445**    Nugent, Frank S.  "The Good Earth."  *New York Times Film Reviews*, February 3, 1937, 27:1.

**B446**    "Old Glamor."  *New York Times*, September 27, 1923.  (Review of "Casanova").

**B447**    Oliver, W.E.  "Acting Is 'Lift' to Drama."  *Los Angeles Herald Express*, October 28, 1933.  (Review of "Alien Corn").

**B448**    "Out of Town Review: 'Romeo and Juliet.'"  Variety, December 5, 1933, p. 55.

**B449**    "Outsider' Grips."  *New York Times*, March 4, 1924. (Review of "The Outsider").

**B450**    Palmer, Rollin.  "Cornell Comedy Proves Inept, Disappointing."  *Buffalo Courier-Express*, December 7, 1950.  (Review of "Captain Carvallo").

**B451**    Palmer, Rollin.  "New Praise Won by Miss Cornell."  *Buffalo Evening News*, April, 1935.  (Review of "Flowers of the Forest").

**B452**    Parker, H. T.  "Review of 'Candida.'"  *Boston Transcript*, December, 1924. (Also in K. Cornell, *I Wanted to Be An Actress*, 219).

**B453** Parker, H. T. "Review of 'The Letter.'" *Boston Transcript*, September, 1927. (Also in K. Cornell, *I Wanted to Be An Actress*, 229-237).

**B454** "Play: 'The Green Hat.'" *New York Times*, September 16, 1925.

**B455** "Plays on Broadway: 'Romeo & Juliet.'" *Variety*, December 25, 1934, p. 48.

**B456** "Plays Out of Town: 'Romeo & Juliet.'" *Variety*, December 11, 1934, p. 56.

**B457** Pollack, Robert. "Cornell's New Historical Role a One-Eyed Princess." *Chicago Sun & Times*, January 22, 1949. (Review of "That Lady").

**B458** "Premiere of Cornell Comedy Wins Only Polite Applause." *Buffalo News*, December 7, 1950. (Review of "Captain Carvallo").

**B459** Rascoe, Burton. "Ancient 'Antigone' Emerges Bright, New." *New York World-Telegram*, February 19, 1946.

**B460** Rascoe, Burton. "Chekhov's Three Sisters Opens at the Barrymore." *New York World-Telegram*, December 22, 1942.

**B461** Rascoe, Burton. "Hardwicke Steals Show in 'Candida.'" *New York World-Telegram*, April 4, 1946.

**B462** Roussel, Hubert. "Katharine Cornell in One-Eyed Role; Lovers' History in 'That Lady.'" *Houston Post*, March 29, 1949.

**B463** Sallie. "The Dressie Side: 'Outsider' Gripping." *Variety* March 5, 1924, p. 7.

**B464** Sennewald, Andre. "The Barretts of Wimpole Street." *New York Times Film Reviews*, September 29, 1934, 12:2.

**B465** Shaw, Len G. "Herod and Mariamne." *Detroit Free Press*, November, 1938. (Also in K. Cornell, *I Wanted to Be An Actress*, 355-357).

**B466** Shaw, Len G. "The Theater." *Detroit Free Press*, November 1, 1938. (Review of "Herod and Mariamne").

**B467** Sheaffer, Louis. "Cornell and Aherne Star in Enjoyable Maugham Revival." *Brooklyn Eagle*, December 10, 1951. (Review of "The Constant Wife").

**B468** Short, Frank Lea. "The Actors' Theater Revives 'Candida.'" *Christian Science Monitor*, December 16, 1924.

**B469** "Shows in N.Y. and Comment: 'Casanova.'" *Variety*, November 4, 1923, 14.

**B470** "Shows in N.Y. and Comment: 'Will Shakespeare.'" *Variety*, January 12, 1923, p. 14.

**B471** "Shows in N.Y. and Comment: 'Will Shakespeare.'" *Variety*, January 19, 1923, p. 17.

**B472** "Shows in N.Y. and Comment: 'Casanova.'" *Variety*, October 4, 1923.

**B473** "Shows on Broadway: 'The Firstborn.'" *Variety*, May 7, 1958, p. 70.

**B474** Stevens, Ashton. "Audience Writes Unspoken Word, Makes 'Barretts.'" *Chicago Herald Examiner*, April 24, 1932.

**B475** Stevens, Ashton. "Miss Cornell Brings in 'The Barretts' a Virtually Perfect Production." *Chicago Herald-Examiner*, April, 19, 1932.

**B476** Stevens, Ashton. "Critic Finds No 'Candida' So Womanly as Cornell's." *Chicago American*, May 29, 1937.

**B477** Stevens, Ashton. "Critic Speaks of Anderson, Cornell." *Chicago American*, May 22, 1937. (Review of "Wingless Victory").

**B478** Stevens, Ashton. "The Green Hat." *Chicago Herald Examiner*, September, 1925. (Also in K. Cornell, *I Wanted to Be An Actress*, 224-227).

**B479** Stone, Percy. "Now That Katharine Is a Producer." *New York Tribune*, February 22, 1931.

**B480** Taylor, Harvey. "Katherine Cornell's New Play Is Poor." *Detroit Times*, December 12, 1950. (Review of "Captain Carvallo").

**B481** "The Barretts of Wimpole Street." *Variety Film Reviews*, October 2, 1934.

**B482** "The Unconquered." *Variety Film Reviews*, June 23, 1954. (Review of Helen Keller documentary).

**B483** "Thirty-seven B'way Shows & Seasons, Peak 'Lucrece' 7 Times, $14,000, in Doubt." *Variety*, December 27, 1932, p. 45.

**B484** Towse, J. Rankin. "'Casanova' is a Rich & Popular Show." *New York Evening Post*, September 27, 1923.

**B485** Towse, J. Rankin. "Clemence Dane's Play & Sundry Comments." *New York Post*, February 9, 1924. (Review of "The Way Things Happen").

**B486** Towse, J. Rankin. "The Play: 'The Enchanted Cottage.'" *New York Post*, April, 1923. (Also in K. Cornell, *I Wanted to Be An Actress*, 195-198).

**B487** "Twenty-seven Thousand Advance Sale for Kath. Cornell in L.A." *Variety*, January 30, 1934, p. 55. (Reviews of "The Barretts" and "Romeo and Juliet").

**B488**   "U.S. Soldiers' Response to 'Barretts.'" *New York Times*, September 17, II, 1944, 1-3.

**B489**   Waldorf, Wilella. "Katharine Cornell Abandons 'Herod and Mariamne.'" *Washington Post*, November 14, 1938.

**B490**   Waters, Arthur B. "The Stage's White Hopes." *Philadelphia Ledger*, January, 1924. (Also in K. Cornell, *I Wanted to Be An Actress*, 206-207).

**B491**   Watts, Jr., Richard. "Charming Revival of Maugham Play. *New York Post*, December 10, 1951. (Review of "The Constant Wife").

**B492**   Watts, Jr., Richard. "Christopher Fry Thinks It Over." *New York Post*, February 24, 1955. (Review of "The Dark Is Light Enough").

**B493**   Watts, Jr., Richard. "Christopher Fry's Play about Moses." *New York Post*, May 1, 1958. (Review of "Firstborn").

**B494**   Watts, Jr., Richard. "Doctors at Bay." *New York Herald-Tribune*, March 12, 1941.

**B495**   Watts, Jr., Richard. "The Playwright and the Actress." *New York Post*, March 18, 1960. (Review of "Dear Liar").

**B496**   Watts, Jr., Richard. "Something Memorable." *New York Herald-Tribune*, April 28, 1942. (Review of "Candida").

**B497**   Watts, Jr., Richard. "Two On the Aisle." *New York Post*, November 23, 1949. (Review of "That Lady").

**B498**   Watts, Jr., Richard. "The Wingless Victory." *New York Herald-Tribune*, December, 1936. (Also in K. Cornell, *I Wanted to Be An Actress*. 333-336).

**B499**   Whipple, Sidney B. "'The Doctor's Dilemma' Magnificently Played." *New York World-Telegram*, March 12, 1941.

**B500**   "William Faversham in 'Old Country.'" *New York Times*, October 31, 1917, 11:1.

**B501**   Winchell, Walter. "Dishonored Lady." *New York Mirror*, February, 1930. (Also in K. Cornell, *I Wanted to Be An Actress*, 252-254).

**B502**   "Wingless Victory." *Variety*, December 30, 1936, p. 51.

**B503**   Woollcott, Alexander. "Allan Pollock Welcomed." *New York Times*, October 11, 1921. (Review of "A Bill of Divorcement").

**B504**   Woollcott, Alexander. "Moreau's 'Joan.'" *New York Times*, April 17, 1921. (Review of "The Trial of Joan of Arc").

**B505**   Woollcott, Alexander. "The Outsider." *New York Times*, March, 1924. (Also in K. Cornell, *I Wanted to Be An Actress*, 208-210).

**B506**   Woollcott, Alexander. "Richard Bird as Marchbanks." *New York Sun*, December 13, 1924. (Review of "Candida").

**B507**   Woollcott, Alexander. "Second Thoughts on First Nights." *New York Times*, October 16, 1921. (Review of "A Bill of Divorcement").

**B508**   Woollcott, Alexander. "The Severe Miss Crothers." *New York Times*, March 3, 1921. (Review of "Nice People").

**B509**   Young, Stark. "The Actor's Theatre." *New York Times*, December 13, 1924. (Review of "Candida").

**B510**   Young, Stark. "Candida." *New York Times*, December 21, 1924.

**B511**   Young, Stark. "Mr. Belasco's Opening." *New York Times*, October 22, 1924. (Review of "Tiger Cats"). (Also in K. Cornell, *I Wanted to Be An Actress*, 214-216).

## Dissertations and Unpublished Studies

**B512**   Moss, Lynda Towle. "A Historical Study of Katharine Cornell as an Actress-Producer, 1931-1960." Ph.D. Diss. University of Southern California, 1974. Ann Arbor: University Microfilm International 35/04Ap2434, Order number DDJ78-11546.

**B513**   Letters from fans. New York Public Library Performing Research Center.

**B514**   Tillinghast, John Keith. "Guthrie McClintic, Director." Ph. D. Diss. Indiana University, 1964. Ann Arbor: University Microfilm, Inc. Order number 64-12,093.

**B515**   McClintic, Guthrie. "Guthrie McClintic." An incomplete draft of a sequel to "Kit and Me," held in unprocessed Gertrude Macy Collection at the New York Public Library for the Performing Arts.

## Collections

**B516**   Katharine Cornell-Guthrie McClintic Collection, in the Billy Rose Theatre Collection, New York Public Library for the Performing Arts, Lincoln Center, New York.

**B517**   Nancy Hamilton Collection (unprocessed), Billy Rose Theatre Collection, New York Public Library for the Performing Arts.

**B518**   Gertrude Macy Collection (unprocessed), Billy Rose Theatre Collection, New York Public Library for the Performing Arts.

# APPENDIX A

# Awards, Honors, Citations

## Awards

**A01    Delia Austrian Medal** (May 17, 1935).  Daniel Frohman presented the bronze medal to Miss Cornell at the annual luncheon in Central Park Casino and 25th anniversary of the New York Drama League for her distinguished performance as Juliet in her own production of *Romeo and Juliet*.  Second and third awards were given to Elisabeth Bergner for her acting in *Escape Me Never!* and Florence McGee for her performance in *The Children's Hour* (B155).

**A02    Chancellor's Medal** (February 22, 1935).  The award was made by Chancellor Samuel P. Capan of the University of Buffalo, in New York, to Miss Cornell for performing a great and ennobling thing which "dignifies the performer and Buffalo in the eyes of the world" and for enriching the life of her generation.  The only honorary award made by the University, it is the first time it has been awarded to an artist and a woman (B226).

**A03    Gold Medal of National Achievement Award** (March 30, 1937).  At a White House dinner First Lady Mrs. Franklin Delano Roosevelt presented Chi Omega Sorority's coveted annual award to Miss Cornell, the first actress to receive it.  Frank Gillmore, president of the Actors and Chorus Equity Associations, sent the following telegram with the message that "...the actors and actresses of America take great pride in the fact that the award this year has been given to Miss Katharine Cornell, our much-loved and much-admired comrade.  Each of us feels a personal gratification and a sense of elation that this outstanding lady of our profession should be so honored" (B234).

**A04    Medal of Freedom** (1945).  The award was bestowed on Miss Cornell for her services during World War II by the United States Government.  Commemorating contributions to "world peace or cultural or other significant public or private endeavors," the Presidential Gold Medal represents the highest civilian honor (B221).

**A05    Antoinette Perry Award** (1948). This award was made for her distinguished performance in *Antony and Cleopatra* while Miss Cornell was touring with the play. The American Theatre Wing chose the recipients of this award (B157).

**A06    Jane Addams Medal** (February 6, 1950). Rockford College in Rockford, Illinois, honored Miss Cornell for a distinguished contribution through her life and work (B198;236).

**A07    Medal for Good Speech on Stage** (May 20, 1959). This award, intended "to draw attention to correct, unaffected and euphonius diction," was bestowed on Miss Cornell by the American Academy of Arts and Letters (B005).

**A08    American National Theater and Academy (ANTA) National Artists Award** (January 10, 1974). For her "acting ability and her theatrical genius" and for having "elevated the theater throughout the world" Miss Cornell received this gold medal. It had been given only once before, in 1972, to Alfred Lunt and Lynn Fontanne. ANTA, which conceived the award, was chartered by the Congress in 1935 as "an expression of gratitude from a nation for continued artistic excellence" (B034).

### Honorary Degrees

**A09    Doctor of Letters Degree** (1936). Dr. Glenn Ford, President of the University of Wisconsin, in Madison, and friend of Miss Cornell, conferred this honorary degree on her while she was touring in *Saint Joan* (B236).

**A10    Doctor of Letters Degree** (June 14, 1937. Elmira College, Elmira, New York, honored Katharine Cornell and Helen Hayes with this degree. Miss Cornell, who was appearing in a play in Boston, could not attend; her father accepted the degree in her behalf (B002).

**A11    Honorary D. Litt. Degree** (June 15, 1937). Cornell University in Ithaca, New York, honored Miss Cornell with this degree (B198).

**A12    Honorary Doctorate of Humane Letters** (June 21, 1937). President W. A. Neilson, of Smith College, Northampton, Massachusetts, presented Miss Cornell with this honorary degree.   Walter Lippman was the commencement speaker at the annual commencement exercises (B135).

**A13    Doctor of Letters Degree** (May 24, 1938). President William A. Eddy of Hobart College, Geneva, New York,  conferred this honorary degree on Miss Cornell for "bringing the highest artistry of great drama, production and acting to the remotest provinces of a nation...." This was the 113th commencement of Hobart College where her grandfather and great grandfather had been trustees (B062; B100).

**A14    Honorary Master of Arts** (June 15, 1938). This degree was awarded to Katharine Cornell by the University of Pennsylvania, Philadelphia. She was one of five persons upon whom honorary degrees were conferred (B225).

**A15**   **Doctor of Fine Arts** (June 4, 1941). Miss Cornell and news commentator Lowell Thomas received honorary degrees from Clark University, Atlanta, Georgia (B112).

**A16**   **Honorary Degree** (1947). Ithaca College in Ithaca, New York, presented Miss Cornell with an honorary degree (B236).

**A17**   **Doctor of Fine Arts Degree** (June 15, 1948). At its 201st commencement President Harold W. Dodds of Princeton University, Princeton, New Jersey, bestowed this honor on Miss Cornell as "an acknowledged leader of the theatre in our time and the embodiment of its highest standard and finest traditions. Her notable career is the product of native ability, tireless industry and an unswerving refusal to be satisfied with anything but the best. Always there is the passionate conviction that art is for the people and the artist is the servant of his art. Every New York success must be taken on tour, regardless of expense, discomfort or personal sacrifice. We cite her here for her distinguished contribution to one of the great arts of all time, and for the pleasure and deep satisfaction she has given us." Also receiving honorary degrees were General Omar N. Bradley and Dr. Raymond B. Fosdick (B190).

**A18**   **Doctor of Law Degree** (December 4, 1951). Katharine Cornell and Brian Aherne each received this honorary degree at the dedication ceremonies for Baylor University's new Armstrong-Browning library in Waco, Texas. As a chief attraction, Miss Cornell and Mr. Aherne recited their lines from *The Barretts of Wimpole Street* (B018).

**A19**   **Honorary Degree of Humanities** (June 14, 1955). The degree was bestowed on Miss Cornell by Rev. Dr. Theodore P. Ferris at the 155th commencement exercises of Middlebury College, Middlebury, Vermont.

**A20**   **Doctor of Literature** (June 11, 1956). Katharine Cornell and Guthrie McClintic were awarded honorary degrees by Kenyon College in Gambier, Ohio.

### Citations and Other Honors

**A21**   **Citation** (1944). While performing *The Barretts of Wimpole Street* for the armed services in Europe, Miss Cornell and her company received a citation from General Mark Clark "for excellence in performance, merit and discipline" (S55).

**A22**   **Special Exhibit** (1950). Eugene Speicher's portrait of Katharine Cornell in the role of Candida opened at the Albright Art Gallery in Buffalo, New York (B213).

**A23**   **Woman of the Year Citation** (December 29, 1959). The Women's Division of the American Friends of the Hebrew University cited Miss Cornell for her "outstanding contribution to the American cultural scene," for bringing "dignity and romance to the theatre" and for linking the warmth of her art with the 'progress of mankind.'" A Katharine Cornell Chair of Comparative Literature, to be endowed for $100,000, was also being established in her honor at the University of Jerusalem (B116).

**A24**   **Tribute** (February 16, 1973). Friends honored her on her seventy-fifth birthday which, to their surprise, was really her eightieth, a deception which began in 1928.

Among those who celebrated with her were her cousin Douglas Cornell and his wife, Nancy Hamilton, Gert Macy, Margalo Gillmore, the Lunts, Anne Gugler, Bill (he restored Association Hall for her) and Lois Katzenbach (B163, p. 517).

**A25  Dedication of Special Library** (April 24, 1974). The New York Public Library's Theater Collection in Lincoln Center dedicated a special room, intended as a reading room, for the Katharine Cornell-Guthrie McClintic collection. Among the reviews, awards and memorabilia was a framed letter from George Bernard Shaw in which he called Miss Cornell "a gorgeous dark lady from the cradle of the human race, wherever that was." Martha Graham, Lillian Gish and Brooks Atkinson made brief remarks in tribute to Miss Cornell. Atkinson said, "the theater becomes electric when she appears." (B205).

# Roles Miss Cornell Did Not Play

## Plays

*The Old Country* (Opened: October 30, 1917)

William Faversham tried to persuade Kit to try out for the leading role in *The Old Country*, in 1917, but she refused because she did not feel ready for the part. Mosel noted in her biography that, inasmuch as Faversham had never seen her act, Kit may have thought the offer was made in deference to Mrs. Wolcott who was helping her get started. Kit's refusal to accept the part was probably fortunate as Faversham's play closed 15 days after its October opening.

The critic in the *New York Times* found the sentimental English play to be thin and not the sort of thing that American audiences appreciated. Faversham played the lead role in his typical manner, which was "graceful, suave, romantically picturesque." By failing to convey the roughness that bitterness and life on the frontier would have etched on the character of James Fountain, the role Faversham played, he had detracted from 'the vigor of the play" (B500).

*Jealousy* (Opened: October 22, 1923)

Al Woods had wanted Miss Cornell and Glenn Hunter to play in this two-character melodrama which he asked Guthrie to direct. Kit did not accept his offer because she did not want to do another play in a European setting. Instead, she bought Margaret Ayer Barnes' dramatization of Edith Wharton's *The Age of Innocence*. The part of Valerie in *Jealousy* went to Fay Bainter. Guthrie McClintic not only directed the play but also replaced Glenn Hunter when he withdrew from the play at Miss Bainter's request. She wanted Guthrie in the role.

The female lead in *Jealousy* when to Fay Bainter, and during the Boston tryout, Guthrie played the role of the husband. Before going to New York, he stepped out of the part, giving it to Richard Bird. It is not clear how John Halliday came to be the lead, but it was noted that it was difficult to find the right actor for the character. In that a play with only two characters is a rarity and a challenge, the *New York Times* reviewer thought that, in this case, it worked.  The play, which was later made into a mediocre movie, bears resemblance to *Tiger Cats*, at least in its theme of marital infidelity and jealousy (B387).

### The Doll Master (Projected: 1923-24)

David Belasco had coerced Miss Cornell into signing a contract to do a play after *Tiger Cats*.  When he did not have a play ready for her at the time *The Green Hat* was offered her, she agreed to do it.  Belasco immediately announced that Miss Cornell would play *The Doll Master*, which was only a title.  The play had not been written.  He finally released Miss Cornell from the contract with the condition that the program state that she appeared "by permission of David Belasco" (B163, p. 195).

### Rosmersholm (Projected:1937)

After *Alien Corn* Miss Cornell wanted to play Rebecca West in Ibsen's *Rosmersholm*.  Several circumstances changed her mind.  The translation she had commissioned was not satisfactory.  Furthermore, she was not getting the support to play the role from Guthrie or friends and advisers who were urging her to do Juliet.  She had also reached a point where she felt she could accept the challenge of Shakespeare.  Moreover, her age (she was then 40, secretly 45) was a factor, so she decided to introduce *Rosmersholm* into the repertory after she did *Romeo and Juliet*.  In 1937, it was announced in the *Buffalo News* that she would do *Rosmersholm* the following season.  Neither plan materialized (B163, p. 319).

Mosel and Macy speculated that, had she played Rebecca West in *Rosmersholm*, Miss Cornell probably would not have done *Romeo and Juliet*, and a "different kind of theatrical career would have followed" (Mosel, p. 320).  Their speculation may have been based on the fact that the plays of Ibsen reflected the trend toward realism, determinism and psychological truthfulness (B128).  Had she gone in that direction audiences would have been deprived of seeing her as Juliet and possibly other outstanding roles.

In 1935, Eva Le Gallienne appeared as Rebecca West in *Rosmersholm*.  Brooks Atkinson of the *New York Times* found Le Gallienne's acting more credible than the play, which did not appeal to him.  He considered it to be "a sort of pulpiteering."  With a leading critic viewing the play as uncongenial, Miss Cornell may not have fared any better in *Rosmersholm* than her fellow actress, Miss Le Gallienne (B282).

### The Ivory Fan (Projected: 1938)

In 1937 Miss Cornell bought *The Ivory Fan* by Gustav Eckstein, a professor in the College of Medicine at the University of Cincinnati.  It was to be one of the 5 or 6 plays in the repertory planned for her world tour which did not come about because of Ray Henderson's death.  After that, when the United States was at war with Japan, the theme was inappropriate (B140).

## Films

*The Barretts of Wimpole Street* (Released: 1934; Metro-Goldwyn-Mayer; running time: 110 minutes)

In an effort to persuade Katharine Cornell to play Elizabeth in the film, Irving Thalberg offered her a handsome sum with the promise that he would destroy the film if she was not satisfied with it. She finally accepted, then, overcome with panic, hastily withdrew her verbal agreement. Thalberg's argument that she would be doing the film for posterity was frightening to her. After Bernhardt's death, she had witnessed the ridicule of *Camille* when younger audiences saw the great actress on film. Miss Cornell did not want to be subjected to that humiliation. She wanted the response of an immediate audience, not a second-hand screen image that could be shown after her death.

Metro-Goldwyn-Mayer filmed *The Barretts* with Irving Thalberg's wife, Norma Shearer, as Elizabeth and Frederic March as Robert Browning. Charles Laughton played the tyrannical Edward Moulton-Barrett. *Variety* thought the production was "ultra, from direction to sound and cameras," but that the lengthy forepart was slow and could have been condensed. *New York Times* reviewer Andre Sennewald thought the shrewd filming and courageous acting had obscured the faults of the play. Making no comparison to Cornell's stage portrayal, he found Miss Shearer's Elizabeth "brave and touching." Special mention went to Flush, whose "almost human and occasionally super-human powers of expression are so remarkable as to cause some alarm for the superiority of the human race" (B464).

Miss Cornell's concerns about film, that it would require a great deal of restraint in gesture and expression, were justifiable concerns. Also, the finer features of Miss Shearer were more adaptable to the screen. The enthusiastic reception of the critics and public to both actresses can only make those fortunate enough to have seen both the stage and film productions richer for the experiences.

In 1957, MGM refilmed *The Barretts* with Jennifer Jones and Bill Travers as the poets. It was about a year after Miss Cornell had made her debut with Elizabeth on television.

*The Good Earth* (Released: February, 1937; Metro-Goldwyn-Mayer; running time: 140 minutes)

Miss Cornell turned down an offer to play O-Lan and the part went to Luise Rainer who won an Academy Award for her performance. Based on Pearl Buck's book *The Good Earth*, the film was "one of the finest things Hollywood has done," in the view of Frank Nugent of the *New York Times*. The filming was plagued with many problems, including revisions, changes of directors and the death of Irving Thalberg, who had supervised the early sequences. The result--sometimes ponderous and slow but with brilliant photography and splendid performances--received high praise (B445).

*For Whom the Bell Tolls* (Released: 1943; Paramount Pictures; running time: 170 minutes)

The role of Pilar, for which Katina Paxinou received an Academy Award, was turned down by Miss Cornell. Despite its length, the movie was one of the best films of the year, according to Bosley Crowther of the *New York Times*. Crowther thought that Sam Wood, who wrote the screen play, and director Dudley Nichols were "overzealous" in their fidelity to Ernest Hemingway's novel. The quality was excellent but the film was too long. Miss Cornell was well suited in appearance and ability for the role of the Spanish woman. Had she accepted it, she would have played with an excellent cast such as she would have selected: Ingrid Bergman, Gary Cooper, Akim Tamiroff and a number of actors who had appeared in her stage casts (B351).

*Since You Went Away* (Released: July, 1944; United Artists; running time; 166 minutes)

Miss Cornell had wanted to play in *Since You Went Away*, a homefront film in World War II, which David O. Selznick was directing. However, Selznick thought Claudette Colbert was ideal for the role and sent Miss Cornell a rejection letter, which is reprinted in *Memo from David O. Selznick*, a book by Rudy Behlmer (B179). The situation is ironic in that everyone in Hollywood for years had been trying to get her to accept a role and she had always declined.

Inasmuch as *New York Times critic* Bosley Crowther judged the play to be "a rather large dose of choking sentiment," in which a double-standard as to the war effort prevails, Miss Cornell's rejection may have been her good fortune. Crowther also thought the play had spent a long time harping on the theme of "lonesomeness and anxiety," a theme all too well-known (B353).

*The Nun's Story* (Released: 1959; Warner Brothers; running time; 149 minutes).

There being several mothers superior in *The Nun's Story*, it is not clear which role Miss Cornell was offered. It was probably Mother Emmanuel played by Edith Evans. The story has the kind of conflict and suffering that appealed to Miss Cornell and she would have been working with a stellar cast. The film was "a brilliant synthesis of idea and pictorial imagery...stunning contrasts in color, tempo and moods" (B352).

*Florence Nightingale* (Projected: 1951)

In 1951, it was announced in the *Washington Times Herald* that Miss Cornell would do the film version of Cecil Woodham-Smith's biography of Florence Nightingale. Later, George Jean Nathan in *Publishers' Weekly* predicted that, if it were made, it would be the "two-a-day, reserved-seat premiere somewhere along in 1958-59." For undisclosed reasons, Miss Cornell did not make that film. She did, however, make a recording entitled "Florence Nightingale."

*The Unconquered* (Released: 1954)
    (Albert Margolies; running time: 55 minutes)

In 1949, Robert Flaherty of the American Foundation of the Blind sought Miss Cornell for a film on Helen Keller. Although she and Miss Keller were close friends, she did not act in a film about Miss Keller. However, she did narrate Nancy Hamilton's inspirational documentary on Miss Keller's valiant fight to live a normal life. Through early photographs, newsreel clips and footage of more contemporary scenes the film retraces much of Miss Keller's life. Because of the depressing aspects of the chronicle of a woman who, in her infancy, was left blind, deaf and unable to talk, *Variety* suggested that the subject matter does not qualify it for general distribution. It was recommended for schools, social welfare groups and women's clubs because of its educational value and example of courage. Throughout the picture Katharine Cornell narrates the commentary written by James Shute.

The technical director of the biopic is Richard Carver Wood. Joe Lipkowitz is the cameraman and the music score is by Morgan Lewis. Miss Cornell's practice recording for the film is listed with the Nancy Hamilton collection in the Library of Performing Arts in New York City (B482).

# APPENDIX C

# Miss Cornell's Articles, Book, Foreword

It is not clear how much of the actual writing of the articles and autobiography Miss Cornell did, for in some cases she told her stories to a writer who was acknowledged as second author. It is assumed that, where no co-author is identified, the writing is hers.

**"Audiences I Have Known"**
(New York Sun, November 19, 1927)

Written when she was playing Leslie Crosbie in *The Letter* Miss Cornell discussed the concern that actors have about the varying responsiveness of audiences. She compared the expectations of opening night audiences who, unlike those who came to see the closing performance, were quite impartial. Actors, she wrote, instinctively feel the support or antipathy of an audience. When support is lacking the actors lose enthusiasm, although they may be unaware of it.

Holiday time, current events, the day of the week, and time of performance affect the emotional spontaneity of an audience. Responsiveness is also influenced by the makeup of audience members, whether they are young or old, quick or slow to catch the lines, dignified or carefree (B049).

*I Wanted to be An Actress: The Autobiography of Katharine Cornell*
(New York: Random House, 1938; also published in *Stage* magazine)

This autobiography was told to Ruth Woodbury Sedgwick Sedgwick, editor of *Stage* magazine in which it first appeared. The life story covers Miss Cornell's career through her apprenticeship, her early Broadway, stardom and actress-manager years to 1937. It includes many photographs as well as reviews and articles by critics and notable authors.

*Time* (4/3/39) reported that the book was acceptable but failed to convey the personality of Miss Cornell. In that respect it was disappointing. It has, however, documented events in her life and preserved critical reviews and has been an invaluable resource (B047).

**"Actress Manager: A High-Point in the Career of the First Lady of the Theatre"**
(*Senior Scholastic*, April 6, 1940: 17-21)

Miss Cornell's article conveys her excitement in finding *The Barretts of Wimpole Street* for which she bought the rights as a present for her husband, Guthrie McClintic. He was delighted with her gift but insisted that she play the role of Elizabeth which she did not feel was right for her. She finally agreed to do it.

The McClintics had been considering the formation of their own company if they could find a play they liked. *The Barretts* seemed to be the right vehicle for this new venture. Urged by A. Conyer Goodyear, Stanton Griffis and Gert Macy, who were to be the financial backers of the company, Miss Cornell became a manager. Henceforth, the marquee would read "Katharine Cornell Presents--."

In an easy, conversational manner, Cornell explained how they worked out the company's structure and found the right actors, especially for Browning and Flush. With interesting anecdotes she gave insight into rehearsals, Guthrie's directing, her opening night stagefright, Gert's training of Flush and meeting Greta Garbo. She also discussed her health problems that necessitated a temporary closing of the play and the final, tearful night of the New York run.

Two photographs are included--one of her as Elizabeth with Brian Aherne as Browning in *The Barretts,* and the other of her and Guthrie. A brief biographical sketch accompanies Miss Cornell's story of becoming an actress-manager (B048).

**"Foreword" in *Curtain Going Up*! by Gladys Malvern**
(New York: Julian Messner, Inc., 1943)

Miss Cornell summarized her career as "twenty-seven years of hard work." She believed that many women who were working hard to become finer beings achieved serenity but never ceased in the their efforts to improve.

The story of her unfinished life would hopefully encourage other young women to follow a stage career. She could not tell them how to begin or how to go about being an actress, for there were times when she needed that encouragement desperately. Reminding them that the work they must do is "unglamorous, exhausting, and dispiriting," she emphasized the importance of conviction and determination. Other essentials are a carefully planned attack, as well as "intelligence, awareness, sensitivity, self-effacement, industry." Physical beauty, while not most important, removes one barrier in their climb. Having no formula for success except that they must forge their own paths, she hoped that her life and career would inspire them. "For now more than ever, when footlights are dimmed in other lands, our own have need to shine the brighter, and new fuel must be added to the flame with which they burn" (B139, p. xi).

**"A Good Play Will Always Find a Good Audience"**
(*Theatre Arts* 38, May, 1954, pp. 27-29)

In this story, as told to Alice Griffin, Miss Cornell discusses the compensations and dispels some of the myths of taking shows on the road. Despite the hardships, and there were many, she believed that taking plays to the people throughout America was the way to build audiences and make "friends for the theatre." Many of her fans, particularly the GIs who had seen *The Barretts* in Europe, consisted of persons who would never have seen a play had she not toured to them. That first experience made avid theatregoers of many.

Her 1932 tour of *The Barretts of Wimpole Street* was the first extended tour of an entire Broadway company with stars. Furthermore, contrary to the beliefs about people in the hinterlands, she found them to be "receptive, eager, critical, and astute."

She compared the hardships that actors underwent in the early part of the century, when theatres were far from adequate, to the conveniences of the 1950s. She noted that audience members, as well as actors, made sacrifices. She was impressed and gratified by the number of people who traveled many miles to see her plays. At the same time she was modest about her role in building a following on the road.

The idea that people wouldn't be drawn to classics was also a misconception she dispelled. She maintained that, if a production was good, it would find an audience. She proved it with *Romeo and Juliet, Saint Joan*, and *The Three Sisters* (B046).

# Index

This index refers to both page numbers and to individual entries in each of the two sections which correspond to Miss Cornell's specific career achievements. Events are listed chronologically and numbered consecutively in each section for cross referencing.

The major events of her career, Stage Appearances, begin with her early, or apprenticeship, years (SO1 through S21) and continue through her early Broadway years (S22 through S34). The remainder of her stage appearances occurred in her actress-manager years which began with *The Barretts of Wimpole Street* (S35) and ended with *Dear Liar* (S66). Radio, Film, Television and Recordings make up the second section of career activities. Radio entries are identified by "R," film by "F," television by "T" and recordings by "D."

The bibliography lists 518 reference sources including those cited in the various sections of the book and additional sources for more information on Miss Cornell. The first 255 sources are annotated. Entries (numbered B001,...etc.) consist of books, journals, periodicals, magazine and newspaper articles. Critics' reviews (numbered B256,...etc.) which appear in newspapers make up the second part of the bibliography, and are followed by dissertations, unpublished work and collections.

The appendices include Miss Cornell's awards and honors (Appendix A), theatre and film roles she was offered or considered but did not play (Appendix B) and the articles, foreword and autobiography that she wrote (Appendix C).

**About the Author**

LUCILLE M. PEDERSON is an Associate Professor emerita at the University of Cincinnati, where she taught in the Department of Communication. Her writings have appeared in *Notable Women in the American Theatre* (Greenwood, 1989) and in journals such as the *Journal of Auditory Research*, the *British Journal of Audiology*, and *Communication Education*.

**Titles in**
**Bio-Bibliographies in the Performing Arts**

Milos Forman: A Bio-Bibliography
*Thomas J. Slater*

Kate Smith: A Bio-Bibliography
*Michael R. Pitts*

Patty Duke: A Bio-Bibliography
*Stephen L. Eberly*

Carole Lombard: A Bio-Bibliography
*Robert D. Matzen*

Eva Le Gallienne: A Bio-Bibliography
*Robert A. Schanke*

Julie Andrews: A Bio-Bibliography
*Les Spindle*

Richard Widmark: A Bio-Bibliography
*Kim Holston*

Orson Welles: A Bio-Bibliography
*Bret Wood*

Ann Sothern: A Bio-Bibliography
*Margie Schultz*

Alice Faye: A Bio-Bibliography
*Barry Rivadue*

Jennifer Jones: A Bio-Bibliography
*Jeffrey L. Carrier*

Cary Grant: A Bio-Bibliography
*Beverley Bare Buehrer*

Maureen O'Sullivan: A Bio-Bibliography
*Connie J. Billips*

Ava Gardner: A Bio-Bibliography
*Karin J. Fowler*

Jean Arthur: A Bio-Bibliography
*Arthur Pierce and Douglas Swarthout*

Donna Reed: A Bio-Bibliography
*Brenda Scott Royce*

Gordon MacRae: A Bio-Bibliography
*Bruce R. Leiby*

Mary Martin: A Bio-Bibliography
*Barry Rivadue*

Irene Dunne: A Bio-Bibliography
*Margie Schultz*

Anne Baxter: A Bio-Bibliography
*Karin J. Fowler*

Tallulah Bankhead: A Bio-Bibliography
*Jeffrey L. Carrier*

Jessica Tandy: A Bio-Bibliography
*Milly S. Barranger*

Janet Gaynor: A Bio-Bibliography
*Connie Billips*

James Stewart: A Bio-Bibliography
*Gerard Molyneaux*

Joseph Papp: A Bio-Bibliography
*Barbara Lee Horn*

Henry Fonda: A Bio-Bibliography
*Kevin Sweeney*

Edwin Booth: A Bio-Bibliography
*L. Terry Oggel*

Ethel Merman: A Bio-Bibliography
*George B. Bryan*

Lauren Bacall: A Bio-Bibliography
*Brenda Scott Royce*

Joseph Chaikin: A Bio-Bibliography
*Alex Gildzen and Dimitris Karageorgiou*

Richard Burton: A Bio-Bibliography
*Tyrone Steverson*

Maureen Stapleton: A Bio-Bibliography
*Jeannie M. Woods*

David Merrick: A Bio-Bibliography
*Barbara Lee Horn*

Vivien Leigh: A Bio-Bibliography
*Cynthia Marylee Molt*

Robert Mitchum: A Bio-Bibliography
*Jerry Roberts*

Agnes Moorehead: A Bio-Bibliography
*Lynn Kear*

Colleen Dewhurst: A Bio-Bibliography
*Barbara Lee Horn*

Helen Hayes: A Bio-Bibliography
*Donn B. Murphy and Stephen Moore*

Boris Karloff: A Bio-Bibliography
*Beverley Bare Buehrer*

Betty Grable: A Bio-Bibliography
*Larry Billman*

Ellen Stewart and La Mama: A Bio-Bibliography
*Barbara Lee Horn*

Lucille Lortel: A Bio-Bibliography
*Sam McCready*

Noël Coward: A Bio-Bibliography
*Stephen Cole*

Oliver Smith: A Bio-Bibliography
*Tom Mikotowicz*